SILENT
THUNDER™
mokurai order

THE RAZORBLADE OF
ZEN

Cutting through the clutter, confusion, and conflict between
extremes of rationalism and theism in the face of man-made
and natural disasters during a time of increasing uncertainty

TAIUN MICHAEL ELLISTON, ROSHI

REDFeather™
MIND | BODY | SPIRIT
4880 Lower Valley Road, Atglen, PA 19310

Other REDFeather Books by the Author:
The Original Frontier: A Serious Seeker's Guide to Zen,
ISBN 978-0-7643-6088-6

Other REDFeather Books on Related Subjects:
The Three Principles of Oneness, Anthony Stultz,
ISBN 978-0-7643-5813-5
Mindfulness Matters, Pax Tandon,
ISBN 978-0-7643-5525-7

Edited by James Young
Designed by Brenda McCallum and Lori Butanis
Cover design by Brenda McCallum

*Cover image © Elina_Li, Landscape with blue misty forest mountains vector
image. Courtesy of Vector Stock*
Type set in Copperplate/News Gothic/Minion Pro

ISBN: 978-0-7643-6526-3
Printed in India

Published by REDFeather Mind, Body, Spirit
An imprint of Schiffer Publishing, Ltd.
4880 Lower Valley Road
Atglen, PA 19310
Phone: (610) 593-1777; Fax: (610) 593-2002
Email: Info@redfeathermbs.com
Web: www.redfeathermbs.com

For our complete selection of fine books on this and related subjects, please visit
our website at www.redfeathermbs.com. You may also write for a free catalog.

REDFeather Mind, Body, Spirit's titles are available at special discounts for bulk
purchases for sales promotions or premiums. Special editions, including
personalized covers, corporate imprints, and excerpts, can be created in large
quantities for special needs. For more information, contact the publisher.

We are always looking for people to write books on new and related subjects. If
you have an idea for a book, please contact us at proposals@schifferbooks.com.

CONTENTS

ACKNOWLEDGMENTS

The Razorblade of Zen is the second in a series of related efforts to clarify the practice of Zen and its meditation, as well as their importance to navigating the stormy seas of change facing the people of the world today, especially the United States. The first book in the series, *The Original Frontier*, was published in 2021 and emerged as a kind of owner's manual for personal Zen practice. Both books were originally part of the same rather unwieldy manuscript that, with guidance from rejection slips and a group of readers, including several volunteer editors, became two—the first about 250 pages, the second present volume a little over 200, admirable for brevity if nothing else. To those whose participation and feedback helped reshape the original texts, I am deeply indebted, but they are too many to mention by name.

Those who helped to see the project through to publication I hope to acknowledge in full here, but the actual dimensions of their contributions will not be captured in full, as they include many months of one-on-one dialogue dealing with copy content, as well as technical issues around the science referenced in addition to arcane matters of crediting citations and other details of publication. It was a group effort, from which they, as students of Zen, claim to have benefitted, and which I hope that you, as the next group of readers, will benefit as well. As part of an ongoing process of refinement of the message and its context, I encourage you to contact me with any questions or comments you may wish to contribute. You never know; your remarks may affect any future revisions.

Special thanks to those who also graciously provided blurbs for the cover and especially to Hoko Karnegis for the foreword. My sincere apologies to anyone who feels left out, but the initial development of this thesis goes back over decades, and some early contributors have been lost to the fog of memory. I invite you to contact me, however, to continue the dialogue.

Hoko Karnegis, sensei, ordained by Shohaku Okumura Roshi, head student at Kogetsu-an in Shiga, Japan, 2005. Dharma transmission, head teacher at Eiheiji and Sojiji, 2012. Vice abbot and successor at Sanshin, 2016. Served as communications director at Hokyoji Zen Practice Community, Minnesota, and interim practice director at Milwaukee Zen Center. Adjunct instructor of Eastern religious traditions, Lakeland College, Sheboygan, Wisconsin; Ivy Tech Community College's lifelong learning program. I am grateful for her incisive and insightful foreword, as my dharma sister (Okumura Roshi performed my formal Soto Zen transmission ceremony in 2007).

Kuya Nora Minogue, resident Soto Zen priest at Sakuraji in Creston, British Columbia, currently training with Mountain Rain Zen Centre. Kuya, the primary editor on the project, got out her purple pen and helped whittle down the 250-plus pages that initially comprised the manuscript, posing cogent challenges to the relevance and appropriateness of certain passages, while adding examples of points made in the text. Could have done it without her, but probably wouldn't have.

Shikaku Paul Manuel Aviles Baker, senior director of research at the Center for Advanced Communications Policy, principal research scientist at Georgia Tech; PhD in public policy from George Mason University; MP in urban planning from the University of Virginia. Master of theology, Candler School of Theology, Emory University. International policy research and collaborative policy networks, issues of technology and usability policy, workforce development and innovation diffusion. Paul (Shikaku) has been practicing meditation for over fifteen years, joining Atlanta Soto Zen Center in 2018, serving as treasurer. But his dedication to Zen may have faced no greater test than educating me on the details of attribution of citations in this kind of text, for which I had no training, and for which I owe him a debt of gratitude.

Steven M Carr, CPhil, PhD, professor of biology and computer science, Memorial University of Newfoundland. Teaches and researches genetics, evolution, computational biology, and the history of biology. Steven is a long-term practitioner and beginner on the path, his own definition. He collaborated extensively on correcting my musings on evolution and its relationship to the development of the human mind in the history of Zen Buddhism. Many bows and kudos in his direction. *The Razorblade* would not be nearly as sharp without his fine-tuned strop.

George Wrisley, PhD, associate professor of philosophy, University of North Georgia, and published author. Provided early and necessary, incisive and clarifying caveats from a scholar's perspective on Zen and philosophy in general, which made their way into both volumes, to the benefit of all.

And the first shall be last. I would like to express my deep gratitude, admiration, and respect for my wife, Diane, without whose tender loving care and patience this project could not have come to fruition.

FOREWORD

By Hoko Karnegis

At about the same time that Taiun Elliston began practicing Zen, a German academic named Heinz Bechert coined the term "Buddhist modernism." It describes a field that looks at the various elements influencing Buddhist practice today, which in the West include rationalism and scientific naturalism as well as Romantic expressivism. Rationalism makes reason the main source of knowledge, while romanticism emphasizes individualism and the emotions. These movements were larger social responses to the karmic circumstances of their times and places, and it seems inevitable that they've also influenced the spiritual practices of Western Zen adherents. For the largely convert Western sangha that wasn't born into a Buddhist culture and may not have practiced in Asia, it's not always clear that practitioners are seeing and experiencing Zen through a set of their own cultural filters that shape not only what they do, but how they perceive what they do.

This book asks: How do we put the practice we've inherited from our Japanese ancestors into conversation with our modern Western influences? It's tempting to try to lift our practice out of any cultural context in an effort to return to a "pure" form that sheds its "trappings," but that's impossible. If we attempt to drop the Asian cultural elements of our practice, we simply substitute Western ones that may be harder for us to see. Before we scornfully toss aside the things we call "trappings"—those things we think of as an ornamental harness on the pony cart—we'd do well to see what human spiritual need caused the arising of those elements, even if we choose to meet that need in some other way based on our own culture that feels more familiar.

In my experience, Westerners trying to put their practice into a modern context tend to lean either toward the "Buddha was a scientist" or the "Buddha was a mystical sage" point of view. It's easy to pick and choose various teachings and practices to reinforce our own conclusions based on whether we're rationalists or romantics. Some would say that the emergence of a psychological Western Buddhism is the middle ground that allows us to be scientific about our emotions.

In any event, as Taiun Elliston points out, exploration of our relationship to both theory and belief, or both rationalism and romanticism, in our practice is really important. Buddha himself urged us to see how wisdom and faith were actually in a fine balance. In his own awakening story, frequently referred to in this book, he shows that both are necessary to stave off hindrances to human awakening, as embodied by the demon Mara. Mara's whole agenda is to keep people tied to the craving and aversion of samsara, and he's always doing recruitment and retention. He appears while Shakyamuni is sitting under the bodhi tree working on understanding the nature of suffering and seems to say a lot of kind things. Oh, poor you. This is too hard. You should give it up and just go about your life in the world of the senses.

But Shakyamuni knows what's going on. He says, No, I see your legions of demon hindrances behind you and I know you're just trying to tempt me away from awakening. He's not getting up from his seat "for I have faith and energy, and I have wisdom too" (Collected Wheel Publications 2014). And, of course, the result was that in the end it was Buddha that sat under that tree and saw the morning star. As Dogen Zenji says, wisdom (understanding the true nature of self) is the basis of faith, and the place where faith manifests is the place where buddhas and ancestors appear (Matsuoka 2006).

We frequently hear from our teachers that there's nothing outside of Buddha's way, or this one unified reality. If so, then there's room for both rationalism and romanticism in our practice, as well as going beyond ideas of rationalism and romanticism, what Taiun Elliston calls "getting beyond belief." We leave behind our stories about whether both we and the Buddha are scientists or sages or both or neither when we engage wholeheartedly in the practice of zazen. In that space, we modern Western practitioners join our ancestors in the complete manifestation of Buddha nature.

Hoko Karnegis
Vice Abbot, Sanshin Zen Community
Bloomington, IN

LIVING IN
INTERESTING TIMES

"May you live in interesting times" is said to be an ancient Chinese curse, as I mention in the introduction to *The Original Frontier*, my prior book (Elliston 2021). "Interesting," here, is the opposite of peaceful or boring. We certainly live in interesting times, currently cursed as we are with a pandemic of historical proportions that has imposed universal, if intermittent, social and travel restrictions upon the most mobile society in history. For many this has resulted in changes in livelihood, exacerbating the have-versus-have-not divide and other forces of polarization in an increasingly interconnected world.

For the first time in living memory for many, we Americans face challenges to freedoms usually taken for granted, both at home and abroad—restrictions we tend to associate with purportedly less enlightened, even despotic, governments. All this in the context of continuous conflict and forever wars around the globe. Or perhaps the reporting has simply gotten better, and things only seem more parlous than ever. As they say, the airplane that goes down gets all the attention. The hundreds of thousands dying from COVID-19 obviously did not get the attention they needed in time. But the rogue physicians pushing unproven cures and pols treating the virus as yet another political football become media darlings. The public's patience and bandwidth, meanwhile, are reaching a breaking point. Viral fatigue runs smack up against short attention span, a quintessentially American, new-normal mindset.

Relating recent events may someday date this text, but it is likely that the emerging sea change—no pun—in humankind's relationship to Nature will continue unabated. By the time you are reading this, COVID-19 may have subsided. But pandemics have occurred before and are likely to occur again, given the intransigent nature of human behavior and that of viruses.

In times of over-the-top, relentless media-based amplifications of anxiety and uncertainty, we turn to tried-and-true resources for resolution, respite, and relief, such as our religious faith. Or we may opt into the cutting edge of science (e.g., the seductions held out by advances in social media, or the most recent must-have exercise equipment). Entertainment also provides temporary sanctuary, losing ourselves in gaming, binge-watching TV series and movies, always-on news, and music piping in earbuds 24/7. Politics itself qualifies as ersatz, if polarizing, entertainment, which it has always provided to a degree. Some escape into books, devouring romance novels, mysteries, sci-fi, and other fiction, along with self-improvement guides and revisiting the Western and Eastern classics, even books on philosophy or Zen. The heavier the book, the safer we feel hiding behind it.

But in the face of such literally earth-shaking developments as climate change fueling ever-increasingly violent storms and flooding, firestorms and drought, along with volcanic activity, and their concomitant disastrous effects upon whole populations, from starvation by widespread famine to ethnic cleansing—indulging such distractions amounts to so-called ostrich behavior. Those who know something about ostriches will tell you that they are not so willfully ignorant as we are. Mother ostriches will defend their nests viciously, with bone-breaking kicks. Mother Nature will do the same.

The current viral plague is only tangentially a consequence of climate change. But its spread northward of the more typical tropical disease reservoirs, into a place like Wuhan, is something that we have been warned of for decades. We cannot forever put off confrontation with reality. It will eventually come calling on our doorstep. So, what to do? Zen offers some ways of coping that the more familiar, traditional approaches based on religion and science do not.

The dire straits in which we currently find ourselves constitute some of the many motives driving me to share my experience and understanding of Zen, my appreciation for its uniquely simple meditation, and how I see the place of Zen practice in our prevalent world culture, most especially the United States. Zen Buddhism's first Pure Precept is the admonition to do no harm, echoing that of the American Medical Association. We can use a lot more of that—doing no harm, that is.

The first book in this series, *The Original Frontier*, was designed as a user's manual for integrating meditation into your personal approach to coping with the pressures of contemporary living. *The Razorblade of Zen* is meant to properly place your pursuit of the benefits of Zen in the spectrum of the other options on offer, from secular scientific sources to the religious community. I will attempt to share what Zen has to offer for living in our interesting times. I suggest reading both texts for a well-rounded view of Zen's relevance in the personal as well as the societal sphere. Until now, Zen has largely fallen outside the visible spectrum of Western culture's coping mechanisms, though meditation has become mainstream. The most obvious and egregious proof of the disconnect between peoples' behavior and the prescripts of science is the deadly debate around vaccination and masking. It is exacerbated by the moving target of safe practices issued by various authoritative sources, including the White House, the CDC, the NIH, the National Education Association, and various schoolboards, and other agency heads. Toss in a coterie of celebrities from sports, entertainment, and government leadership circles refusing to conform, and nobody knows who is on first, or when the next variant will come out of left field. Turn to religious leaders, and they are queuing up to take sides in the fray as well.

Zen offers an island of sanity in the sea of confusion that is our world, a kind of sanctuary in which to take stock of our inventory of viable options, and to evaluate which of them we might exercise for the sake of ourselves, friends, and families—all the while embracing reality.

Another reason for writing this text is that many Westerners, perhaps including yourself, still harbor gross misconceptions about Zen in spite of the glut of published material now available. These include the assumption that Zen is something ancient and archaic, exotic and foreign, pessimistic or nihilistic, or simply inaccessible, unrelatable, and irrelevant to our times. On the other hand, many more Americans are now benefitting from the mainstreaming of meditation, including wider dissemination of Zen communities throughout the United States. In spite of this increasing exposure, or perhaps because of it, I would like to try to clarify the real Zen as I understand it from direct experience, along with its relevance to our American culture as I see it.

Designing a Zen Life

My perspective on Zen is formed by my background in professional design, including graphic, industrial, and environmental applications, as well as my career in fine arts. Growing up in a musical family that emphasized improvisational jazz also contributed a certain sensibility. Teaching at university level beginning in my midtwenties, including developing art and design curriculum, along with consulting and market research for innovation in the private sector, has informed my appreciation of Zen's traditional protocols and highly refined method of meditation. It has also helped to mature my personal and practical assessment of the applicability of Zen to our modern maladies. Much like design, Zen is basically a problem-solving process, directed toward defining the most basic problems of life. I hope to develop a third text exploring this relationship in some detail.

The intersectionality of design-thinking and Zen may not be readily apparent. It has to do with our human proclivity for creativity. My professional career has helped me to understand the creative process, which cultivates deep intuition. Zen training provides the ultimate method for tapping into our innate talent for solving life's problems, which may largely be considered problems of design intent: how we design, and redesign, the process of our own lives. Approached as a work in progress, living design process becomes crucial to our survival, and to any hope of real happiness, especially in context of the complex circumstances in which we find ourselves. The reassurances of faith and religious belief on the one hand, and the promises of technology and science on the other, appear less effective and diminishingly attractive in light of overt pressures of living in the twenty-first century.

Sharpening the Razor's Edge

When you hear Buddhists proclaim "the middle way," you may suppose that they mean simply practicing moderation in all things. Colloquially, this trope suggests a kind of lackadaisical, Caspar Milquetoast way of living: avoiding conflict, taking the easy way out, following the path of least resistance. But from a Zen perspective, Buddhism's Middle Way prescribes an aggressively proactive embrace of life as it actually is, warts and all. It means striking a balance between the competing forces that pull us in every direction, much like gravity. Immersed in gravity, we resist gravity, like a juggling tightrope walker on a high wire keeping all the balls in the air at the same time.

The middle way in Taoist-influenced Zen means not harboring preferences, especially for pleasant over unpleasant circumstances: easy to say, but difficult to follow. My Zen teacher, Soyu Matsuoka Roshi, taught that this middle way of Zen is the most extreme position of all, precisely poised between opposing tensions in each dimension of everyday life: the razorblade's edge of the Zen mind.

Zen's sitting meditation helps us to cut through personal and cultural biases, offering a direct approach to determining and taking compassionate action in any situation. Anyone, anywhere, anytime, can adopt this method to developing Zen's outlook, without unduly disrupting their demanding daily routines; indeed, the very demands of daily life fuel the process of practicing Zen.

Zen can be disruptive to your status quo, but in the most positive sense. What it disrupts is our habitually hapless way of coping with the vagaries of life. The very things that bedevil us come to be seen as the content of our Zen practice. They become the necessary grist to the mill that refines our ability to understand meaning in life. As such, Zen represents a radical, even revolutionary, approach.

When we hear, for instance, the current comforting message that "We are all in this together," or "We will all get through this together," we don't really buy into it. These tropes suffer from the same threadbare overuse as "Our thoughts and prayers are with you." The rising death toll from the pandemic is all the evidence we need to know that we will not all get through this. Following the money reveals that we are certainly not all in it together on any basis of equality of cost-benefit analysis. Social and financial inequality have become key driving factors, leading to the poorer segments of society and Third World countries being the most negatively affected by the virus, especially from inadequate distribution of medical supplies and equipment, primarily vaccines. Meanwhile, polarization in the political arena and the stress of racial and social injustice are reflected in frequent mass killings and police shootings, predictably followed by protests, triggering pushback from lawmakers, amplified in the daily news feed as equal-opportunity shills for ratings. These kinds of inequities have led to revolutions in the past, and it seems we are heading full tilt in that direction today.

It is important to remember that while current events and emergencies are compelling and demanding of our undivided attention, threats to our health and happiness have ever been thus. The fundamental causes and conditions of existence—aging, sickness, and death—have not changed substantively since the time of Buddha. But the stunning scale of affected population in the billions, and the geometric expansion of resultant chaos, constitute a phase-shift of an order of magnitude. Safety in numbers no longer applies.

The practice of Zen emphasizes moderation in all things in the best sense of the phrase, regardless of the immediate Sturm und Drang of circumstance. But Buddhism has never been about fomenting revolution or overthrowing the powers that be. It is about modeling a different approach, a third or middle way, that neither depends upon government nor undermines it. Moderation in Zen does not suggest a kind of laissez-faire attitude of simply letting things take their own course. But it does recommend a more spontaneous approach to mitigating our compulsion to control events, and our tendency to overthink everything. In the context of American society this idea amounts to an extreme position. But extremism in the pursuit of moderation is no vice. No apologies to Senator Goldwater.

In considering what follows, I dearly hope that you are prepared to moderate any expectations and preconceptions you may harbor about Zen. The text may also challenge some fixed ideas you may have regarding claims of rationalism, those aspects of your worldview based on logic. It may also call into question some beliefs of theism, those aspects of your worldview based on your faith. But the point of this book is not to debate objective truths of rationalism, nor subjective truths of theism. Instead, it is meant to give you a perspective on Zen in the modernist context of both institutions, as well as others of the social-political sphere. Zen calls upon us to suspend our ordinary judgmental mind and to set aside our cherished opinions in order to assimilate its deeper secrets. An open mind is necessary to examine and embrace the teachings of Buddhism under the microscope of meditation.

But penetrating the deeper secrets of rationalism or science also requires going beyond the limits of logic, according to one of its high priests, the venerable Dr. Albert Einstein, who is famous for a lot of sayings, including one given on the occasion of Max Planck's sixtieth birthday (1918): "There is no logical way to the discovery of these elemental laws. There is only the way of intuition, which is helped by a feeling for the order lying behind the appearance."

Dr. Einstein is beginning to sound a lot like a Zen master here. Einstein described his famous thought experiments as a visceral kind of process, a gut-level creative visualization of the imagination, rather than an investigation pursued through ordinary analytical thinking, whether in the language of words or numbers. A person steeped in the philosophy of science might suggest an approach more like that suggested by Thomas Kuhn, based on his theories in *The Structure of Scientific Revolutions* (1970), namely that intuitive insight mainly provides the hypotheses for testing by methods of normal science. Intuition does not magically arise from deductive or inductive processes, any more than relativity simply fell out of the mathematical equations.

To a veteran practitioner of Zen, and a relative novice in the realm of rationalist thought, Einstein's "way of intuition" sounds a lot like Zen meditation—in Japanese, zazen. Relinquishing our usual reliance on analytical discursive thought is definitely recommended while sitting in Zen. Zazen is also about discovering "elemental laws" (i.e., what is called buddha-dharma). Both processes lead to insight, perhaps of a different order, and both require going beyond logic but are within the reach of intuition.

The most dramatic, early proof of the import of Einstein's intuitive insights was revealed in the form of the atomic bomb. The year 2015 marked the seventieth anniversary of the first use of the bomb dropped on Hiroshima and Nagasaki in World War II. Einstein himself apparently deplored this action, though he had warned FDR that the Nazis were racing to get the bomb.

Matsuoka Roshi immigrated as a peaceful emissary to America during this period of international conflict. It is a great irony that he grew up near Hiroshima, one of the targets of the only nuclear Armageddon ever visited upon the human race, at least thus far. He originally arrived on these shores in 1940, when the bomb was barely a gleam in Robert Oppenheimer's eye. It, the Bomb, must have been a profoundly personal source of grief for him. But this barbaric act did not dissuade him from bringing Zen, a peaceful form of Buddhist practice, to Japan's enemy. His loyalty, both to his adopted country and to his mission of propagating Zen, I take as a mark of his great compassion, foresight, and wisdom. Ironically and illogically, Oppenheimer was apparently a devotee of Ahimsa, the ancient Indian principle of nonviolence. Difficult to see the compassion or wisdom in nuclear devastation.

There is certainly no logical way to understand such horrific global events, or to assimilate them into a "feeling for the order lying behind the appearance." Zen cannot explain everything, including the worst excesses of human behavior, other than as examples of profound ignorance. But any meaningful understanding of Zen begins with thoroughly examining the workings of your own mind. Relying solely on logical analysis without engaging intuition is likely to prove futile. In Zen, as in the far reaches of science and higher math, we must rely on an intuition that is deeper, and more fundamental, than discriminative thinking alone. Zazen keeps the razorblade of intuition sharp.

Being Happy with Nothing Special

The pandemic and its side effects have brought a couple of realities to the forefront, notably the trope that "that which does not kill us makes us stronger" from Friedrich Nietzsche. Christopher Hitchens, dying from cancer, vigorously refuted this idea in his last series of essays for *Vanity Fair*. That which does not kill us immediately can also make us a whole lot weaker in the meantime on societal and economic fronts as well as our personal health and well-being, exacerbating an already difficult situation. Buddha learned this lesson during his ascetic period. He declared the extreme paths of self-gratification and self-mortification to be equally unworthy and unprofitable, with the latter being painful into the bargain. This lesson framed his defining of the Middle Way. It is tough enough.

This truism reinforces the Zen view that we are not in control of everything and, in fact, not much of anything. In spite of the advances of modern science, Nature enjoys hegemony over our health and happiness, and we will live to regret it if we ignore her voice. Or we may not live to regret it, both individually and as a species. In either case, the world will proceed on its journey unfazed, according to science fiction writers, and science speculators such as Dougal Dixon in *After Man*, a prediction of the zoology of life on Earth some fifty million years after the disappearance of *Homo sapiens* (1981).

But where the rubber meets the road for most folks is exemplified by the enormous scale of the impact Nature's haphazard intervention—in the form of a microscopic life-form—can have on our personal, immediate goals and daily objectives in pursuing the good life. Yet its disruptive force is not based on any malicious intent. From a rigorous scientific perspective, the current virus itself is not exactly an independent life-form, as it cannot survive with, or apart from, its host. In many ways, it is just a beautifully designed little mechanism that illustrates evolution on a finely focused scale. The mRNA vaccine is likewise a beautiful invention. Note that we are playing on the terms "design" and "invention" liberally in an evolutionary and human context, sans connotations of creationism.

But the fact that our political leadership can be woefully inadequate to the task—emphasizing the economy over human health is short-sighted; and the pleasure-seeking of fame and fortune is pretty much a waste of time—are realities pragmatically embraced in Zen, though not exclusively Buddhist. Their saliency has been made clear by the body slam the virus has delivered to the body politic.

One limited upside of the pandemic that many have discovered is that they do not really need to commute to work. And that quiet mornings, clear skies, fresh air, and clean water can indeed be the norm. It raises a fundamental question about "getting back to normal": Do we really want to?

However much you may personally enjoy the surfeit of products and services, entertainments and cultural arts that are on offer, particularly in the wretched excess consumption-based societies of the First World, with the United States still the leading poster boy, Zen asks the iconic and ironic question: Is that all there is? Design asks a corollary question: How much is enough? The same question applies, perhaps to a lesser degree, to the Second World and Third Worlds. Or do we, by now, have a Fourth?

Interesting times have historically produced anomalous fringe societies, sometimes following the pursuit of pleasure as a strategy for evading the more depressing dimensions of living in civilization. But the middle way of the Buddhist Order in Buddha's India, and that transmitted through the countries of origin down to the community of practitioners today, was not, and is not, that.

Zen's monastic lifestyle countenances owning only seven items, including a few robes, sandals, a straw hat, a monk's bag, and a set of nesting bowls for eating, called oryoki bowls. The largest one was for begging. Their historical business model was mendicancy, depending on the kindness of strangers, the local villagers. Oryoki, Zen monastics' formal way of eating, connotes "just enough," another expression of moderation. In the meal chant, we are reminded that we regard greed as the obstacle to freedom of mind; we regard this meal as medicine to sustain our life. Compare to the movie character Gordon Gekko: greed, for lack of a better word, is good. In Zen, greed is reduced to its ultimate simplicity, manifested as consuming more rice or gruel than you really need.

The creature comforts of modern civilization are certainly preferable to the alternative: grinding poverty, leading to desperate diasporas from war zones and accompanying death, disease, and destruction plaguing many of the Third World corners of the globe today. But we cannot help but harbor a suspicion that relativity is at play: poverty for the many is codependent upon extreme affluence for a few. With international commerce and travel providing ready vectors for spreading disease, and mass migrations stoking fears of emerging conflict in more peaceful areas, with the worst of these disasters further exacerbated and fueled by predatory politicians, no one can feel safe anymore. Not that anyone ever could feel absolutely safe anywhere or at any time in the prehistory and history of humankind. But by now we should be able to do better, one would think.

In such a sour pickle, it is understandable that we would turn to traditional sources of succor relied on in the past, ranging from family and friends to humble fellowship, or resorting to the glittering and glitzy promise of modern technology. Some turn, or return, to their faith: church, synagogue, temple, or mosque, seeking shelter from the storm (shout out to Master Dylan 1975). Some find solace in the rarified heights of philosophy, or more prevalently these days, in their political caucus. Some embrace positivism, bilateralism, and diplomacy, hoping that we can (and will) rationally solve the global problems ostensibly driving local conflicts. And equally hopeful that a superhero from science, or calvary, or the cavalry itself, will arrive just in the nick of time to fend off inevitable and irreversible catastrophe.

But even the politics of hope often turn out to be less-than-satisfactory in delivering hoped-for results. The failures, sellouts, and outright betrayals that we see in our leadership—not only of the political class, but also of the scientific, medical, religious, business, and educational sectors—indicate that they do not always have our best interests at heart. Titular spiritual leaders are often caught up in the same mad pursuit of wealth and power that characterize the worst excesses of classist society. Just as Buddha confronted the inequity of India's caste system in the sixth century BCE, we confront our own slightly less blatant version of class warfare in our time. The social sphere can and does impact the personal sphere negatively, as well as positively, perhaps in equal measure.

While we may admire, secretly or overtly, the upper 1 percent of the haves for their material success in life, we suspect that it comes at the expense of the have-nots in a casino game that is rigged in favor of the former. We invest (read "gamble") our dollars and hopes on lottery tickets as a hedge against the hopelessness that might ensue if we unsentimentally calculate the overwhelming odds against winning. We despair at news of suicide rates, deaths from poverty and overdoses, and various other canaries in the coal mine, sending increasingly urgent, alarming signals of something gang agley.

We are faced with a situation that looks like it may never get much better, despite our natural and national tendencies to optimism. In fact, it seems to be getting so much worse on so many fronts: to wit, the latest pandemic at center stage, with sideshows of daily protests against the latest outrages of injustice, perceived or real, and the mounting effects of climate change accelerating human and wildlife migration waiting in the wings.

Our response to irrational times is not likely to be all that rational. What to do and how to cope within this cacophony of causes and conditions is our daily koan, Zen's illogical riddle applied to everyday life in contemporary society.

But the personal sphere is where we live and it is not separable from the social, the natural, or the universal spheres, as it turns out. We are often severely impacted by surprise incursions coming from far reaches out of the blue, as well as from more immediate social influences. Can anyone say COVID? Asteroid? Or comet? Solar flare? Earthquake? Crimea or Ukraine?

It is natural and human that a kind of dismay, even despair, threatens to set in. Worse than the "national malaise" that notoriously helped derail Jimmy Carter's campaign for a second term for president, casually dropped in one of his ersatz FDR fireside chats, cardigan and all. Intended to calm and encourage the populace, it backfired politically and predictably, an overreaction to merely pointing out such a pessimistic, if ultimately realistic, observation. He said the quiet part out loud.

With so many threats to our comfort level impinging on all sides—from the constant shock tactics of the numbing daily "breaking news" cycle to the disturbing events in our own neighborhoods, where do we turn for relief?

I propose that one answer, for myself the first-and-foremost fundamental answer, lies in Zen. Its famous "nothing special" take on the ultimate peak experience of Buddhist insight extends to the ordinary ups and downs confronted in daily life. Instead of Job's famous lament "Why me, Lord?," we ask "Why not me?" What's so special about myself that I should not suffer the same slings and arrows of fate that others do?

Zen can help to temper the worst excesses of your disappointed expectations, while informing an aspiration to the deeper meaning of life in all its imperfections, and more to the point, in spite of them. This fundamental attitude adjustment finds verification in zazen, where we find what we are missing from the bigger picture of our worldview. Don't sweat the small stuff, and it's all small stuff redux.

In the following section, we will compare some of Zen's principles to conventional worldviews from rationalism and theism, placing Zen smack-dab in the middle of our choices for addressing and reducing, if not eliminating, the stresses of living in the real world today. May you live in interesting times, and "The times, they are a-changin'" (Dylan 1964) on steroids. Zen provides the playbook for developing a strong offense, and zazen the method for balancing out your natural defenses.

Reading This Book

These days I think it unrealistic to assume that anyone will read an entire book at one sitting, even one as brief as the present text. You may want to take it at your own pace, as recommended for Zen meditation. It may be advisable to browse through the chapter titles and subtitles first. You may want to absorb my observations in small bites, like strong spices, giving them time to digest. Like most discussions of Zen, a given section of this text may restate similar points from a different angle. But all of Zen's teachings bear repeating.

The sections are subdivided by subheads such as Reading This Book to allow for quick and easy scanning. This will enable you to complete whole sections in a single session, or to find reasonable stopping points you can remember and quickly restart. It's a book. It will still be there when you come back to it.

Of course, you are free to read this text in any way that suits you. Taking it up occasionally to scan a topic that appeals to you at that moment may be more balanced and effective than reading straight through in linear fashion. I recommend alternating bouts of reading with sessions of meditation as in *The Original Frontier*. The reading can reinforce and encourage your meditation, and your meditation may help clarify what you are reading.

Nonetheless, I have attempted to lay the text out in a reasonably logical sequence. First, Zen is examined in the context of conventional contemporary American worldviews, contrasting it against those of rationalism and theism. Then I present some ideas about the impact and implications of living a Zen life in today's world. I hope the simple logic of this facilitates your assimilation and application of the content but beware the substitution effect. Reading about Zen does not replace sitting in zazen.

COMPARING RATIONALISM, THEISM, AND ZEN

This book is a heartfelt expression of my personal confidence in the demonstrable effectiveness and appropriateness of Zen training for our times. But casual readers and even longtime Zen practitioners may not share my enthusiasm. It pays to exercise a healthy skepticism in matters concerning our deepest aspirations, especially when considering a matter as seemingly alien and strange, novel and foreign, as Zen. But Zen practice begins with a reexamination of the familiar, focusing directly on our own present reality.

Positioning Zen as an alternate social view—against the familiar tenets of scientific rationalism and those of devotional theism—may help to clarify what Zen is by exemplifying what it is not. By placing Zen in the context of conventional or received wisdom, its unique position on the spectrum of options for action may become clearer, its tenets more accessible. The fundamentals of Buddhism are not like objective scientific hypotheses, theories, or laws. Nor do they qualify as subjective beliefs.

But Zen teachings may be safely regarded as more theoretical than faith based, as they do not conflict with the findings of science. Many teachings of Zen will challenge the familiar belief systems of theism, but some of its general underpinnings, such as that life is a kind of test or challenge to be overcome, are compatible with certain religious doctrines, including those of Abrahamic Judaism, Christianity, and Islam. Zen's compassionate embrace can accommodate all but the most extreme religious or philosophical viewpoints. Anyone of any faith can usefully practice zazen. Zen is for everyone and is always contemporary, as my teacher would often say.

Zen and zazen partake of both spirituality in its outlook and empirical observation in its method. It occupies a kind of middle ground between extremes of religious fundamentalism on one end and secular reductionism on the other. Thus, Zen offers a middle way for negotiating pitfalls of our current highly polarized culture, a distinct alternative from conventional coping strategies found in Western society. On the spectrum ranging from accepted dictates of rationalism to established beliefs of theism, Zen stands out as a third attitudinal and operational way. My exercise in comparing the three fields examines distinct differences in eight specific dimensions which all three have in common. I have laid out selected examples in a chart for clarity of comparison and contrast (figure 1).

A caveat: being in no wise an expert on theism nor trained as an exponent of rationalism, my treatment necessarily represents an oversimplification of those two fields. But for the main purpose of placing Zen in its modern context, my relatively superficial survey will suffice.

Of course, this approach is fraught with potential misunderstanding. For example, you may be a devout Christian, a professional scientist, or simply a person who tends to side with one or the other of these two sometimes-opposed world-views. We live in a highly polarized, often fractious, public space these days.

But clarifying Zen is worth risking some conflict and confusion. In its unique design and method, Zen is up to today's challenges, relying as it does on personal investigation in meditation and bringing the results of that intensive research—findings, conclusions, and recommendations—into daily life.

You may find my choice of terms and resultant comparisons between the general tenets of Zen, rationalism, and theism to be unexpected, somewhat inappropriate, and even unwelcome—not the choices you would make. But by contrasting Zen with familiar concepts, however inept or incomplete the comparison, such memes act as foils to show where Zen differs substantially, positioning it in the nexus of contemporary American and Western culture in general. Hopefully.

I hope you will find profiling Zen in this simplified way useful to refining your worldview. It should clarify where Zen departs from prevalent cultural approaches and assumptions, especially those of contemporary religion and science, not to mention the political arena. Contrasting with our culture and customs should yield a meaningful perspective on Zen theory and practice for the novice as well as the experienced practitioner.

The new and unfamiliar is best set against the old and familiar if we are to elicit where and how they differ.

In figure 1, eight dimensions selected as archetypal are compared and contrasted across fields of rationalism, theism, and Zen as worldviews. Comments on rationalism and theism are gleaned from public sources amended by expert collaborators. Those on Zen stem mainly from personal experience.

DIMENSION	RATIONALISM	THEISM	ZEN BUDDHISM
1. Questions asked	How?	Why?	What?
2. Problems defined	Chaos	Sin	Ignorance
3. Attitudes nurtured	Perseverance	Faith	Doubt
4. Entities trusted	Evidence	Savior	Self-Nature
5. Methods employed	Experiment	Prayer	Meditation
6. Truths claimed	Verification	Belief	Identification
7. Goals pursued	Knowledge	Salvation	Vow
8. Conclusions drawn	Evolution	Creation	Coarising

FIGURE 1. Comparing and Contrasting Rationalism, Theism, and Zen Buddhism

For the sake of simplicity, we proceed by first addressing general but salient distinctions between the three fields, followed by examining each of the eight dimensions in more detail as they appear to function within each of the three fields of endeavor. Beginning with analyzing the different classes of questions addressed in each, proceeding through central problems identified by their proponents, the various methods employed, and so on, my commentary wraps up with an exemplary conclusion drawn from each field. It goes without saying that any such inventory cannot claim to be exhaustive.

Couching Terms and Caveats

The selected dimensions and attributed categories are chosen for purposes of illustration, rather than as expert or definitive. They are offered as context to shine some light on where Zen differs. If your worldview is theistic, you may note that "scripture" is not included, though it could readily fit within one or more of the dimensions. If you are a scientist or self-identify as a rationalist, you may prefer a more definitive term such as "control," rather than "knowledge," as a key goal pursued in science.

Other latent dimensions come to mind such as "values." One of which, for rationalism, might be expressed as "predictability," since a theory or proof is not valuable, and may not even be true, if it does not provide a certain degree of replicability under varying circumstances. In theism, the highest value might be expressed as something like abiding in a "state of grace," or entering into the presence of God. We often differentiate between social groups and national cultures by insisting that they don't share our values. This take on "values" has become one of many political footballs being kicked around in today's seemingly endless political campaigns and debates. The highest values in Buddhism might be regarded as the Three Treasures: buddha, our original (awakened) nature; dharma, the (compassionate) teachings; and sangha, the (harmonious) community.

You are invited to accept my terms for now and to rework the exercise in your own words. For the sake of discussion, they will serve as talking points, hopefully illuminating where Zen comports, or parts company, with some of the specific mindsets or biases of rationalism and theism.

REFLECTING ON RATIONALISM

I must admit to some trepidation in commenting upon a subject that has so many complex facets, and which has been discussed so eloquently by the great thinkers of the Enlightenment and of the Western tradition in general. I will attempt only to sketch an outline of the conventional wisdom I have assimilated from the cultural milieu and my limited investigation following popular resources on science and philosophy, along with a little help from my friends. I hope the treatment is sufficiently comprehensive and rich enough to indicate the scope of the rational worldview, as well as some of its limitations. This will serve to provide a framework for comparison to the theistic mindset, but more importantly to that of Zen as a worldview.

In broad strokes Zen may be compared complimentarily to rationalism, especially in its emphasis on the empirical method, relying directly on our own experience and the evidence of our senses. Theism does not compare to Zen nearly so well since it relies on belief systems or doctrine for understanding the world.

Experience and Belief

We have to be careful in defining "experience" in relation to Buddhist insight or to belief systems or doctrines in general, whether religious or cultural, as well as to insights from empirical observation. On the one hand, our experience may be uncontaminated by belief or doctrine: a direct apprehension of reality prior to the development of related beliefs or concepts. On the other hand, some experiences require background beliefs and concepts in order to convey any determinate content—for example, experiencing an event such as the Fourth of July or feelings of a particular quality, such as patriotism.

The first "pure" kind of experience may be reasonably argued to be false or nonexistent, since most experiences register as what they are only in cultural context: background concepts, assumptions, and beliefs. Their meaning would vary depending on context and custom. Most of our experience is not self-interpreting or unambiguous but is conditioned by theory or preconceptions—sometimes referred to as the "theory-laden-ness of experience" (Boyd and Bogen 2021) by acolytes of the philosophy of science.

For example, when we stand on the shore with Christopher Columbus and watch a boat sail away, it begins not only to get smaller but apparently begins to sink. If you believe that the Earth is flat, then there is only one option: your experience of the boat is that it is sinking. If on the other hand you believe—in the sense of knowing—that the Earth is spherical and that there is no good reason why the boat would sink, then you experience the boat as sailing over the horizon. It is clear then that experience is not only clouded by prior knowledge, conceptions, and perceptions, but formed by them.

Another example: if a streak of light occurs in a cloud chamber, the observing scientist may say, "There goes an electron!" But a scientist's experience of an electron is dependent upon a background understanding about how electrons interact—as electrons are not directly observable to the senses—as well as how a cloud chamber actually works. Similarly, photons are not individually observable to the senses. Yet we see light. A related example from the history of Zen (Chang 1971):

> A monk called Hung Chou came to visit Master Ma Tsu and asked, "What is the meaning of Bodhidharma's coming from the West? (implying What is Śūnyatā, emptiness?)" Ma Tsu said, "Bow down to me first." As the monk was prostrating himself, Ma Tsu gave him a vigorous kick in the chest. The monk was at once enlightened. He stood up, clapped his hands and laughing loudly, cried, "O, how wonderful this is, how marvelous this is! Hundreds and thousands of Samādhis and infinite wonders of the truth are now easily realized on the tip of a single hair!"

The kick to the chest theoretically triggers in the monk a direct experience of the answer to his question, obviously on a nonverbal level. But outside the context of Zen Buddhism—including all of its concepts, tenets, and practices, et cetera—how would such a kick likely be experienced? An apprehension of reality as it is? That is, as emptiness? It is demonstrably true that the meaning of experience and the context of belief, in the conventional sense, cannot be separated absolutely. In this case as in all other anecdotes of the transmission of buddha-dharma, the experience depends 100 percent on the sincerity of the student and his trust in the teacher, which may be considered a kind of belief or faith. However, this kind of faith should not be conflated as a false equivalency with blind, nonevidentiary faith.

In this regard Zen places the emphasis on experience over belief or doctrine, especially when the former contradicts the latter. Zen also gives primary importance to the experience over the expression of it, which comes full circle to the notion of a different order of experience—one that is beyond expression, beyond theory-ladenness, and certainly beyond belief.

A final caveat: rationalism, I am told, is so broad that it might be better to focus more tightly on what is called the "scientific method" which, unlike the hoary history of rationalism, is regarded as a relatively recent development. The Enlightenment beginning in the fifteenth and sixteenth centuries raised an appreciation of reason to a level coequal with religion. During the seventeenth century (see: Bacon, Descartes, Galileo, Newton), religious belief in God was slowly replaced by methodological reliance on Science, capital S. The eighteenth century continued the trend through a time of revolutionary turmoil on the political front, notably in America and France. By the early twentieth century, this was a done deal. World War I and the Bolshevik Revolution followed. Today we appear once again at the brink of revolution, caught between science and religion, facing such unprecedented apocalyptic change that the very term "unprecedented" has become meaningless. But, as we say in Zen, every moment is unprecedented.

THINKING ABOUT THEISM

I am even more reluctant to comment on theism than on rationalism, for obvious reasons. Closely held faith-based belief systems represent broad and deep worldviews that are even more inaccessible to compromise than those of the defenders of reason. True believers assert and defend their beliefs with vehemence. This is totally understandable, as much more is at stake than mere professional standing or income. One's very soul hangs in the balance, after all. But I hazard a commentary on theism for the same reason that I dare to examine rationalism: to establish the salient cultural context for Zen in our world of today. I "believe" in Zen, in a manner of speaking. That is, I believe in the efficacy of its method and the relevance of its teachings. Zen offers an alternative to relying solely on faith-based religion or reason-based science in coping with reality. Zen is actually complementary to the two worldviews. It offers a way of bridging the secular and the sacred.

Buddhists generally do not engage with non-Buddhists in debate or disputes over its teachings. There are hopeful signs that such ancient sectarian quarrels between Abrahamic religions are abating. Pope Francis recently renounced the longstanding crusade of converting or attempting to convert Jews to Christian beliefs, embracing for the first time in history the idea that faiths other than Christian Catholicism and Protestantism can be routes to salvation.

What little understanding I have of faith-based religion stems from early exposure to Sunday school and church sermons. More recently I have garnered some insight through participation in interfaith dialogue, through a series hosted at the Zen Center, including a year as cochair of the Fulton County Interfaith Coalition in Atlanta, Georgia, and as a panelist in an online interfaith world peace initiative headquartered in South Korea. I have come to see certain commonalities between other faiths and Buddhism on practical, if not soteriological, terms. Intrinsic to all is the universal quest for understanding and some sort of salvation, as well as tried and true methods for finding hope and practicing compassion in the face of an incomprehensible world of suffering. This need to know the unknowable, the transcendent, was the impulse and intent behind Buddha's quest for spiritual insight. The driving force for discovering his birthright in meditation was to cope with suffering and his need to understand its existence and meaning, which seems to be the general focus of all religion.

Contemplating Tradition

Whether Jewish, Hindu, Muslim, Christian, or Bahá'í, many ministers, rabbis, and priests recognize that somewhere in the ancient past of their faith there was a tradition of contemplation or meditation. Contemporary versions may take the form of centering prayer or simply entering into silence and thus the presence of God, as in Psalm 46:10: "Be still and know that I am God."

Not to argue the point, but it should be noted that those of us who have spent some time in meditation know that it can be anything but silent, and that stillness is the key to centering. But most faiths have lost the thread of this original practice. The interest that interfaith leaders have in zazen often revolves around a question of how precisely to meditate, how it might complement their boilerplate forms of worship and rituals, and how it might possibly inform, or challenge, their beliefs.

We are often asked how Zen relates to theistic religions. But a more fruitful starting point might be the various beliefs of theism, and how they relate to Zen praxis. Zen is the meditation sect of Buddhism, which is regarded as one of the world's four great religions. But some practitioners consider it a kind of category error to define Zen as religion. Salvation in soteriological systems often depends upon the intercession of a deity, saint, or savior. In Zen, it depends upon direct insight from our own efforts. This is not an egoistic attitude but merely assuming responsibility for our own existence. We are not responsible for life itself—we are not God—but we are responsible for what we do with it. The most responsible thing is to attempt to penetrate to the true meaning of existence itself.

Second, we might clarify the relationship of Zen, with its emphasis on zazen, to Buddhism itself, some sects of which do not emphasize meditation. Some assert that Zen is not really Buddhism, or that it constitutes a significant departure from its strictly devotional branches. I disagree. Zen claims to transmit the essential teachings of buddha-dharma through its direct medium of meditation. This claim is supported by the record of early teachings that, necessarily through the medium of language, attempt to point to what Buddha himself discovered in meditation, which is essentially beyond words.

Third, we might consider how Zen practice and theory compare to other nontheistic practices and beliefs, but this would be a project for another time. Here, we merely want to establish how Zen differs from theism in general, as well as from that other beacon of contemporary society, rationalism.

Believing in Buddhism

Common misunderstandings of Zen are revealed in such frequently asked questions as: What do you believe? Or, Do you worship Buddha? Buddhism is neither a belief system nor a form of worship. Anyone can come to understand how salvation in Buddhism differs from that of belief-based faiths, but only by practicing the way of meditation taught in Zen, preferably with guidance from an experienced teacher. Basically, we save ourselves from our own ignorance. A little coaching can help.

Buddha was not a Buddhist any more than Jesus Christ was a Christian. Buddha's initial insight from his direct experience in seated meditation formed the foundation for his teaching. "Do thou likewise" is sagacious Zen advice. We do not reject all forms of belief, of course. Conventionally speaking, we "believe" that Buddha experienced something transformative and that all humans have the potential to experience something similar. Beliefs or tenets of Zen are dependent upon our ability to prove them to ourselves in our own direct experience: the taste of the pudding, as it were.

We also "believe in" the efficacy of Zen, particularly its meditation. We believe and revere Buddha and his recorded teachings. But revering is not the same as worshiping. We don't believe in Buddha.

Buddha was a human being much like you and me. But he transcended the limits of human personality, including its many attachments and aversions, by coming to terms with the suffering of aging, sickness, and death on a very personal level. This insight led to his being greatly admired in his own time as "Buddha," Sanskrit for the "fully awakened one," an honorific derived from a root term meaning "awake." But even in his own time he was not worshiped. There were even those who took issue with his teachings. His own cousin, Devadatta, tried to assassinate him, according to the story.

Perhaps uniquely among world religions, Zen Buddhism is a program of personal activism. We are each encouraged to undertake direct action in order to overcome our own ignorance through our own direct experience, mainly via sitting upright in zazen. We do not rely on an intermediary in the form of a savior or saint, priest or pastor, scripture or doctrine. Action in Zen consists primarily in meditation practice, secondarily in study, and thirdly in community service.

Communal Zen practice includes rituals supportive to meditation, but does not overemphasize devotional worship or fellowship, as do many faith-based congregations. We practice the golden rule to the extent possible, including a reluctance to proselytize, or to engage in religious debate.

Zen literature consists primarily of the surviving record of teachings from Buddha (Sanskrit: sutra), and commentaries (S. shastra) by ancestors in India, China, and Japan. Liturgical chants amount to testimonials of the ancestors' personal insights, from that of Buddha on down to the present day. They are all speaking with one voice, if in different milieus—various fingers pointing at the same moon. In Zen liturgy, we recite these teachings repeatedly in order to fully assimilate them. This includes devotional recitations expressing reverence for Buddha, various bodhisattvas, and Zen ancestors in the lineage (S. bussorai), but not as worship or prayers for intercession, with rare exceptions for certain verses considered to have protective powers (S. dharani) to prevent disaster.

These traditional homilies take their deeper meaning from what we personally discover in our own zazen. The Heart of Great Wisdom Sutra (S. Prajna Paramita Hridaya Sutra), the most frequent daily chant in Zen centers, is mainly a testament to the "emptiness" (S. shunyatta) experienced in meditation at its deepest level. Other liturgical chants and written commentaries point to metaphysical and social implications of this legacy of spiritual insight handed down and entrusted to us by the Zen lineage.

As with rationalism, theism is also very broad, its history dating from prehistory, so to speak. The Western evolution of religion shows perhaps as much change as that of science, roughly paralleling developments in recent centuries. It was a central impetus, or excuse, for the colonial powers bringing so-called civilization to the world at the point of a gun and played a major part in the purported rationale for revolutions to follow. Those who are writing about the role of religion today, from a scholarly, philosophical, and historical perspective, will find plenty to criticize in my pedestrian commentary. But please remember that I bring this up only because so many are finding reasons to turn elsewhere for answers to increasingly difficult challenges to belief, whether of science or religion, that we are facing.

The recent Hollywood production *Don't Look Up* is only the most recent parody of the intransigent, self-destructive, and self-defeating ignorance seemingly inherent in the human condition. It follows on the history of such dystopian classics as *Dr. Strangelove*: funny, but not really. Buddhism is relevant because from the beginning it has offered a way (i.e., Zen) to face life—and, especially, to confront death—directly, whatever the prevailing causes and conditions.

ZEROING IN ON ZEN

While I feel much more comfortable commenting on Zen than I do about theism or rationalism, I harbor reservations that any attempt to explain it will prove futile. This is a known issue. A famous poem in Zen liturgy ends with something like: "Words! The Way is beyond language for in it there is no yesterday, no tomorrow, no today." The experiential is extremely difficult to express in words. It is difficult enough just to describe the surrounding physical environment, or a mental or emotional event in our lives. How much more so to articulate a process promising to lead to transformative insight?

The cursory survey of selected conventional memes of rationalism and theism should render my comments on Zen more meaningful than if they were presented in a stand-alone essay. But any true appreciation of Zen will come mainly from your own zazen.

Meditation Rules

Zen is known as the meditation sect or branch of Buddhism.deity-based religions appear to rely on doctrinal studies and devotional practices, or the preaching of a messiah, prophets, or saints, aimed at helping followers to come into alignment with the commandments and will of God. Certain schools of Buddhism emphasize study and devotional practices as much as, or more than, they do meditation. Such historical influences as Taoism stress coming into harmony with the Way, which resonates with Zen. But Zen assigns a decidedly peripheral role to such practices as incense offering, bowing, chanting, repentance and reading scripture, ceremony, and ritual services. The central effort in Zen is directed to our foremost responsibility: experiencing our own insight, as did Buddha.

This attitude does not derive from hubris, nor does it imply any disrespect for the founder, Shakyamuni, or the ancestral lineage holders of Buddhism, with their vast, recorded legacy of teachings. It stems from the simple fact that followers of Zen are not satisfied with secondhand experience, nor content with merely subscribing to culturally conditioned beliefs about the meaning of our existence. Zen is the ultimate in do-it-yourself.

In this regard, Zen meditation would find an affinity with the saints, seers, prophets, and holy men and women of other religions who claimed to have experienced direct revelation but were not always treated kindly by their fellow believers.

Ancestors of Zen are generally held in high esteem as deeply enlightened exemplars. Contrast this to the suspicion, contempt, and fear with which some visionary religious figures such as Joan of Arc were treated. Or Meister Eckhart, the great Christian mystic censured in 1389 by Pope John XXII, who issued a papal bull in which Eckhart's statements were characterized as heretical. This censure was not lifted until 1910. Existential fear has a long memory, but being burned at the stake is irreversible.

The known ancestors of Zen, like the saints of other systems—and Jesus Christ himself—are regarded as bodhisattvas: enlightening beings who dedicate their lives to the spiritual salvation of others. To qualify as an authentic teacher of Zen (Japanese: daiosho), each individual must personally have had an epiphany, an insight into the awakening that Zen points to, realizing essentially the same spiritual truth discovered by the historical Buddha. This event is just as deeply meaningful at any time in history.

Certain Christian sects might argue that Jesus, already being God at birth, could not have gone through any such transformational change. Other doctrines may differ. But the story of Buddha's awakening is one of simply recovering his original nature, not one of mystical transformation, or some sort of magical alchemy. Siddhartha Gautama was already Buddha at birth. As are we all. He just didn't know it. Likewise for us.

Again, Buddha and the ancestors are not worshiped in Zen communities. Nor are they called upon to intercede on our behalf. While prayer and meditation may share a parallel function—that of aligning adherents with the deepest aspirations of their faith—Zen does not subscribe to a personal connection with a cosmic Buddha or bodhisattva as an object of worship, or as an appeal to salvation.

Zen meditation does offer adherents of any faith a personal method of immersion, an intense absorption in unfiltered consciousness. It is holistic, involving the whole heart, body, and mind. This natural meditation cannot be limited to Buddhists nor considered exclusive to Zen.

But as a cautionary aside, some experiences that may rise to the level of consciousness in deep meditation may not conform to, and may indeed challenge, one's closely held beliefs. Buddha's experience contradicted the contemporaneous belief in the atman, the Hindu concept of an indwelling self or soul. This wide belief was embraced at that time, and, one supposes, yet today. Buddha originated and taught the doctrine of anatta, paraphrasing: no separate entity of being, self, or a soul. This atman should not be misconstrued as identical with the Christian concept of the immortal soul. Christianity did not yet exist at the time of Buddha's teaching.

Where Zen Differs

Unlike scientific rationalism, Zen does not claim, or even attempt, to define an objective universe devoid of an observer. The inseparability of observer and observed, self and other, mind and body, is a basic tenet or finding of Buddhism. Of course, science recognizes that observers affect that which is observed, no matter how diligently other variables are controlled in the design of the study.

Zen may differ most clearly from conventional rationalism in general, and scientific empiricism in particular, in its meditation. Zazen focuses directly upon the sensorium and its processes, calling into question the very data received from the senses, including its interpretation by the thinking mind. In doing so, the Zen approach is not unscientific, but arguably partakes more of the soft sciences such as psychology and sociology than it does of the hard sciences such as physics and biology.

Buddhism's cluster of Six Senses is biased in favor of survival, the external five acting as a distant-early-warning system, our DEW line of self-defensive survival. The five "portals," as they are sometimes referred to, report data to the mind-brain, the internal overseer function. On the most primal level, we need to know whether the grizzly bear is charging us or running away.

But as the sixth of the senses, thinking itself is not at all autonomous. The automatic functioning of the discriminating mind—constantly judging good and evil, right and wrong—is also biased by preferences favoring the pleasant, and averse to the unpleasant. Our vaunted faculty of discrimination must be left behind, in order to enter into the inmost nondual sanctum of consciousness, bridging inner and outer worlds like our personal wormhole. The discriminating mind is fully capable of discriminating against discrimination itself.

Unlike theism, Zen does not attempt to explain the unexplainable by reference to a divine will. Nor does it distinguish between or prescribe a "holy" life over the ordinary life of a layperson. There is said to be no "stench of holiness" around Zen. Living a Zen life does not require giving up our ordinary everyday way of living—unless it is unhealthy or otherwise destructive—and taking up the lifestyle of a monk or nun. Lay practice is the most normal way of integrating Zen into normal life for most normal people. Life in the monastery is for the very few, relative to the population. From a talk Matsuoka Roshi gave (2006):

> In Zen, the purpose of the religious life is to find the truth about life in this world and then to live with this knowledge. Instead of hoping to obtain some material thing or fortune from a supernatural being, in Zen we live in order to enter into the true life. We do not even desire to become a Buddha, for doing so takes the emphasis off the present moment of life and puts it into the unpredictable future. Instead, we live this moment to its fullest and so act as to develop the potential to be a Buddha which lies dormant in each of us.

If asked, you would probably not casually claim that the purpose of your life is to become a buddha. But remembering that the term simply means to wake up fully, you might reconsider. If you consider what it means to wake up, in every sense of the phrase, it is something worthwhile to aspire to.

The fact that Matsuoka Roshi considered the aspiration to Zen to be religious in character is both an artifact of Japanese culture, where religion does not occupy the same niche as in the West, as well as of his cogent discernment of societal and cultural considerations in propagating Zen in the West. He understood that most of his audience in the middle decades of twentieth-century United States would regard Zen as a branch of Buddhism, as basically a religion. Many of its early adapters did not see it as such but more of a philosophy, a way of life, or even a kind of psychotherapy—none of which are adequate to capture its true nature or its niche in today's context.

In Zen's traditional worldview, people do not need to do anything special to change their circumstances in order to enter into a religious life, but only to incorporate Zen, primarily through the practice of zazen. There is no value in pretending to be monastic or anything other than what we are: layfolk.

CONTRASTING
THE EIGHT DIMENSIONS

With this brief overview of similarities and differences between the worldviews of Zen, rationalism, and theism, let us now turn our attention to each of the eight dimensions as they appear to function for followers in each field: (1) the kinds of questions they each ask; (2) the important problems, as they define them; (3) the attitudes they attempt to nurture; (4) the various entities, real or imagined, in which they invest their trust; (5) the methods they employ; (6) the truths they claim to be self-evident; (7) the goals they pursue and aspire to achieve; and (8) some of the salient conclusions they have drawn.

I will endeavor to treat rationalism and theism as fairly and completely as possible—within the limits of my current understanding and within the limited scope of this essay—in order to set the contemporary cultural context for revealing where Zen differs. As we will see, Zen falls somewhere between the extremes of rationalism and theism.

A final caveat: at the risk of repeating myself, I want to be crystal-clear that the main reason for selecting this context and making these comparisons is to establish a simple framework of familiar but formative received wisdom in contrast to the proper place of Zen in our modern milieu. I fully realize that a thoroughgoing analysis of rationalism, theism, or Zen itself cannot be given justice here. I will leave it to others to attempt a broader scope, a more scholarly exegesis, or a more accurate historical analysis. My intent here is simply to offer a springboard—from the relatively familiar world of conventional science and religion—to a dizzyingly deep dive into the relatively strange, but curiously familiar world of Zen. Strap on your oxygen tank.

DIMENSION 1.
QUESTIONS ASKED: HOW? WHY? WHAT?

Granted that these three types of questions actually overlap considerably, I ask you to allow for the moment that those posed by the rationalist mindset (i.e., How?) are clearly distinct from, if not totally at odds with, those of the theistic mindset (i.e., Why?). In return, I will endeavor to make the meaning of the relevant Zen question (i.e., What?) as clear as possible, in contradistinction to the other two.

Rationalism, especially in the form of scientific endeavor, tends to address the "how" of things, whether theoretical or practical. Generally, science explores how things exist and how they work, scrupulously avoiding the existential question of why it is that all things, including human beings, exist. Philosophy is not within the scope of this text, but the majority of its proponents likewise give the nod to rationalism, often addressing the "how" more so than the "why," when they expound upon how humanity and its societies work. Or at bottom, how they should work.

Generalizing, we use the term "theism" as a catchall placeholder for various doctrinal religions that profess an abiding faith in a personal God. Christianity may be the most familiar faith for the majority of the United States, myself included. I certainly benefited from my limited exposure to Protestantism, primarily in Sunday school, as a child. But we are all exposed to the predominant conventional Christian worldview through public institutions, including the educational establishment as well as the commercial media. There are even those who insist that the United States was founded as a Christian nation.

In broad strokes we may say that all theistic religions, including Christianity, seek to answer the "why" questions, whether theological or philosophical. Why does the universe exist? And why, indeed, do we humans exist?

In a TED talk I came across on YouTube literally titled "Why Does the Universe Exist?" the speaker, Jim Holt (2014), called the title the ultimate "why" question. In the introduction he profiled a theistic view as expressed by the Christian philosopher Leibniz, who said that God created the universe out of nothing: creation *ex nihilo*. End of story. No mystery here. Most contemporary Christians would endorse this view. God plus nothing equals the world. It got a big laugh from the TED audience.

But then he went on to describe the Buddhist view as similar, that the world equals nothing. That to a Buddhist the whole world is just a big cosmic vacuity. In the aforementioned Heart of Great Wisdom Sutra, a recap of the basics of Buddhism, the materialistic idea of any form having permanent self-existence is negated by the famous formulation: form is emptiness; emptiness is form (Shumucho 2001). But declaring that given emptiness, there is no form, feeling, thought, impulse, or consciousness does not literally mean that there is nothing whatsoever, that our normal world is all delusion. It means that the material world appears precisely by virtue of its essential emptiness: impermanency, imperfection, and insubstantiality of all that exists. Emptiness, as the essential dynamic underlying the appearance, is meaningful only relative to form, its manifestation. Both are coarisen and interdependent, like matter and energy, in Buddhism's model of the Twelvefold Chain. This is the "what" of nonduality.

Had Buddha stated only half of his formulation, stopping at "form is emptiness," this speaker might have a legitimate point. But the rest of the story is that "emptiness is form," which reclaims the reality of living in the material world. In Buddhism the world is certainly not nothing. But this is one of the popular memes about Zen, concerning which Mr. Holt, a speaker of exalted position and reputation attracting nearly three million viewers, should know better.

A Zen student and I were invited to speak about Zen to a Protestant congregation where we were treated to, and sandbagged by, an official video produced by the denomination's headquarters touting this same idea. That Buddhism, compared to Christianity, offers only nothingness. The point was driven home by the star of the film, a charismatic minister, when he dramatically snuffed out a candle. This egregious mischaracterization based on ignorance, along with half-a-dozen other misconceptions the minister solemnly intoned, gave me the talking points for my address, which followed immediately. I took notes and welcomed the opportunity to clarify Zen. My younger attendant was not so forgiving.

These are a few of the many discomfiting examples of self-proclaimed "experts" on one side of any given issue presuming to know what they are talking about, when referencing or ridiculing tenets of the other side. It is better to land in the middle, remaining discreetly agnostic, especially regarding things you don't understand, until more fully informed.

Fortunately, serious efforts are being made in worldwide interfaith panel discussions to draw out the common threads between religions, instead of opposing them in yet another ideological debate. I am privileged to participate in one international online world peace movement, whose premise is that if religious leaders can come to some degree of rapprochement, political leaders may finally follow.

When any group or individual, whether scientific or religious, claims to have the answer to both the "how" and the "why" of all things, we may reasonably regard such presumption as the height of arrogance. The long-running and largely settled faux debate between the proponents of "intelligent design" and those of the traditional theory of evolution is a case in point. The former, in touting their beliefs on human origins, and refuting scientific theories, display a certain lack of humility, or honesty, in the face of overwhelming evidence of the latter, which they try to dismiss as "just a theory." Another example is the asymmetrical tug-of-war between politicians and professional educators over religion in public schools, a smoke screen for instituting Bible study. Abortion is another of the hotter belief-versus-science buttons that keep coming back like a bad penny. In most cases, the science does not support the belief. And nothing is so obvious as that which is hidden, especially a hidden agenda.

"Why" Is Sometimes "How"

A semantic clarification may be in order. Colloquially asking "Why is something so?" sometimes acts as a stand-in for a "how" question. In the vernacular, "why" sometimes means "how," depending on what we mean by "why."

Take the collapse of a bridge, a real-world concern gaining traction with our crumbling national infrastructure. A person might reasonably ask why it collapsed. There are at least two ways to interpret this usage of "why," one having to do with causes, the other with ends or purposes. That is, the question might refer to functionally how the bridge collapsed (i.e., what caused it to collapse). One possible answer: dynamiting the support structures. Or faulty construction. Or inadequate maintenance.

Another possible answer would concern the end result, the purpose behind the collapse. If it was dynamited, then someone placed the explosives. Why? Perhaps because it was old and needed to come down for safety reasons before a new bridge could be put up in its place. Dynamite is the proximate cause for the bridge collapse, but the purpose is replacing a dangerous bridge with a safe one. Or a terrorist group may take out a strategic bridge. But both purposes, replacement versus an attack, are legitimate answers to the "why" question. The answer addressing the "how" question is also a reason why: dynamite.

If you ask a scientist why something behaves the way it does (e.g., why the Earth orbits the sun) and not the other way around, the explanation may seem to answer the "why" question. Earth orbits the sun because it is in thrall to a greater gravitational field. "Because" expresses the "why" of causality.

But if we look more closely, the explanation is more about how the solar system works, not why it is so. "Why" questions beget ever more "why" questions in an endless regress, like trying to satisfy the curiosity of a child. Well then, the child says, Why does the sun have more gravity? Because it has more mass. Why does the sun have more mass? Et cetera, ad infinitum.

With that hair fully split, and for the sake of this discussion, we return to the chart, treating "how" questions as eliciting causes and methods, and "why" questions as addressing intents and purposes.

Rationalism: How?

Simplifying for the sake of argument, the professional proponents of rationalism in general, and science in particular, explore questions of the "how" class. How—not why—all things including sentient beings exist. How they came to be the way they are and how they work at present as well as how they interact with each other, synergistically and symbiotically. Scientists develop hypotheses about how reality functions and design experiments to test their ideas. Then they produce, measure, document, and interpret the evidence.

If important and consequential enough, other experts duplicate or approximate the experiments in a peer review process to verify the findings. When verified by third parties (e.g., through replication of measurable results), hypotheses solidify into theories. Buttressed with sufficient evidence over time and proving dependably predictable, a theorem may be elevated to the dizzying height of physical law. We might say that this is the scientific nut, in the shell of creation. All such theories or laws, however, are subject to revision upon discovery of contradictory evidence. They are not holy writ.

The scientific method may be regarded as the ultimate application of the rationalist worldview, though the cognoscenti may rationally object to such a characterization. Many scientists claim to share the beliefs of theism, including that God exists, in some form or fashion. Others may point out that the scientific method is not entirely devoid of the irrational, including the role of chance or coincidence, or that of intuition. Any such generalization, of course, will suffer from logical limitations and inherent contradictions. Nonetheless, rationalism may be usefully employed to contrast with Zen.

The Religion of Science

A child approaches reality with a sense of awe and wonderment, a mode of inquiry closely akin to Zen investigation, which has been likened to peeling away an onion one layer at a time. Each discarded layer reveals another underlying layer. At bottom, the onion falls apart, revealing the emptiness at its core. And there can be a lot of tears along the way before reaching the center.

In Zen, as in science, the questions asked are often more important than the answers. An old saying holds that the difference between world-class and mediocre scientists is that the former ask the more important questions. Zen practice likewise may help resolve trivial issues in relatively short order, but the more intractable problems of daily life take longer. Any answer to any Zen question is typically an even bigger and deeper question, pointing to the mystery of existence itself.

No matter how complete and thorough a scientific explanation, up to and including the elusive holy grail of the standard model of physics, a "grand unified field theory" or theory of "everything," the rationalist view can never fully answer the "why" questions. Science cannot explain away everything.

When science elevates its understanding of how the universe works—or that part of it presently under the microscope—to the level of why it is so, it enters upon the slippery slope of scientism, defined as an excessive belief in the power of scientific knowledge and techniques, which is tantamount to establishing a religion of science. We do not believe in science any more than we believe in Zen.

Theism: Why?

Speaking broadly, the questions raised in theism seek to explain the meaning or fundamental purpose of existence, and of humankind's place in it. In other words, the "why" of things. Theology seeks to comprehend the nature, or at least to discern the will, of God and to prescribe the dynamics, or rules, of our relationship to that higher power. This dynamic requires defining what is fundamentally wrong with human existence, and how to right it in order to fully live the faith and ultimately achieve salvation. Like the endlessly curious child, religion asks and attempts to answer the cosmic question "Why, oh why?" over and over. Faith leaders try to provide meaningful answers, referring to scripture, and prescribing devotional practices such as prayer.

When religious thinkers respond to the fundamental "why" questions with answers framed as "who," the result is theism or deism. Paraphrasing liberally, the dictionary distinguishes theism from deism by defining theism as the belief that a creator is actively engaged in day-in-and-day-out activity of our world. Deism similarly posits a creator, but one that is no longer involved in everyday micromanagement of the creation.

Job's lament: Why me, Lord? portrays the downside of blind faith in a deity, slavishly following commandments and assuming that such devotion will be enough. Job questions why we can still suffer so terribly while assiduously adhering to the rules of our faith. His is a case study as to why religious leaders feel called upon to deliver doctrinal answers to otherwise unexplainable realities: why bad things happen to good people and good things happen to bad people.

It is of course overly simplistic to subsume all questions of theism under the rubric of "Why?" All religions devote a great deal of doctrine to problems of how to live faithfully in everyday life, for example. Living in accord with the gospel is often rationalized, not just by the obvious personal and altruistic benefits of living compassionately in one's social milieu, but also with the promise of being reborn, either spiritually in this life, or physically resurrected in the next. Believing that our reward is in heaven may go a long way to alleviate the suffering of daily life, but it is not enough in Zen, and apparently is losing its appeal in general. We want to know how to live fully in this life, to actualize our spiritual potential. Zen promises to point the way.

Encountering Suffering

Job's dilemma finds a parallel in Buddha's extreme estrangement from earthly existence owing to the unconscionable, ubiquitous suffering he had witnessed from childhood into early adulthood. He is said to have been profoundly affected as a toddler, witnessing the agony of dissected earthworms writhing on the freshly plowed soil. Later came the famous story of the Four Sights: seeing an aged man, a sick person, a corpse, and a monk, encountered over four successive nightly forays from the palatial compound on his horse, Kanthaka. Based on this reality check, he resolved his life's direction.

These encounters only reinforced his view of life as inherently entailing suffering (S. dukkha). The potential of following a path to salvation in the face of the inconvenient truths of existence was triggered by the last sight of a spiritual seeker of the time. These visions inspired his First Sermon, outlining four aspects of sentient existence as constantly changing: birth, aging, sickness, and death. This event is the first recorded instance of the Three Gems—buddha, dharma, and sangha—coming together. The "why" of existence may have still been speculative, but the "what" and "how" were now clear.

Imagining God

Some doctrines of theism hold that human beings are made in God's image. As corollary, God is visualized as the spitting image of humanity, writ large. This belief amounts to a kind of circular logic, an internally consistent loop. It provides the rationale underpinning the belief that human beings are so special that we occupy THE central and critically important place in creation, having dominion over all creatures of the Earth. Unfortunately, this self-serving prophecy is often enlisted to excuse all manner of unreasonable treatment of the rest of creation, as well as the followers of lesser gods.

In monotheistic religions, God often represents perfection, omniscience, and omnipotence. But humans, God's paramount creations, are imperfect and limited, born into sin originally committed by their primogenitors, Eve and Adam, eating the fruit of the tree of knowledge of good and evil. Yet with all our imperfections, we are still subject to God's will. This dichotomy is promulgated by clergy who are also human: imperfect and fallible, including the Pope du jour. In Abrahamic doctrine, the fall from grace is akin to Buddhism's take on human ignorance, in both innocent and willful flavors. Our insistence on reifying self and our own opinions is part of the problem, including our image of God.

The proposition of inerrant perfection implies an inconsistency within the internal consistency. If God is perfect, how can his creations be imperfect, unless by divine design? And if the latter is the case, their very imperfection must be, by definition, perfect—determined by the will of God. On the plus side, aside from the logical dichotomy, this premise of innate human imperfection sets up the proposition that we must all strive to do better, which is surely a truism of all religions and philosophies. This premise certainly comports with Zen Buddhism's general principle of imperfection as characteristic of all existence, alongside impermanence and insubstantiality.

Perfection versus Imperfection

Both images—that of the perfection of God and that of the imperfection of humanity—appear to be opposite sides of the same coinage, exercises in self-referential and preferential discrimination. The comparison may amount to a harmless and ultimately positive goad to self-improvement if it fosters humility rather than hubris. But a bias built in to an underlying belief in perfection versus imperfection, when unexamined, tends to distort our perception of reality, much like selective memory. If we always and only see things through multicolored eyeglasses of conditioned preconceptions or unconscious precepts, we can never register any evidence to the contrary. Hello, confirmation bias.

This bias holds true whether you self-identify as a rationalist thinker, a theistic believer, or a Zen zealot. Zen suggests that apparent imperfection is not really opposed to absolute perfection, but that both exist only in the mind of the observer. In any case, they form a complementarity, not an opposition.

Paradoxically the notion that the human form reflects God's image and vice versa represents theism's perhaps unwitting cooptation of humanism: anthropomorphizing the creator while simultaneously projecting an anthropocentric slant upon creation itself. Presumably shared human attributes idealized as being "of God" reflect deeply human aspirations to something greater writ large. But these impulses may also derive from less than divine inspiration. They may stem directly from our supposed imperfections, which are always in and of the eye of the beholder.

The proposition that reality is an imperfect reflection of an imagined perfection seems hopelessly circular, and too easily dismissed as irrational, if hopeful, thinking. It is not altogether irrational to invest a certain amount of faith in a belief, especially in the face of irreconcilable conflicts within our own rational experiences. We witness unnecessary human suffering wrought by increasingly severe natural disasters, amplified by malfeasance of human stewardship, or lack thereof, whether witting or unwitting. Bridges also collapse because someone cut corners to make a buck.

Closed-loop, belief-based thinking does not rise to the level of critical analysis necessary to distance ourselves from emotional attachment to our own cherished opinions, to which we so readily give the benefit of the doubt. The predictable result is that beliefs devolve to self-fulfilling prophecies, lobbying against taking the action necessary to preempt unintended consequences, such as refraining from stubbornly rebuilding housing in recurring flood zones.

Explaining the unexplainable with a facile "God moves in mysterious ways" dodges the question of causality, with its demand for scientific rigor. Such expressions attempt to explain away events that do not conform to the definition of, and belief in, a loving and caring God. The increasing devastation of Nature's wrath on vulnerable populations living in areas below rising sea levels, zones prone to earthquake and tsunami, drought and flooding, volcanic activity, and so on, beggar belief in a humancentric deity. Theism's default position amounts to a kind of religious reductionism: all causes devolve to a First Cause, rationalized as part of God's Plan.

Such claims are made without resort to evidence, other than the testimony of the canon and that of fellow believers ensconced in the echo chamber known as the gospel. This view tends to privilege survivors over victims in any given tragedy. If a judgmental deity is in charge, one can only conclude that the reason a tornado selectively levels every other house in the community, leaving others untouched, is that the occupants of the former must be sinners, while those occupying the untouched homes must be the chosen of God. These are admittedly extreme views, shared by few.

A parallel corruption of Buddhist teaching holds that those who suffer calamity are simply getting the karmic retribution they deserve. Both are examples of confirmation bias gone berserk. But Buddhist imperfection is not a respecter of persons. No one is exempt from interdependent causality.

Secular Humanism

Secular humanism as a rationalist philosophical system of thought privileges humankind as being at the center of worldly existence, a view similar to that of theism. But it pushes back against the belief that a creator is in charge, let alone that humans are formed in their image. Ancient Greek and Roman worldviews can be thought of as humanistic, as they countenanced a pantheon of gods who all too often exhibited all-too-human characteristics. Those remaining agnostic on religious matters, presumably including many scientists, may self-identify as humanists, preferring to land in-between strict believers and outright nonbelievers. With its emphasis on human beings having the inborn capacity for awakened buddha-nature, while yet remaining admittedly imperfect, Buddhism would probably land in this column, as a humanistic-leaning spiritual practice, certainly not as a deity-based faith.

But when the "why" of theism arrogates to itself the "how" of rationalism, we enter onto another slippery slope, the ersatz science of religion. Explanations of the world's workings as manifestations of God's will may be the default hallmark of deity-based doctrine, but such beliefs are often touted as evidence of intelligent design, with humanity at its pinnacle. But human organs do not always perform as well as those of so-called lower animals, one standout example being the olfactory range of your average pet dog. The point in Zen is not to argue with the beliefs of theism, nor the accepted laws of science, but to make the simple case that there are many things that we simply do not, and cannot, know. It is far better to confess to our ignorance and confront the mystery of existence honestly, than to feel that we have to have a ready answer to every question—especially facile answers to the "why" questions.

Zen Buddhism: What?

If you can accept my broad-brush correlation of the "why" questions with theism and belief, and the "how" questions with rationalism and reason, you may be ready to consider the central categorical question of Zen. The fundamental inquiry in Zen is not a matter of "why" or "how," but may be best expressed as "What?" As in: What is this, in front of your face?

We don't try to answer the "why" questions in Zen. We don't even ask: Why are we here? Where did it all begin? Or: When will it all end? These are considered hopelessly speculative and, more to the point, irrelevant to the problem at hand. Wise Buddhists avoid overindulging in rank conjecture, focusing instead on immediate and practicable action. Zen may be defined as promulgating a philosophy of principled action, pure and simple.

You may argue that the "who" questions, such as "Who am I?" would be most relevant to Zen—as distinct from "Who" questions, capital W (i.e., theology). But cultural connotations of "who" are already too personal, too entangled with gnarly preconceptions and entanglements around self-identity. We want to study the self, yes, but only in order to forget the self. Better to contemplate what we are, rather than who we are. It is a more objective and scientific inquiry, less philosophical or psychological. Keep it simple.

How and Why Zen?

If you are at all acquainted with Zen, you may argue that certain "how" and "why" questions are, indeed, important to its praxis. They come into play in terms of method or technique, in instructing others in how to do zazen, for example. "How" questions are also useful on a social level, as in how to employ skillful means in clarifying the dharma, and in sangha relations. Why we sit upright and still, rather than relaxing in just any posture while meditating, is also admissible. Why should we practice Zen at all? is a question germane to this day and age, with its many distracting alternatives on offer in the spiritual and self-improvement marketplace. Historically the question was relevant for other reasons.

"What" questions fall somewhere between those asking "why" or "how." Many "why" questions may be purely speculative, but most "how" questions are functionally actionable. "What" questions, on the other hand, point to the concrete reality beyond the beliefs of theism, and more immediate at hand than the working hypotheses or theories of rationalism, which require a certain arm's-length objective distance.

A famous Chinese Zen master asked a visiting monk: What is it that thus comes? This "what" indicates the actual reality of the living being, directly pointing to the ineffable true self. The monk in this case could muster no immediate response, apparently having never encountered his true self. After training with the master for many years, he finally responded by saying something like: to name it would be to miss the mark. This inconclusive statement was accepted by the master as confirming evidence that this monk had finally had a genuine insight into his self-nature.

But even if we can agree that Zen's ineffable truth—here identified as the "what" of reality—can be experienced directly, it does not follow that the "why" of it can be explained. And certainly the "how" of realization itself remains a deep mystery. How this mysterious transformation of the self comes about is described, paradoxically, as a process of forgetting the self, Or being actualized by all things. Or becoming free of delusion. This indicates a kind of negative process in reverse, not the usual linear set of positive incremental steps to learning something new. Zen's method of zazen may be seen as an intimate process of unlearning what we think we already know about our own self, our original mind.

A familiar Zen admonition is to not mistake the finger pointing at the moon for the moon itself. The "what" of Zen points to the concrete reality, the actual moon, not what we think it is. The word "moon" is a reference to that reality. That we call it the "moon" is a matter of mere agreement. If you speak French, it is called "lune." The term itself represents no more than a verbal finger pointing at the moon, not the moon itself. This is true of all verbalization but is especially apropos of Zen teachings. Words necessarily fall far short of the reality.

According to Wikipedia, there are between 5,000 and 7,000 languages spoken in the world today. There are also any number of nonverbal languages such as music, dance, theater, and art, as well as gesture and sign language. For each and every sense—seeing, hearing, smelling, tasting, and touching, and even thinking itself—there can be a distinct language, or several. Every meaning on the spectrum of intent—from loving kindness to hateful spitefulness—can be expressed, from a slap of the hand to a caress. But the intent is not always obvious. Compassion can sometimes look like cruelty, as in the current appreciation for "tough love."

What the concrete reality of our existence really is cannot be captured in words, nor in any other abstract framework of language. But we cannot resist indulging in finger-pointing. What Zen is pointing to is the "what" of the matter.

DIMENSION 2.
PROBLEMS DEFINED: CHAOS,
SIN, IGNORANCE

You were probably taught at an early age to look at life situations as problems to be solved, primarily through the application of logic. You were challenged by parents, peers, teachers, and colleagues to develop a solution or multiple solutions for the ever-changing problems at hand. Much of what passes for education amounts to exercises in problem-solving. Many forms of entertainment such as board and computer games, puzzles of all kinds, Rubik's Cube, and some television and radio shows such as *Jeopardy* and the *Wheel of Fortune* and their many imitators, amount to challenges to our playful problem-solving proclivities. Everybody likes to play games, especially those with large payouts.

But we are also encouraged to codify methods for solving life's problems dependably and repeatedly, and if possible predictably, as they arise, applying Zen's "skillful means" on a daily basis. Preventive problem-solving has moved higher on the agenda in the shadow of the pandemic. How can we keep this from happening again? is the common catchphrase when a tragic accident or natural disaster occurs. Problem-solving is also central to standard methods of measuring intelligence. Public education pays tribute to this assumption by teaching to the test. Measurable IQ reigns supreme, if controversial, as a cultural value. Intelligence and problem-solving are thought to be linked.

Problem Definition

In the professional design approach to problem-solving I learned in college under the rubric of the Bauhaus method and later applied in business, the first step toward any viable solution is developing a thoroughgoing definition of the problem. But thoroughly examining a given problem includes challenging its conventional definition. In professional consulting, this often means revising the clients' definition of the problem they are paying you to solve. In personal cases we are often too close to the problem to see it clearly. This process of challenging assumptions often leads to a fundamental redefinition of the identified problem itself. The more comprehensive the definition of a problem, the more likely the success of the solution.

When pursued thoroughly, this process may transcend the initial problem altogether, sometimes replacing it with a more pertinent definition, one of broader scope. To illustrate, we might take up the problem of designing a better automobile. In brainstorming we may broaden the context to include consideration of alternative transportation systems, thereby eliminating the need for a better automobile altogether. This specific problem forms the crux of the current debate on funding mass transit, versus extending highway and expressway systems, not to mention the advent of self-driving vehicles, one of many such developments challenging the status quo. The emergence of the COVID-19 virus and the resultant isolation and distancing of the pandemic promises to disrupt and reconfigure the entire paradigm of public transportation. When the dust settles, the results will become clearer.

Culturally Incorrect

Perhaps a similar, outside-the-box reconsideration of culturally incorrect or unwelcome problems as routinely identified—such as chaos, sin, and ignorance—could allow us to transcend unsatisfactory solutions as proffered by contemporary leaders of rationalism and theism, not to mention politics.

Chaos, in the general sense of the term, not the technical theory from mathematics, might more helpfully be universally recognized as a higher form of order, rather than an evil to be eliminated. Strategies for anticipating, embracing, and accommodating chaos as a natural force might then emerg, which follows on Dr. Einstein's suggestion that intuition is "helped by a feeling for the order lying behind the appearance." Designating phenomena as "chaotic" masks the underlying order, prompting inappropriately fearful responses, such as the panic and coverups we have witnessed on a worldwide basis in reaction to the coronavirus.

Likewise, what normally may be regarded as a moral or mortal sin, such as abortion, might be acknowledged to be a relatively minor mistake from which we may learn something valuable rather than an eternal stain requiring divine intervention to redeem. "Sin" might then appear not so final, so deserving of retribution, and so threatening to human civilization or even to one's personal salvation as it is conventionally regarded. Indulgence in illicit sex might not be so irresistibly attractive to the hypocritical moralist, struggling to walk the walk and not just talk the talk. The taboo of sin as intrinsically evil may explain the downfall of some of our more self-righteous preachers. Temptations of sex, drugs, rock-and-roll, and libertine lifestyles of the rich and famous, proscribed by fire and brimstone preaching, may arise precisely or partly because they are presented as such absolute taboos.

It is a perverse aspect of the heart to desire what is verboten. In worst-case scenarios of so-called religious justice rampant in certain theocracies around the globe, petty thieves are mutilated; wives stoned to death for infidelity; sisters and daughters murdered in the name of familial honor. In the ostensibly enlightened West, we may regard such infractions as forgivable, if not condoned.

From a rational secular humanist perspective, we may regard chaos, of either the manmade or natural disaster variety, as simply things gone terribly awry rather than as God's vengeance against a targeted group of sinners, as sometimes portrayed by self-righteous Western televangelists. Sin is often wielded as a club, a convenient label for selected behaviors defined as aberrant in the eye of the wielder. It is usually paraded as concern for the sinner, but it is actually intended to impose social control.

Universally Imperfect

From the standpoint of Zen, castigating certain behaviors as irredeemably sinful, or defining chaotic events of the world as the work of Satan—or conversely, the will of God—ignores a universal truth of Buddhism: reality is inherently imperfect as well as impermanent and insubstantial. Humanity itself, and attributes of human society, are equally subject to these traits, if on a distinctly different scale.

Buddha and his followers dedicated a great deal of time and effort to defining the problem of human existence, as did their counterparts in the West. Abrahamic religions, those of the Middle and Far East, Vedic and Hindu traditions in India, Taoism and Confucianism in China, as well as indigenous religions in all corners of the world including Native Americans, share a similar mission, if differing definitions of the problem: all seek to solve suffering and to realize some sort of salvation."

What we call "history" may be regarded as one big problem-solving exercise carried out over millennia, beginning before the beginning of recorded time. Otherwise, we might not be here today. Creation myths attempt to answer questions of how it all began and how it will end. Buddhist cosmology instead embraces the cosmos as beginningless and endless. Buddhism focuses more on the present reality than on speculation about first causes and ultimate finalities.

Theistic religious leaders often disagree on, and debate these questions, to which the default answer is often a "Who," as in John 1:1: "In the beginning was the Word . . . and the Word was God." Science reverse-engineers the current dynamics of astrophysics, back-plotting the Hubble constant rate of expansion of the universe to a single point of origin, the placeholder for which is the Big Bang, or the Big Bounce. Both postulations beg the childlike question: What happened before that? Neither science nor religion answers satisfactorily. Zen resolves the dilemma by insisting that the question itself has little or no relevance to the immediate problems of the living.

Rationalism: Chaos

If you are a scientist, any definition of top-of-mind problems commanding your attention would probably vary widely, and from those of other scientists, depending upon your specialty. But the overarching nemesis of the rationalist worldview may be generalized as a tendency toward chaos or disorder, that of unbridled nature as well as that of human society. The fears we face in everyday life are heightened by a sense that things are spinning out of control, either of our own limited resources or those of the powers that be. Examples of the latter would include anarchy and lawlessness on the social level, which seem always on the rise, perhaps owing to the current worldwide 24/7,

365-day obsessive reporting. Unbridled nature similarly generates anxiety over chaotic systems such as climate change and its effects on local weather patterns. On the strictly personal level, existential anguish—primarily prompted by the aforementioned cardinal forms of suffering: aging, sickness, and death—bridges both the natural and the societal in one fell swoop. Pandemic stands as proof of concept.

The rationalist approach attempts to anticipate chaos and to develop solutions that serve to prevent or limit resultant suffering for which the onset of local chaos is the proximate cause. This underscores an urgent emphasis on predictability in the earth sciences, as well as in the social realm.

The scope of scientific endeavors toward these ends is expanding exponentially along with advancing technologies to address disruptive emergencies of the world. Natural ecosystems along with national and world economics play increasingly critical and interactive roles. Public health threats such as pestilence, crop-failure-driven famine, as well as pandemic and epidemic outbreaks, represent the interface of human and natural disasters. Maintaining social order through enhanced crowd-control techniques, policing actions, and military defense increasingly challenges the resources and agility of governance worldwide. Where we cannot prevent disaster, the thrust is toward greater predictive ability and faster, more efficient and more effective first-response teams.

In the context of this degree of complexity, exacerbated by the increasing rate of change, we might suggest "control" rather than knowledge as the primary goal of rationalism. Control over circumstances necessarily depends upon knowledge, both of the causes and potential solutions of specific problems as they emerge. While gaining knowledge may be interesting in and of itself, its value is increasingly driven by our common need to control nature, including human nature.

Recent expansion of the use of remote-controlled drones is only one of many double-edged examples. They can be used for good or evil, depending upon their operators and the mission. Like all machines, they are subject to operator error. Control and chaos, as parodied in the 1960s television comedy *Get Smart*, may still be seen as two main competing forces of the world. But there is nothing funny about it. Young recruits in middle America fly drone sorties in the Middle East like an electronic game, but one that inflicts terror, death, and destruction on "enemies" on the ground nearly 10,000 miles away in a modern iteration of forever warfare. When will they ever learn? as the folk song plaintively asks.

One serious limitation of rational thought may be seen in our tendency to define chaos from a strictly human-centric point of view. This is in servitude to our hardwired survival instinct, and an innate preference for the comfort of perceivable order. But this impulse comes with negative consequences to other species. Factory farming is the predictable result of rapacious demand for cheap meat in our daily diet.

Indentured to Self

Our logical-thinking mind (S. citta) cannot perceive or easily conceive the nonseparation of self and other. Consequently, we seem forever stuck in egotistical maneuvering and self-centered manipulation. Or we find ourselves in outright denial of the aforementioned inconvenient truths in order to justify pursuit of ever-more lavish lifestyles and creature comforts.

The rationalist imperative married to our desire for comfort means that much of what we see promoted in the media as solutions to perceived discomforts have little or nothing to do with survival. But they wield enormous appeal to our preference for physical, mental, and emotional pleasure. One standout example is the ubiquitous cosmetics industry, including products promising to make us appear younger, for both men and women. Matsuoka Roshi would often declare: Zen keeps the men younger and the women more beautiful! But he did not mean in the cosmetic sense. The Four Horsemen of the Apocalypse—disease, famine, pestilence, and war—symbolize archetypal threats to human society and to the long-term survival of the species. Nowadays you may have noticed that they comprise more of a thundering herd than a quartet. And that some of the wildest and potentially most destructive horses hail from science itself. These include such bogeymen as the aforementioned atomic genie, angst-ridden prospects of genomic manipulation, controversial harvesting of stem cells, and the daily onslaught of prescription medicines with evermore fanciful names, and ever-longer litanies of potentially damaging and deadly side effects, plus distractions such as billionaires in a space race diverting needed resources from more immediate earthbound needs.

Enslaved to Mammon

Unintended consequences of rational experiments—based on good intentions married to profit motive—add to the anxiety. Past use of DDT to control mosquitoes in malaria prevention resulted in unintended consequent harm to other insects, fish, and birds, finally working its way up to humans at the top of the food chain. This cataclysmic downside, belatedly recognized in spite of such early warning alarms as published in *Silent Spring*, by the sainted Rachel Carson, has shifted our focus from chemical agents to targeted genetic engineering (e.g., of malaria- or zika-resistant mosquitos). This type of scientific engineering may have unknown, equally negative and long-term side effects. Increased attention to self-regulating holistic ecological systems promises a more intelligent approach to human needs, one that not surprisingly is in better balance with the needs of all life-forms.

But when knowledge of ecological constraints rubs up against self-preservation, bottom-line profits, or even mere inconvenience, the result is often unintended consequences. We continue to engender such tragedies as birth defects resulting from prenatal contact with toxic chemicals, such as antiquated lead poisoning, nearly ubiquitous in some urban environments. Loss of species and deforestation can be traced to inefficient modes of transportation, however convenient. Water and air pollution, contamination and disease of livestock, stem from industrial farming practices. This is our world—eight billion and counting—in which the balance inherent in Zen's all-inclusive worldview is needed more than ever. The current pandemic amounts to a blip on the screen in this context.

A Life Worth Living

Other scientific endeavors offer solutions to human suffering through medical prowess in developing life-, health-, and comfort-enhancing technologies, which, though neither foolproof nor final, are mostly welcome, a majority of us would agree. But extreme methods of prolonging life—which science seems increasingly able to develop, and healthcare systems increasingly able to provide, if at an exorbitant cost—can be less than welcome and sometimes repellant, bordering on the irrational. For its ostensible beneficiaries, institutionally imposed extended care often appears arbitrary, and beyond the control of any one group or person. The threat of imminent death may trigger panic and appear chaotic in its arbitrariness. But death is, after all, a natural phenomenon. Viruses are eminently natural.

Eventually, if we continue down this road, human mortality itself may come to be categorized as a medical problem rather than as a natural consequence of life. As things stand, birth inexorably leads to death. But fear of death—both its inevitability and frequent haphazardness—triggers whole movements aimed at promoting longevity, even aspirations to immortality, such as cryogenics and cyborg-inspired replacement parts. As of the most recent audit, nearly 70 percent of the human body has become replaceable with manufactured or transplanted parts. This fact raises existential questions with implications bordering on science-fiction. Recently a COVID-19 patient underwent a successful transplant of both lungs. With accelerating research, can 100 percent replaceability be far from an achievable goal? What part of the body is ultimately irreplaceable? Where are "you" in the middle of this?

In this context, what constitutes "chaos" or "order" becomes a judgment call—definitely in the eye, ear, nose, tongue, body, and mind, of the beholder.

A Higher Form of Order

Phenomena not directly caused or produced by the efforts of humanity, such as natural disasters, usually regarded as examples of chaos, may perhaps more usefully be regarded as manifestations of a higher or subtler, more complex definition of underlying order. But it is difficult to get a positive "feeling for the order lying behind the appearance" in the face of disaster. Attributing such human tragedies to the will of God implies that Nature, ostensibly designed by God, is not necessarily a respecter of persons, as we might hope God would be. Recognition that humans, individually or in the aggregate, may not be the apple of the eye of the universe after all, is the beginning of true humility. The sublimely complex order of the universe ostensibly revealing the mind of God, as some would have it, including Charles Darwin, may necessarily appear as chaos to us mere mortals.

Human beings may be able to recognize only those patterns of order that are preprogrammed into the human nervous system, such as our newborn propensity to recognize faces. If so, to see chaos as order, one would have to be chaotic oneself. We would have to embrace our own self-nature as intrinsically chaotic. To do so we would have to transcend our built-in bias favoring an oversimplification of the complexity of existence into graspable patterns of perceived order. This implies that to recover our original mind, we have to go out of our normal, self-defensive mind.

This view comes close to that of the self in Buddhism. Our so-called self, notably chaotic in at least a few aspects, is not taken for granted in Zen. In zazen, the sense of self is subject to intensely critical and direct examination. The self is a specimen to be dissected under the microscope of Zen, but with great care and compassion. The constructed self may not survive, but the true self will.

Tyranny of Reason

Also worthy of critical examination is the unimpeachable status in which the power of reason is held in secular circles, particularly in the West. Robert Pirsig in *Zen and the Art of Motorcycle Maintenance* (1999) relates a lecture given by the persona of Phaedrus in which he refers to the university as the "Church of Reason." Reason is elevated to the status of a deity and never questioned critically. There is a certain prejudice in modern society to see university credentials as having higher value—reflected in higher access, privilege, prestige, and wages—than the accumulated wisdom of personal experience. For example, the advice of a professional psychologist or counselor with the requisite backdrop of certificates and degrees is given more weight than that of an elder tradesman or a humble housewife. Even though the young psychologist or counselor may be operating based on learned theorems rather than a backlog of experience. Or from youthful irrational exuberance, rather than sage wisdom.

Embracing chaos and the limits of reason, our rational exercise of compassion—or simply doing the right thing, over above and beyond simply serving our own enlightened self-interest—means that critical decision-making and taking decisive action become immensely more complex and demanding. Overweening rational concern for oneself or one's country is counterbalanced by an all-embracing transcendent concern for all the others party to the transaction: universal compassion. This engenders a much more nuanced understanding of international issues, suggesting the development of humane crowd control methods, for example, or addressing the roots of protest and terrorism, rather than resorting to violence or waging war first rather than last, as a default position.

The Just War

The subject of war brings up an anecdote from the life of Buddha. He is said to have once been consulted by a tribe whose leaders were contemplating waging war on a neighboring tribe. Rather than endorse or condemn the proposed aggression outright, he suggested that if both sides would be better off after the conflict, the action may be considered a "just war." Apparently, it was left to the tribal leaders to decide how to know for sure whether both sides would be better off in the aftermath.

Resorting to waging war as the endgame strategy for problem-solving, even to the extreme of genocide, betrays an ingrained resistance to confronting the chaotic complexities of residual intertribal and emerging international conflicts from a perspective of compassion. "Compassion" literally means a willingness to "suffer with." Warfare is the most egregious example of problem-solving gone seriously awry. It admits to an abject failure of diplomacy, not to mention of basic human decency.

Of course, military research and funding programs have resulted in advancements providing material improvements to society, such as synthetic rubber, jet airplanes, nuclear power, and various medical treatments, notably prosthetics, largely in the service of questionable geopolitical objectives, and at a terrible cost in human lives and suffering.

But other examples, such as the fair-trade movement, suggest the potential for positive, win-win outcomes. Simplicity is a value in Zen, as it is in design and other dimensions of life. Simple solutions to even simple problems are often extraordinarily difficult to achieve. But the present prevalence of the oversimplification of complex human situations, based on not-so-hidden agendas, is a disaster not waiting to happen. As the late Vietnamese Zen master Thich Nhat Hanh has said, paraphrasing: to work for world peace you must be world peace. You cannot have a dog in the hunt. You cannot harbor preferences or take sides.

Theism: Sin

Any definition of the central problem of existence—What, if anything, is fundamentally wrong with this life?—is predictably quite different from the point of view of theism as compared to one based on rationalism, and perhaps even more so from the standpoint of Zen. In Christianity, the root problem is sometimes expressed as being born into sin starting with the original fall from grace, or the work of the devil. These concepts are entangled in a firmly held belief in the concrete existence of evil as symbolized by Satan or Beelzebub, the deceiver and tempter. Sin is defined as violating the precepts of God's emissaries on Earth, codified as the Ten Commandments, and characterized by estrangement from the intrinsic good, embodied as the grace of God.

Doctrine rationalizes the suffering condition of humanity as being bereft of God's grace, owing to original sin committed by our primordial ancestors. Eve's eating of the fruit of the tree of knowledge of good and evil started all the trouble. Or rather the snake who tempted her, presumably acting at the behest of the Creator. The primordial prototype couple had been taught what is good and what is evil. They knew the difference. It was the act of willfully experiencing the forbidden—becoming aware of, conceiving of evil—that was the original sin. Initiated by Adam and Eve's actions, humanity has continued to do likewise ever since.

Sin, as defined by the dictionary, constitutes a transgression against divine law. This may not be so far removed from the meaning of chaos in rationalism, or of ignorance in Zen. Each depends upon its own kind of ignorance, whether willful or inborn. Good and evil are in the eye and gut of the beholder, whether informed by scientific evidence or doctrinal belief. The only true evil may stem from an entrenched belief in evil, as an existent reality.

The issues here are admittedly complex, but there is a sense in which the simplest solution is probably the correct one, an article of faith in math and science. Coleridge's ancient mariner's "eye of the beholder" (1798) holds true. What people take to be hateful, good, or evil often varies, depending on the person and the situation. But from this it does not necessarily follow that good and evil are nothing but concepts or opinions.

The concept of sin finds its closest parallel in Zen in the willful ignorance exercised by "monkey mind" (S. citta). Suspending judgment, setting aside all opinions of good and evil and right or wrong, is fundamental to zazen, according to Master Dogen, founder of Soto Zen in thirteenth-century Japan.

Christians are purportedly motivated primarily by concern for the future fate of their immortal souls. Evangelists are ostensibly driven by the apostolic imperative to spread the gospel, and thereby save as many souls of others as they can, and not merely their own. This is similar to the ideal of the bodhisattvas—enlightening beings in Buddhism—who work to save all others in this world of Samsara, before allowing themselves to cross over to the other shore of Nirvana. After you, ma'am.

Saving Others

In Zen we do not attempt to save sinful souls, we only help to free living beings. No one can actually save anyone else, but only hope to help them save themselves through insight into buddha-dharma. This is in line with the precept urging us to not spare the dharma assets. We and our fellow-travelers are not saved from perdition, an eternity in hell, but only from our own innate ignorance, which may be likened to the idea of original sin. The evangelistic rationale for aggressive efforts at conversion is captured in the phrase "Hate the sin, love the sinner." But the sin they claim to hate is not always to be found in the eye of the identified sinner that they claim to love. We all define sin in our own way.

For secularists, atheists, and members of other religions, crusades of salvation via conversion, though well intended, come across as presumptuous and condescending, and essentially demeaning to the targeted convert. The attitude—that unless you understand sin as we do and redeem yourself according to our way, you are doomed—is the most egregious meme of the evangelical movement.

Yet many evangelizing Christians are also actively engaged in real-world problems of survival in their own neighborhoods, as well as all around the world. Evangelists and Catholics especially are known for their charitable works on behalf of the disadvantaged, saving bodies as well as souls. Many of these crusaders put their own lives and well-being at risk. They walk the walk, though you may not agree with the talk they talk. In doing so, they are perhaps, in their own minds, motivated by the expiation of their own sins. If so, their reward is surely in heaven, as they are often excoriated on Earth.

Ironically, evangelist Christians seem to be among those most likely to be caught up in various conspiracy theories broadcast by their professed representatives in political office and amplified by the online echo chamber, notably those who purvey the antivaccination mantra. Estimated at 100 million strong, they are apparently among the most intransigent of antivaxxer holdouts, potentially making the achievement of herd immunity in America a nonstarter, or more accurately, a nonender.

In stark contrast to this kind of salvation and on a more earthly plane, a rational secularist may be moved to pay back society by developing tangible solutions to widespread problems, thus providing a better life for all. Motivated perhaps by a sense of gratitude, or even guilt, for their personal position of privilege, nonetheless the outcome may benefit others. The generalized mission of science—to bring order out of chaos—is thus closely linked to religious efforts to mitigate suffering in the present.

Bodhisattvas in the service of humanistic Buddhism are motivated to save others, along with themselves, from the fundamental ignorance that is at the heart of unnecessary suffering rather than saving sentient beings from natural suffering of aging, sickness, and death, not to mention the daily discomforts built into the fabric of life. Zen is not about avoiding suffering at all costs.

Good and Evil, Right and Wrong

The degree of evil inhering in any situation, behavior, or occurrence depends upon the particulars. This reflects the discipline of applied ethics, the source of traditional rules and regulations of Buddhist monasteries (S. vinaya; J. shingi) and indeed the rule of law of society at large. On one level there is the adolescent who lies to his parents about the booze, drugs, or porn they found in his closet. And then there are the likes of Hitler, Mussolini, or Idi Amin. It would not do to tell the spouse of a murder victim, the survivors of a school shooting, or serial killing spree, or a victim of rape, to name a few instances, that evil is only in the eye of the beholder.

There is good reason that certain actions of body, speech, and mind must be condemned as evil or at least deeply harmful, if people are to live in civilized groups. It is in communities or tribes that humans flourish. Murder, theft, and lying are all detrimental to group cohesion. And therefore must, in some sense, be considered to be evil on a societal level. This does not suggest that there are no instances in which lying, theft, and even murder may have to be committed for the greater good.

Salvation and sin cannot be separated, as may appear to be implied in some doctrines of theism. The former comes only through confession and repentance of the latter. One's salvation can also depend upon taking refuge in a savior, following a prophet's teachings, or absolution by a priest. A human intermediary ostensibly can intercede on our behalf between the provocations here on Earth, the promise of heaven, and the threat of hell—while one's soul hangs precariously in the balance.

This latter rather startling and unabashedly paternalistic promise of absolution is completely antithetical to Buddhism. We may genuinely forgive others their transgressions against ourselves, but this act of compassion and generosity does not mitigate their karmic consequences. In Zen, we practice confession and repentance, but not in order to avoid suffering, or the consequences of past actions, predictable and unintended. The process is internalized. We pay it forward in mitigating our tendency to react poorly to adverse circumstances as if they are not our fault, including knee-jerk blaming of others for our misfortunes. But no one, not even Buddha, can absolve you of your karma.

Zen Buddhism: Ignorance

In Buddhism, the fundamental problem of human existence is most narrowly defined as Ignorance, with a capital I. According to this principle, all existence, including that of human beings, arises from a kind of universal ignorance, not willful but innocent, a primordial not-knowing. We and all other living beings come into this world not knowing what we are getting into. If we did know a priori, and had a choice, we might choose not to be born at all. This idea is implicit in Buddhism's Lesser Vehicle (S. Hinayana), that the objective is to escape the wheel of birth and death. The Greater Vehicle (S. Mahayana) rejects the idea of individual salvation. The Supreme Vehicle of the bodhisattva resolves the conflict through action.

As we gradually become aware of the full extent of the givens of sentient existence outlined as the Four Noble Truths in the First Sermon attributed to Buddha (see figure 2 below), it becomes clear that this life includes some downsides that we did not bargain for, at least as far as we can remember. Whose idea was this, anyway?

Ignorance is the first link in Buddha's comprehensive and foundational model of the dynamic cycles of sentient existence, the Twelvefold Chain of Interdependent Coarising (see figure 4 below). However, this ignorance does not rise to the level of a First Cause. But it does precede and lead to birth, according to this model. While sequestered in the womb there is not yet any conscious awareness of knowing, or exceedingly little. All is inchoate arising, abiding, and decaying. We register only subtle, subliminal sensation, with notable exceptions such as the cravings of a mother who suffers from addiction. But as embryos we are generally all unaware, embedded in a state of fundamental ignorance, floating in a surrounding cocoon of warm amniotic fluid.

Zen embraces and honors this simple not-knowing as the fundamental characteristic of the "don't-know-mind," our built-in original and natural state of innocent awareness. This is not the willful self-serving ignorance of "ignorance is bliss." Most of us enjoy a combination of the two: innocently not knowing and not really wanting to know. We prefer the comfort of shutting out the suffering of a chaotic world to the discomfort of critically examining our assumptions about it, or admitting our complicity in contributing to its ubiquitous suffering.

Innate ignorance is not merely the self-centeredness that emerges after birth. All sentient beings are born through this ignorance, an ambient condition that precedes birth. Being innately self-obsessed is a natural result. Self-centeredness is a symptom, not a cause, of human existence.

But this is not the same as being born into a "state of sin." In Zen, we are born free of the overlay of existential guilt associated with some religious worldviews. However, we are responsible for our own existence (i.e., responsible for what we do with it). We are born into total ignorance, driven by our primordial desire for existence itself. Our birth is not God's fault, nor is it our parents' fault. We assume at least 50 percent responsibility for our own life.

Be careful what you ask for.

In this view even a newborn infant is not entirely innocent, being guilty of the desire to exist. But Zen is forgiving, as we all share this degree of guilt. Buddhism does not add an overseeing judgmental God on top of these constraints, holding us accountable to a set of rules or commandments. The challenge to work out our own salvation is enough. Morality is self-imposed in Zen. Our ignorance is not an irredeemable condition of depravity, but a deficit that can be overcome. But it can only be overcome by distinctly different means than the absolution of sin by others. It is our personal responsibility to overcome our own ignorance via our own intuitive insight, primarily in zazen.

Overcoming Ignorance

Your ignorance or mine does not amount to a personal fatal flaw, but is part of the universal condition of all sentient beings, whether human or not. Knowing arises incipiently in the womb, explodes exponentially with birth, is modified through individuation and throughout our formative years, and matures with aging. Often the tape is eventually rewound, returning to not-knowing with the onset of gerontological and neurological decline such as Alzheimer's. But even while young and robust, our own consciousness, shaped by experience, becomes key to either exacerbating or mitigating our inborn ignorance. In Zen, we confront ignorance without intermediary by studying the self in meditation.

According to Buddhism the most problematic consequence of ignorance is our unexamined belief in what Zen calls the "constructed" self. As Socrates by way of Plato reminds us: the unexamined life is not worth living. Just so, the unexamined self is not worth reifying. Most human problems—those we inflict upon ourselves as well as upon the rest of the world—stem from our belief in this imputed self. The human tragicomedy is played out through projection of our self-centered biases onto all aspects of daily life. Overcoming innate clinging to this false self is the initial problem-solving task assigned to us by the prescripts of Zen.

The Zen solution to living happily, compassionately, and wisely is not to be found solely in rationally controlling external conditions to the degree possible in an uncaring universe. Nor is salvation guaranteed via expiating our sins through contrition, confession, and redemption in the eyes of a forgiving God.

In Zen both external and internal sets of conditions—the surrounding chaos and our error-prone biology-and-psychology-driven impulses—are regarded as the "givens" of existence. The central problem is our own intransigence, not the particular temporal, environmental, and biological circumstances in which we find ourselves. On the behavioral front, Buddhism's prescriptions and precepts include the notion that unwholesome, self-centered actions generally bring unwholesome and unwelcome results, while wholesome or selfless actions bring wholesome results. However, there are no guarantees. What goes around does not always come around, at least not in timely fashion, and certainly not as an equal and opposite reaction. Karma is not Newtonian. And we do not control it.

Surrendering the Self

The most meaningful control in Zen is self-control. To a greater degree than we may find comfortable, we must relinquish our fantasy of total control over our circumstances. Clinging to the delusion of control is one of the main impediments to realizing our birthright: the wisdom and compassion of the buddhas. It also goes against the teachings of religions such as Islam and Christianity, which require belief in a self or soul that we surrender to a higher power, so that we can enter into the divine presence of God, or the tender embrace of his prophets and only begotten son, Jesus Christ.

In Buddhism we are to surrender the very belief in a self-existent self or soul. This is considered to be the most charitable, the most selfless, of all actions. Like all forms of charity, this process begins at home. In Zen it is actualized on the cushion, embracing the human condition, and our individual place within it, with humility. If we are able to do so, others may be encouraged to do the same.

By extension, questioning the integrity of the self argues against imposing our will upon others in our personal orbit. Or on the international level, forcing our vaunted cultural and societal customs upon other peoples of the Earth. In a postcolonial world, it is even more important to put one's own house in order first. If we can form a more perfect union in our own backyard, others may be inspired by our example. This true holds on both personal and social spheres of influence.

But Buddhism goes further and deeper. All beings, all of Nature, and indeed the planet itself must be nurtured, embraced within the Magnanimous Mind (J. daishin) of Zen. This is the main message of the Loving Kindness Sutra (S. Metta Sutta) chanted frequently in Zen centers (Sotoshu 2001):

May all beings be happy.
May they be joyous and live in safety,
All living beings, whether weak or strong,
In high or middle or low realms of existence.
Small or great, visible or invisible
Near or far, born or to be born
May all beings be happy

It would be difficult to find a more all-inclusive, warmer embrace of all living beings than this excerpt from a teaching attributed to Buddha. Every conceivable and inconceivable form of life is cited. But we should understand that Buddha was not being sentimental. He is suggesting that all beings be happy with life as it is, not as we might fantasize it could or should be. The natural suffering of aging, sickness, and death included. This message was addressed to human beings, of course. Bearing witness to and embracing the suffering of all is Buddhism' prescription for mitigating our own personal suffering. Helping oneself by helping others becomes all the more obvious during a pandemic.

There is said to be a backstory to this teaching. Buddha and his growing community had gathered in the local forest. Through his enhanced situational awareness, Buddha realized that the trees around them were "unhappy." The impact of such a concentration of human population must have overstressed the natural environment. This teaching may be the first recorded sermon on stewardship of the ecological landscape. It goes to the Buddhist principle that all life is interconnected. Mother Nature ain't happy, ain't nobody happy, as we are learning once again to our chagrin, from the disastrous global damage and disruptions of climate change.

Resisting Suffering

In order to find personal release from suffering, we must first recognize the problem and overcome our own ingrained resistance to suffering. This resistance is not capricious or arbitrary. It is based on survival, including that of the species. Many of the discomforts we frequently experience, particularly those that are physical in origin such as acrid tastes and smells, or loud noises, may signal threats to our safety and survival.

But Zen's teachings assure us that as human beings, unlike animals in thrall to raw instinct, we are uniquely capable of surrendering the grasping, paranoid self and awakening to realization of our true self. That we can, indeed, not just in thought, transcend the fundamental ignorance from which all existence arises. But more specifically, we can disabuse ourselves of the blind ignorance of Buddha's foundational teaching, his original analysis of the problem of suffering in this life. Unless, of course, we continue willfully ignoring these disorienting truths.

Willful ignorance finds its apogee in our futile insistence that we are in total control of our fate. This stubborn trait places us in denial of the teachings of buddha-dharma, particularly in regard to the first of the Four Noble Truths, which proclaims the ubiquity and inevitability of suffering, inexorable change, in any and all corporeal existence. Buddhism defines the origin of suffering as obsessive craving or thirst and holds out the promise of realization of its cessation. Then comes the prescription for an effective approach to navigating the dimensions of daily life, the Eightfold Path (figure 3). As examples of semantic modeling, the figures illustrate the interconnectedness of the constituent components and also function as mnemonics. (For further examples of Mahayana Buddhist teachings, see foldout poster in jacket pocket.)

Like the noble gases, The Four Noble Truths are inert. They do not interact with causes and conditions, and do not vary with circumstance. They are ennobling when we come to see them as simply describing reality, and what we may do to live harmoniously in the face of natural suffering.

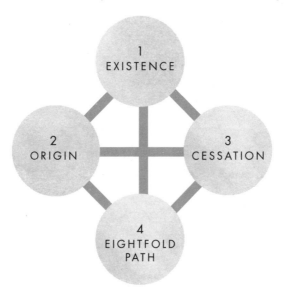

FIGURE 2. Four Noble Truths

This fundamental teaching diagnoses the sickness of the world of humanity. Buddha first defines the existence of suffering as our reactive dissatisfaction with the inevitability of intractable change. Things insist on changing when we want them to stay the same. Other things stubbornly refuse to change when we desperately want and need them to do so.

Then he pinpoints the primary source, the exacerbating origin of suffering: our own personal craving or thirst. The most common examples of human craving and the suffering it brings stem from our dissatisfaction with the changing circumstances of our daily lives, ranging from our inheritance, both genetic and material, to our present livelihood and beyond.

More central to ultimate well-being is our craving for living existence itself. We celebrate birth but mourn death. You may argue that we do not control aging, sickness, and death, and you would be correct. But a Zen practitioner would retort that birth is the leading cause of death. You can't have one without the other, notwithstanding faith claims to the contrary, such as the ascension of Christ.

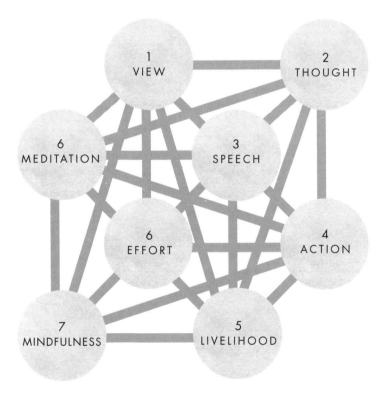

FIGURE 3. Eightfold Path

Third, Buddha offers a prognosis: we are to abandon craving as the bitter medicine we must take in order to effect its cure, the potential cessation of suffering. Relinquishing craving, however, does not result in its disappearance as a central driving force of our life. Craving is built in. How we react to it is the key. The cessation of suffering does not equate to the cessation of craving. Intentionally inflicted suffering, the kind we inflict upon others, upon ourselves, and upon the natural world, can come to an end. Feelings of craving, however, much like the experience of aging, sickness, and death, cannot come to an end, being built into existence itself. Even pursuing enlightenment is going astray.

Fourth, Buddha prescribes a thoroughgoing therapeutic regimen for total physical, mental, and emotional health and maintenance: following the Eightfold Path in daily life, beginning and ending with the practice of meditation (figure 3). Buddha is sometimes regarded as a physician, or the first psychologist. In diagnosing our disease, he shone the light of wisdom on the primary sickness of the world: self-centered striving, based upon a witches' brew of primordial and willful ignorance. Then he made a prognosis, offered a prescription, and developed a therapy for treating what ails us holistically. Following doctor's orders is up to the patient. Take your medicine.

Ignorance of all kinds, natural and intentional, innocent or willful, drives the universal conjoined principles of karma and rebirth. Karma is based on a root word meaning "action." Karma is usually oversimplified in its popular interpretation to resemble Newton's third law of motion: for every action there is an equal and opposite reaction. Of course, it is not all that simple. But in karmic theory, consequential reactions are not necessarily equal or opposite. Further, they may carry over from past actions to the present and from the present to future lifetimes. Whether karma is true or not is unprovable, but it would be wise to come down on the side of caution, avoiding such actions as may boomerang to our woe.

Ignorance also underlies humankind's inhumanity to humanity, as well as to other sentient beings. We err at our peril when we ignore the interconnectedness of all living beings. Individual states of ignorance, manifesting as your unique karmic consciousness as well as mine, are the root of the problem.

Ignorance is the predictable result of our attachment to ego, the self-constructed self. It can be overcome only by surrendering our grip on this false self. When ego is completely relinquished, the true self stands revealed. This is called "dying on the cushion": somewhat akin to being born again, but without the mystic overlay. In Zen, we begin by alleviating our ignorance of the nonexistence of the self through brutally honest self-examination, on the cushion and off.

Embracing Karma

If we engage in willful ignorance of Zen's basic facts of existence, our misguided actions as well as inactions will simply weave an ever more tangled web of karmic consequence. Every day we add threads to our very own Gordian knot of the causes and conditions of future suffering. According to classical Buddhism, if we do not take care of business in this life, the consequences will inevitably revisit our karmic descendants in future lives. We really have no choice in the matter. But we can choose to take care of business the easy way or the hard way.

Our aversion to suffering leads us to reject the very idea of karmic causality. Isn't it enough that we suffer the indignities—Hamlet's "slings and arrows of outrageous fortune"—from this lifetime? Do we really need to pile on with yet more guilt and self-shaming from possible former lives? Is past inevitably prologue? Current variations on this question may be found in the debate over teaching critical race theory (CRT) in public schools, and the issue of reparations in general. The impelling fear underlying the anti-CRT charge, bogus or not, is that impressionable students in their formative years will be damaged by exposure to the reality of their ethnic ancestors' past racist behavior, feeling shame and guilt as a result. Reparations for past inequities is more clearly a transactional proposal, but one which also entails admitting to a kind of karmic carryover, triggered not by individual actions, but those of the collective cohort. Karma is conceived as shared. It comes bundled with the operating system, not solitary in either its origins or its outcomes.

But Buddhism urges us to accept that not all karmic consequences are negative. They can be positive, or even neutral. Just breathing or not breathing for the next five minutes has the consequence of dying or not dying, or possible brain damage. Whether you regard this as karmic, or feel that it is positive, negative, or neutral, depends on proximate causes and conditions. For persons on their death bed, five minutes can represent an agonizing prolongation of unnecessary suffering. For the young and healthy, five more minutes of life may amount to a net positive. In the desert, water becomes such a scarce commodity that one person's thirst-quenching drink can be another's death. In the case of desperate immigrants trapped and suffocating in an abandoned tractor trailer, just breathing may mean that others are deprived of life-giving oxygen.

Karmic results are not always explainable as reactions to known actions, committed within this lifetime. It is not simply a matter of "what goes around comes around." The theory of karmic consequences following unidentified actions addresses Job's nagging question: Why me, Lord? It might also help embrace the suffering that such a question raises. Karmic theory would ask you to ask: Why not me? What makes me so special that I should be exempt from the laws of causality?

Known Issues

Most of the problems we face today as individuals in communities, across nations, and in international relations stem from the same sources as those prevalent in ancient times. According to Zen, it all begins with the mistaken reification of the self, and the ramifications of that misbegotten belief, representing the nadir and zenith of ignorance. In other words, this is the mother of all known issues.

The horror stories that currently comprise our daily informational diet, fed by news media across our ever-shrinking globe, are largely outcomes of this same ignorance, identified so long ago as clinging to the self and its extensions. They are further fueled by secular religion in the form of culturally approved belief systems, which attempt to substitute a concept of reality for reality itself. Our mission of propagating authentic Zen practice in a theistic cultural context may have something to learn from the history of its spread from India through the disparate cultures of China and Japan.

The social milieu in which Buddha originally taught was shaped by prevalent influences such as Hinduism and ancient Vedic traditions. In clarifying the difference in his teachings, he necessarily had to be mindful of this context, referencing the prevailing memes and received wisdom of the time. A cursory reading of the early transcriptions of sutras may sound like Hinduism warmed over, but the sutras actually comprise a reformation of the earlier teachings. Later, as Buddhism spread to China, it assimilated aspects of Taoism as well as Confucianism, including redefining the panoply of gods, notably Quan Yin (S. Avalokiteshvara; J. Kannon) aka the bodhisattva of compassion. When Zen reached Japan, it cultivated harmonious relationships with indigenous religious customs, rather than competing with them. Zen's zazen kept it agile and vital, enabling it to fit into various cultures.

In recent times, adherents of nondharmic religions are sometimes open to differing viewpoints and practices such as those of Buddhism, mainly in the context of interfaith dialogue. Some are inclined to experiment with meditation, especially when presented as a form of centering prayer. But since most religions are based upon strict adherence to doctrinal belief, it is understandable that their leaders would tend to be somewhat closed to any idea or practice that may seem to contradict or threaten those beliefs. But this very close-mindedness, which is often regarded as a virtue and keeping the faith, can become an inhibiting force in the lives of the flock. When dogma or slavish devotion to the dictates of the group's leadership is privileged over personal experience, it may prevent individual members from exploring their own spiritual insight. In extreme cases, this kind of groupthink can result in a cult.

Cult of Self

The other major religions of the world appear to regard Zen as the meditation sect of Buddhism, as a kind of harmless cult. But Zen communities are typically the opposite of a cult. We train everyone who is willing, ready, and able in Zen's uniquely simple method of meditation. All sincere seekers are welcome to consider entering the formal path to priesthood, though we do not promote the idea as a goal or objective. We employ modern skillful group decision processes to manage the operation of the organization, usually as a not-for-profit corporation, with full transparency.

On the personal front, Buddhism points to the present reality before your face as the first principle of Zen, rather than a belief-based or philosophical concept of that reality, however much our peers may pressure us to join a consensus. This emphasis on the individual is intrinsic to Zen's vitality.

Rationalists in general and scientists in particular appear to be somewhat more open-minded than religious leaders, as might be expected based on their claims to objectivity. But many nonaligned novices, when exposed to Zen teachings, prefer to ignore Buddhism's stringent prescriptions for living. They just want the "Zen part," not what they regard as its cultural trappings. This is a symptom of how deeply ingrained our cultural ignorance, or tunnel vision, really is. The social and personal spheres cannot be cast asunder, any more than can the sacred and the mundane. We constantly pile self-serving, willful ignorance on top of our natural burden of simply not-knowing, which is why Zen meditation typically requires so much time. We carry a lot of personal baggage belonging to the self.

The social self is assailed by the rancorous tenor of the times, exacerbated by emerging hegemonies of quasi-religious factions, technologies of social media, and hardening ideologies of political parties. The availability of military-style weapons has amplified to a frightening degree the amount of damage that a single misguided individual, or a small minority, can and will inflict upon large numbers of innocents. Mass murders on an international level and school shootings at the local level have dictated a new normal level of stress in daily life across the globe, and especially in the United States. Combined natural/ manmade disasters such as the current pandemic unpredictably pop up, impelled by the interconnectedness of all beings. Internationally, the nuclear genie threatens to escape the bottle again.

According to traditional Buddhism, these horrific attempts to terrorize, dominate, and exact vengeance on others, and the endless cycle of retribution they fuel, can do nothing to balance out the karmic consequences of the past. In fact, they only exacerbate them and, according to Buddhism, lead to rebirth for those who have lost their lives in the carnage, and potential retribution in future lives.

While this proposition from traditional Hindu and Buddhist sources may seem a reach, Zen is not alone in attempting to comprehend the incomprehensible. Any proffered rationales for these horrific acts fail the test of common sense. The most absurd may be that the very commission of such atrocities opens the path to a promised heavenly reward through martyrdom, as some purportedly believe, and whose leaders preach such fantasies. This is not the first case in history where doctrine was distorted to fit a secular objective. Holy warfare, whether in the Abrahamic or Buddhist context, is a personal, and not a social, struggle. All religions and most philosophies agree that this life is a testing ground.

Such bellicose actions seem to do little to bring about the much-ballyhooed apocalypse of self-destructive dystopian beliefs, but only concoct a wishful temporal caricature of that fatal fantasy. It certainly looks like Armageddon. But it is just a passing foolish fancy. Then the next generation fecklessly, mindlessly, and endlessly repeats the process of retribution. But they come by it honest. It is their legacy from their lineage. When will we ever learn?

From the machinations of our own ignorance, we fabricate heaven or hell right here on Earth, and unfortunately, predominately the latter. People cause most of the world's troubles, primarily owing to ignorance, both willful and innocent, of the simple truths of buddha-dharma. Surrendering the self through Zen's meditation process, or living according to the selfless example of Jesus, or following the actual teachings of Muhammad, is the only hope for a sustainable peace in this world. Zazen is the most we can do to take action in resolving the personal with the social. It takes a community, not a cult.

DIMENSION 3.
ATTITUDES NURTURED: PERSEVERANCE, FAITH, DOUBT

Just as "why," "how," and "what" questions cannot be completely separated, likewise whatever attitudes, qualities, virtues, and disciplines people nurture to cope with life also overlap, like a Venn diagram.

Whether Atheist, Christian, Muslim, Jew, Buddhist, or other faith, the exercise of perseverance and faith, as well as doubt, occurs not in a vacuum, but each operates in concert with the other two. In an imperfect world they often manifest in pairs, rather than as a balanced triad.

Whipping up a frenzy of faith and perseverance absent any reasonable doubt, the combination can foster a dangerous zealotry, whether secular or religious. A healthy dose of doubt can have a tempering effect upon the tendency to become overzealous in our beliefs, ideology, theories, and delusions.

Wallowing in doubt, on the other hand, with no leavening effect of aspiration—or perversely persévering in spite of doubt, but totally lacking in faith—can lead to skepticism, and end in profound cynicism. If, instead, we simply career from doubt to faith and back with no real perseverance, we fall into endless vacillation. This is probably the most unstable of the three combinations of unbalanced pairs, leading to terminal indecision.

Perseverance pays in all three fields: rationalism, theism, as well as Zen. And it is perhaps equally important to each. In rationalist endeavors, proof of concept requires a trial-and-error process. In theism, having a theology relevant to modern times involves revising, or at least rephrasing, early interpretations of doctrine. Each of us has to reinvent Zen for ourselves, which does not come easily.

We have all witnessed countless examples of these out-of-balance syndromes in the passing pageantry of public life. With any one of the three missing, they function about as well as a two-legged stool. Perhaps you have found yourself unwittingly stuck in one of these lopsided combinations, especially during the pandemic. You can't spell pandemic without "panic." But don't panic.

Rationalism: Perseverance

Nurturing an attitude of perseverance needs little or no explanation. Perseverance pays, as we say, if not always. It is a central trait of the scientific method, and for that matter, of all rational endeavors. If you are a scientist, you are committed to persevering through experiment after experiment, despite inconclusive results. A premature "eureka" moment of insight experienced in the theoretical phase often turns out to be invalid when you do the math or put it to the test in the lab. Or so I am told.

Our first glimmering of understanding in any experiment, including Zen's meditation, has to stand the test of time. We are forever going back to the drawing board, the chalkboard—or nowadays the keyboard—in most of our creative endeavors. A scientist faces at least four prospects:

> Believing a hypothesis to be true when it is indeed true.
> Believing it to be true when it is actually false.
> Rejecting it as false when it may actually be true.
> Rejecting it as false when it is indeed false.

What the final resolution turns out to be depends primarily on perseverance.

The main difference between a world-class scientist and a mediocre scientist is said to be the ability of the former to recognize the futility of a line of inquiry more quickly than the latter and thus more quickly cut your losses and turn to a more promising prospect. The same may be said of any complex field of endeavor. Persevering down blind alleys is not valued in the arts, though it may appear to be to an outsider. Nor is indulging in trivial pursuits encouraged in Zen. Tilting at windmills is probably not considered a virtue in theology either.

All would agree that perseverance itself cannot be the sole or even the key determinate of success of any rational enterprise. More important is the choice of experiment (i.e., its relevance to focusing on the current most critical problems). Asking the right questions is crucial to meaningful inquiry and to developing significant useful results. Whether in the arts and sciences or in theological or philosophical inquiry or in Zen, the quality of the questions asked is the best predictor of the quality of the answers.

A frequent finding in research is that the subject "needs more study." Which finding necessitates more funding? Which meets one of the objectives of any study: to continue to dig deeper and evolve as further discoveries are made? Degree of completion is like the proverbial rainbow, forever receding from our grasp. In implementation phases of design, this phenomenon is known as "scope creep."

Persevering in Zen

In Zen, persevering in questioning the question itself is difficult and may lead to analysis-paralysis. But it is absolutely necessary to the spirit and depth of any inquiry. This is the starting point for Zen: the question itself. We continually return to the initial question on the cushion, namely: What is this? What am I doing? Or what is actually happening? Scope creep in Zen is a naturally deepening inquiry.

Theism: Faith

No one can presume to understand the depth of meaning that their faith may have to someone else. What another person means by their faith may be entirely different from what you mean by your faith. It is undeniable that a great many people frequently rely on their faith to meet the vicissitudes of life. Our intent is to characterize faith faithfully, in its conventional interpretation as it is used, or misused, in the vernacular.

In theistic religious doctrine, faith is not readily separated from belief. The terms "faith" and "belief" can be applied interchangeably, often expressed as: What is your faith? Or, What do you believe? Implied in this use of faith is an adherence to specific doctrines: for example, the divinity of Christ, inerrancy of scripture, intercession of the savior or saints, and access to God through prayer. In Hinduism, active faith may be vested in Shiva or Vishnu as aspects of the Supreme Parabrahman. Or one may profess faith in the Greek Earth Mother Gaia manifested as a living planet, nurturing all forms of life in her stewardship. One person's faith may be another's superstition, and vice versa.

Faith is often defined as absolute, rock-solid, an unshakable confidence in the verity of beliefs. Believers continue to rely on faith in the face of, and in spite of, a complete lack of evidence, even massive evidence to the contrary, contravening closely held beliefs. Blind faith of a generalized sort can be held up to the same rational criticism as particular beliefs, as woefully lacking in evidence and completely devoid of logic as well as potentially threatening to the integrity of rational society. The ongoing resistance to wearing masks in the face of a global pandemic smacks of this kind of irrational faith.

Testing Faith

Witnessing a miracle is sometimes cited as primary evidence proving a given belief, or the tenets of a faith. Such evidence comes in the form of personal testimony. Its credibility relies on the credentials of the person testifying as "expert testimony" or on the corroborating testimony of others if available. But memory is known to be unreliable and malleable. Mass hypnosis looms as a possibility, even in the testimony of multitudes.

Faith can be severely tested by dire circumstances. Intense suffering witnessed by or visited upon true believers can challenge their faith. The upside is that it can shake us out of our complacency. One downside is that it can undermine an unshakeable faith in a just God. This is particularly true of the kind of absolute faith that leaves no room for doubt.

You may be familiar with a story about Mother Teresa. The great Sister of Mercy received a lot of attention in the press, both before and after her death. The posthumous publication of her journals revealed a deep and long-term crisis of faith. Like most serious people, she began to harbor certain doubts, perhaps manifested as no longer feeling the presence of God, which she kept to herself while living. Such a crisis of faith is certainly understandable, especially in her case, given the unrelenting suffering she witnessed on a daily basis in her ministry in India. The local Sisters of Mercy mission is a few doors down from our house, and my wife attended when Mother Teresa visited. The great spiritual exemplar gave her a sound smack on the forehead.

In the cauldron of daily life, religious convictions are likely to be tested, leading some to question their own fundamental worldview. When one's faith is severely tested, it may trigger a life crisis, the resolution of which might go either way: total denunciation of prior beliefs, or an epiphany as to their deeper meaning.

Faith may be said to be reliable if it can survive the challenges of lived experience (i.e., suffering). The litmus test is the inevitable onset of aging, sickness, and death, Buddhism's classic benchmarks of sentient suffering. But worse yet is the unnecessary suffering inflicted upon ourselves through self-loathing, and upon others by the very act of "othering," even upon our closest, most beloved ones, through harmful speech and actions, intentional or unintentional. As the old country music standard reminds us: you always hurt the one you love. If one's faith or belief system can withstand the slings and arrows of misfortune, both natural and man-made, it can be considered a true faith.

Faith in Science and Zen

In rational endeavors such as scientific research and development, faith may be defined as confidence, or trust. We have faith in the empirical method, in the ability and integrity of colleagues and associates, and in the body of evidence accumulated over time by professional execution of the specialty's disciplines.

In Zen, we have faith in the Ancestors, fully confident that they were not charlatans. And we have a certain amount of faith in the praxis they have passed on to us, in spite of stark differences of our present circumstances. Zen practice leads to finding faith, or spiritual confidence, in life itself. The earliest tract on Ch'an Buddhism recited in Zen liturgy yet today translates as "Trust in Mind." This is trust in Buddha-mind, or the original mind, as opposed to the untrustworthy monkey mind.

Competency in driving an automobile may imbue us with a certain confidence that we can learn to drive a truck, though we may harbor serious doubts about the challenges a long-haul tractor trailer would present. But confidence in the reliability of the original mind is not dependent upon any specific competency. Buddha-mind is not limited to any particular situation or set of circumstances.

Through Zen practice we can become more accepting of our existential reality, embracing our own limitations as well as those of our present situation. We develop faith in the methodical process of zazen. This practice cultivates patience with ourselves, enabling us to become naturally patient with others, which pays dividends in any stressful or challenging situation. We develop a faith that outside our comfort zone and level of competency, we can engage with confidence. We have nothing to lose.

Zen Buddhism: Doubt

You may find it contradictory to suggest that any spiritual practice worthy of the name would intentionally nurture an attitude of doubt. Doubt does not feel reliable. But the doubt spoken of in Zen is of a different order. Faith and doubt—and to a lesser degree, perseverance, as they function in Zen—do not fit neatly into rational scientific, theistic, or cultural definitions.

Zen's exercise of faith is not faith in a system of beliefs, nor is it conventional professional confidence in one's personal competency. Doubt does not jeopardize Zen practice but reinforces it. Perseverance in Zen is in the face of doubt, not attached to a known, preferred, or hopeful outcome.

Yet another trio of terms—teaching, practice, and enlightenment—were introduced in an early American Zen classic, *Three Pillars of Zen*, by Philip Kapleau, Roshi (2013). He also discusses faith and doubt, along with determination, rather than perseverance. I choose to emphasize perseverance over determination as the latter implies too high a degree of purposeful intent. Perseverance simply means never giving up, one of my teacher's frequent encouragements. All three legs are considered necessary to the practice of Zen. Absent one leg, the stool is rendered unstable. To propose doubt as essential to stability may seem doubly oxymoronic.

In Zen, faith and its complement, doubt, occupy differing but central positions, the yin and yang of emotion. Doubt is the emotional content of faith, the way faith feels viscerally. Faith cannot exist separately from doubt. The experience of doubt tests our faith. The more doubt we feel, the more faith we are called upon to exercise—much like courage, which is not the absence of fear but the ability to act in the presence of great fear. Faith is the ability to persevere, to take wise or compassionate action. To do what is necessary in the face of nagging doubt. In Zen, faith is not blind, the total absence of doubt, but quite the opposite. Faith in the dharma and its masters is not absolute, but to be examined on the cushion.

There are two basic kinds of doubt broadly defined by Zen thought. One is insidious doubt, characterized, for example, by a lack of trust in Buddha's teaching. Or by an unwarranted suspicion of one's teacher. Or even by a sense of personal inadequacy. You may be familiar with this kind of doubt. Its variations on a theme are to be recognized, engaged, and examined thoroughly, rather than suppressed. But then they are to be set aside or overcome through Zen practice.

The other kind is called Great Doubt, capitalized to emphasize the reverence in which it is held. Great Doubt comes about through the contemplation of all that we do not know and cannot know. Contemplate not in the intellectual sense, but in the directly concrete sense. Buddha himself sat down in desperation at the end of his six-year spiritual quest. Recognizing in all humility that in spite of his great erudition, he did not know what he fundamentally needed to know. Great Doubt subsumes all.

Doubting Self

Intentionally engaging in self-doubt is prescribed in Zen: not in the sense of wallowing in feelings of personal inadequacy, but rather in deploying a healthy skepticism regarding the falsity of the constructed self. Doubt sharpens our penetration of the nature of the senses in zazen, illuminating the true self. Doubt tempers and informs our own opinions of all the above. Doubt is our friend.

Self-doubt of this kind is the natural focus of our Zen meditation practice, where it is nurtured assiduously. An old saying admonishes Zen practitioners: keep your doubt at a keen edge. Zazen is the sharpening stone. Zen itself is the razorblade, cutting through everything without discrimination.

Sharpening the edge of doubt focuses our effort on doubting the validity of our own self and our own opinions, rather than doubting others. Of course, we do not blindly follow others, abandoning common sense. But projecting doubt onto others may be misplaced, a kind of evasive maneuver. When our self-doubt is nurtured, it grows, eventually subsuming everything into its sphere of influence. This is the ever-expanding arena of inquiry in Zen, eventually becoming universal in scope.

Confronting Great Doubt

The entirety of our existence ultimately comes into question when we deeply challenge our own cherished preconceptions about reality. In its full-blown manifestation, ordinary doubt accumulates to become all-inclusive Great Doubt. Existence—the whole universe—becomes one big question mark. Zen regards this kind of doubt as the necessary prerequisite for plumbing the depths and assaying the breadth of Buddha's truth. His tongue is said to be "broad and deep." Great Doubt is the true antecedent of genuine spiritual insight, to borrow a term from the discipline of critical path management. This all-encompassing doubt is synonymous and simultaneous with the arousal of the "don't-know mind," the humble opposite of the know-it-all mind.

A growing comfort with and deepening trust in this type of doubt, nurtured in zazen, fortifies our patient acceptance of the ambiguity inherent in existence. This increasing power of patience has a halo effect upon our daily life, where we are often challenged with ambiguous situations. This does not, however, lead to an unthinking acquiescence to whatever comes our way. Zen does not turn you into a welcome mat. But developing patience with the foolish self, as witnessed on the cushion, gives us the grace to practice greater patience with the foolishness of others. When we manifest patience, others are enabled to reciprocate in kind, suffering fools a little more gladly, including our foolish self.

Our burgeoning ability to live with doubt helps us to refine the skillful means necessary for coping with everyday stress, and to develop the resolve necessary to exercise true faith. The hallmark of the exercise of faith is the ability to engage in compassionate action in the face of emotional doubt. It relies upon living with and nurturing the question, rather than craving, and settling for, pat answers.

Asking the most salient questions is of key importance in Zen, as in all rational pursuits. Great scientists ask the great questions. To state the obvious, asking questions is an admission that we don't know the answers. But this does not mean that we should stifle our natural urge to ask, to investigate and inquire. Not knowing the answers is the antidote to doubt, especially when it comes to the central questions in life. Ultimately, we cannot know what we cannot know. And that's okay.

Zen's Trusty Tricycle

Zen models confidence—mental and emotional stability—physically, in the posture of its meditation, whether sitting cross-legged, kneeling, or on a chair. Zazen emulates the tetrahedron of geometry, the simplest and most stable of the primary solids: three-point base, head at the top. Think of zazen as a three-legged stool in motion, more like a tricycle, more balanced than a bicycle. No need for training wheels.

Zen's faith is confidence in our original buddha-nature, which we are seeking to rediscover, or recover, in zazen. This forms the lynchpin that keeps the wheels from coming off, as we persevere in the face of doubt. Faith and doubt are inseparable in Zen, mutually defining.

Zen also finds balance in the interplay of the Three Treasures: Buddha, dharma, and sangha, as necessary to complete the Zen Way. This is a tricycle we can trust to take us safely to the other shore of awakening. Tricycle also designates the three times in Zen: past, future, and present. We strive to maintain the Three Treasures throughout the cycle of the three times.

Buddha is our experience in meditation. Dharma is the recorded guidelines from our lineage. Sangha is the community of Zen folks in history as well as today. This trio comprises the trifold praxis of Zen: meditation, study, and community. We can practice meditation on our own, even in forced isolation, as during the pandemic. But eventually we want to rejoin others in the community. We can practice Zen without studying, but eventually we seek clarification of our own experience in the written record, or living experience of teachers and peers. You cannot get rid of the three, whether wheels of the tricycle or legs of the stool. You have to find your own balance between them.

As we age, it becomes more hazardous to ride a bicycle. With our sense of balance deteriorating, the danger of falling becomes a serious issue. Walking meditation (J. kinhin) helps greatly with this. But with the third wheel of an adult-sized tricycle, the danger is much diminished. Saddle up on the trusty tricycle of Zen meditation. You will enjoy the ride.

DIMENSION 4.
ENTITIES TRUSTED: EVIDENCE, SAVIOR, SELF-NATURE

Though similar in meaning to faith, trust differs in that it is invested in something or someone specific whereas faith may reflect a generalized embrace of doctrine or worldview. Trust in others can be disappointed, as we all know all too well. Trust can be manipulated. It can be misplaced, in a group or an individual in a position of leadership. Cult leaders are the poster boys for this truism. But it may also be true of your local religious and political leaders, or your remote-learning mentors and teachers. No field is exempt from incompetent and dishonest, or merely negligent figureheads.

Placing too much trust in any one member of our family, our network of friends or, most egregiously, in our political leaders who campaign and are elected based on our trust, may lead to betrayal, intentional or not, of that very trust. Persons fulfilling critical roles in your life as parents and guardians, family and friends, colleagues, priests and ministers, doctors and nurses, are after all fallible human beings. We cannot and should not trust them for everything, particularly not for our birthright in Zen, the pursuit of spiritual insight. Matsuoka Roshi used to say: my enlightenment is mine and yours is yours. I can't get yours and you can't get mine.

Trust, along with its darker siblings mistrust and distrust, is most often associated with the motives of another person, or those of a group. Proponents and opponents of the popular cause du jour, often harboring not-so-well-hidden agendas, undermine trust in our public discourse by engaging in disingenuous dissembling or outright deception.

There are too many examples to treat at less than book length, but immigration is an obvious one. No one would disagree that a nation needs to maintain reasonable control of its borders, nor would a reasonably informed person deny that immigration proves to be an economic net asset in the long run. But such issues are easily turned into political footballs for the purpose of affecting election turnout, doing the right thing be damned.

We may even distrust our own motivations, or at least not know clearly what they are, in certain ambiguous situations. It is known to be difficult to convince someone of the truth of a proposition when their pocketbook or their self-regard depends upon their not getting the point. Similarly, it is not easy to see the inappropriateness of nepotism when it comes to our own beloved family members.

We often experience ambivalence in what should be trusting relationships. It is said that the most difficult dharma is the dharma of marriage. Read: committed relationships or family in general.

But karmic entanglement is not limited to the human species. A famous standup comic described that cute and cuddly, newly adopted puppy dog brought home for the first time, as a little 10-pound bundle of grief, as opposed to a bundle of joy. We typically outlive our pets in the best of situations and the pain of their suffering, which can be excruciating for their owners, is something we cannot avoid feeling. How much more so for human-to-human relationships? They do not always end well.

Scientists must trust in their own training and intuition, and in the verification of impersonal proof developed via the empirical method. Theistic or religious people place their trust in the inerrancy of scripture and entrust the salvation of their very soul to their savior or to God. Whether you are engaged in a rational business, a scientific enterprise, a theistic congregation, or a Zen community, your trust is initially placed in your boss, colleagues, members, leaders, and mentors. In the formal priesthood transmission documents in Zen, the teacher "entrusts" the dharma to the student, who becomes their "dharma heir." But eventually our trusting impulse must come to reside in something other than another person or a group, however deserving of it.

Rationalism: Evidence

For those in scientific professions, the meaning of evidence comes close to the definition given in the dictionary: something that gives a sign or proof of the existence or truth of something, or that helps somebody to come to a particular conclusion. Hard evidence of the validity of a theory is usually proven in the replication of results and/ or determined with the language and logic of mathematics. Most people have no idea how higher math works, so it truly seems magical, mystical, or at least mysterious, that such indirect evidence arising out of mathematical equations would be capable of revealing or confirming hard facts of reality. Evidence in law differs in kind, of course, but is still largely based on logic. Even the manipulation of witnesses and juries is logical, psychologically. In the ongoing investigation of possible malfeasance in the political world, documentary evidence—the paper trail—is becoming ever more determinative and even more dispositive than live testimony in determining the tick-tock, the timeline sequence of events, with the caveat that the trail is virtual now and no longer physical paper. Literally leaving no traces is trending difficult to impossible.

Nowadays, with the ongoing exercise of oversight of the legislative branch over the executive, and the recalcitrant refusal of the latter to cooperate with the former, particularly the probe of the January 6th insurrection at the Capitol in the last national election, the importance of evidence in the form of a paper trail of documents, elicited mostly from nonpaper digital media such as smartphones, is becoming ever more prominent in prosecution. In lieu of direct or corroborating testimony, one can be hoisted on one's own virtual petard of indiscrete texting, tweeting, and emailing.

If you work in the soft sciences, expert testimony and statistical correlation may be the extent of evidence required to pass muster and perhaps the only dependable kind available. I have read about a related hopeful movement in political science, proposing that policy be based upon evidence of measurable results, rather than on ideology. Good luck with that.

In certain findings of science, such as Darwin's elegant theory of the origin of species (1859), hard evidence collides with certain religious beliefs, notably those of proponents of intelligent design. Claims that the "irreducible complexity" found in natural organisms bolsters their case for a hidden designer is but one of many examples of hopeful but irrational thinking. The proposition is that many functioning structures in living beings are too complex to have evolved via natural adaptation, independent of any outside guiding intelligence. They must have been intentionally designed. By whom? By God, of course, by default.

The human eye is offered up as a prime example of fiendishly complex design and ingenious assembly which could not have happened "by accident." Your eyes and mine stand as irrefutable evidence, proof positive of the intent and engineering of an unseen designer. But innumerable sentient beings have some form of visual faculty which, it can be argued, represent simpler versions or prototypes of the human eye, whether or not we regard the human being as the last and most refined of God's or Nature's design-build project on Earth.

But what makes this idea irrational? Aside from the implicit forgone conclusion that a process of design in nature requires the existence of a designing entity separate and apart from the item under consideration, the scientific community has argued that the very notion that there is such a thing as irreducible complexity in biology is false. In countering this assertion, scientists point to a whole spectrum of photoreceptors throughout nature, particularly the animal kingdom, but also including photosynthetic plants. These illustrate the manifest reducibility of the visual faculty to relatively simple organic mechanisms sensitive to the presence of light, a whole host of simpler versions of variations on the human eye. Some can even distinguish color and form on a par with or even exceeding that of humans, like the tricolor vision of some birds. "Eagle-eye" is not a meaningful trope for no reason. Dogs see a limited color spectrum compared to humans, but better than we do at lower light levels. Certain shrimp are known to have a broader spectrum of color acuity. The human eye, on balance, may not even be the top of the line.

Evidencing Irrationality

But that a given claim can be demonstrably false does not, by itself, make it irrational to believe in it. Technically speaking, such a belief would be irrational to the believers only if they agreed that the evidence falsified the claims made. And yet in spite of agreeing, insisted on believing them anyway. We see this syndrome in play not only in religion but most exasperatingly in today's political arena, where human venality holds sway over widespread claims of voter fraud, denying the legitimacy of open and fair elections. But it may appear less than obvious in areas of scientific investigation.

Embracing the notion of irreducible complexity would not be irrational if one believed that it is indeed supported by evidence based on testimony of those taken to be experts. Evidence need not always be first person, but only the accepted testimony of those we trust. So if we are misled by our leaders in areas of expertise for which we do not have the time or inclination to do the research for ourselves, our confidence in them is not a matter of irrationality, but naïveté, plain and simple.

This definition of irrationality reduces to a dispute over whose testimony is most trustworthy. Most of us tend to side with those who agree with our predispositions, which may be socially rational, but would be scientifically irrational. One tell, as the conmen say, is the expression "I believe in . . ." (something as being true), rather than the more prosaic "I believe that . . ." (something is true).

The former betrays an innate precept or preconception. The latter expresses only a conventional conjecture, whether based on evidence or not.

In the public arena, especially in political and religious circles, conversation often turns on what a person "believes." For example, what they believe will be the likely result of a government policy or decision affecting their life. The confusion arises when religious beliefs are conflated with beliefs based on evidence. A scientist declaring "belief in" a theory amounts to sloppy language, just lazy syntax. Belief that a theory is a fact represents a conviction that it is indeed true, but always subject to revision when confronted with evidence to the contrary. Not so much for religious, or self-centered beliefs.

Simplifying Irreducibly

In Zen we come down on the side of irreducible simplicity. Science and higher math seem to concur that the simplest, most elegant of several potential solutions is most likely to be the correct one.

Please indulge an oversimplification. By analogy the human mind and its processing of sensory evidence may be likened to a computer. Computers, like other highly refined instruments, may usually be depended upon to faithfully perform tasks as they are intended, designed, and programmed to do. But the output is already biased by its very genesis from humancentric input. Same with the mind. Something similar may be said of design intent regarding scientific experiments in general. Preprogramming must necessarily reflect any biases harbored by those conducting the experiment, however unconsciously. Like viruses, biases infect incoming data subtly but inevitably, distorting outcomes. Double-blind testing and other means of screening minimize this kind of un-witting influence. But we have to allow that even accepted scientific evidence is subject to interpretation and thus to human fallibility. What is accepted as canonical is often a matter of reaching a critical mass of peer agreement, much as in less rigorous disciplines such as religion, philosophy, and the arts.

Peer review is meant to provide a remedial last resort to prevent unintentional misrepresentation of findings and conclusions as well as policing for the occasional intentional fraud. But the peer process itself can also be flawed for all-too-human reasons. These amount to practical precautions for scientists not to place too much trust in the self, that first-person arbiter of evidence.

Instead, ethical scientists turn to colleagues and peers to fact-check and confirm their discoveries. These checks and balances are brought to bear for reasons beyond devotion to truth for truth's sake. A lot is at stake, including reputations and careers and the all-important access to uncertain and diminishing resources of funding.

Independent investigation of a range of scientific studies has shown that scientists often harbor an unconscious bias, rendering them incapable of registering any data that contradicts it. This finding would presumably prevail in so-called soft, as well as hard, sciences. It would no doubt hold true in the professions as well, such as business, design, engineering, jurisprudence, medicine, and psychiatry. There is no reason to believe that those in the business of propagating Zen would be exempt. The unexamined life may not be worth living. Likewise, unexamined biases are surely not worth harboring.

Empirical versus Scientific

Not all empirical evidence rises to the rigor of scientific evidence. An increasingly common example in the postdigital world with a smartphone in every pocket: video footage of a thief caught in the act may be convincing evidence of his behavior, but it does not constitute what is meant by scientific evidence. The video documents certain facts: the thief's presence and actions at the crime scene. But it does not corroborate a general hypothesis or theory about crime. Not in the same sense that the recent detection of gravitational waves further confirms Einstein's theory of relativity.

This is one aspect distinguishing scientific from empirical evidence, whether of our own eyes and ears, or that of others. Science subsumes specific cases of phenomena under general principles of causality, so that any instance of that class of phenomena is likewise explained and thus predictable.

This kind of evidence outstrips that of the video of a thief. Capturing a person robbing a particular store on video may evidence that the thief did it and how, but it does not explain how robbery of any and all stores happens in general or will in all future cases. One particular case experience does not allow us to extract the general principle (shout out to R. Buckminster Fuller and Kuromiya 1981).

Depending on evidence in the form of third-party verification and requiring predictability is at once a strength and a weakness of rationalism and science. A given experiment can never be exactly duplicated in every dimension, and it may be impossible to control for certain variables. In the direct study of consciousness, the focus of Zen, it is a difficult, perhaps impossible, standard to apply.

Theism: Savior

Caveat redux: my comments may serve more to betray an admitted ignorance of theism and the gospel than to provide context for comparison with Zen, my stated purpose. Apologies in advance to any who may be offended and an earnest plea, not a cop-out, to take my misconceptions as examples of the general confusion rampant in the public arena, which you may hope to correct.

Adherents of theism presumably place their trust in a just, merciful, and loving God. Christians entrust their lives to his son, Jesus Christ. Many rely on prayer and the benevolent oversight of saints, as well as living priests, ministers, and other messengers of the faith, to bring grace and salvation. Certain Catholic saints, such as Mary, the Mother of Christ, and canonized former popes, play a soteriological role. They may be called upon to intercede on behalf of the supplicant, or for loved ones, for the souls of the deceased, or simply for assistance in worldly affairs.

But the God of the Bible, especially of the Old Testament, is also represented in scripture as jealous, wrathful, and vengeful—not so much to be trusted as feared. The phrase "God-fearing" is used as an admiring endorsement of the true believer. Nonbelievers, however, may consider it a pejorative. Why would one be afraid of one's own God?

In the face of such an all-consuming fear, it is natural to long for unearthly or divine intercession, preferably through a figure that has some sympathy for our plight, a personal savior. This leads to a seemingly absurd proposition: that embracing Jesus will save us from the wrath of his father, who after all has the final say in whether we are forgiven our sins. A cynic might remonstrate with this as nepotism on a cosmic scale. Of course, individual adherents may vary widely in regard to such beliefs.

Devout Christians invest Jesus Christ with their total trust as the "only begotten Son of God" and as their personal savior. Christ is called upon through prayer and embraced as the sole way to salvation. By accepting Christ and repenting sins, salvation is guaranteed, and you will dwell forever in God's presence. If you are not a believer, you might reasonably presume that belief in an afterlife cannot be verified before death, though those who are born-again might argue the point. The same may be said for belief in reincarnation in Hinduism, or even the principle of rebirth in Buddhism.

Absolving Afterlife

As mentioned above, one tenet of Catholicism that Zen followers would find troubling argues that a priest can absolve members of the flock of certain of their sins, acting as a moral and mortal intermediary between heaven and earth. This not only goes against the Buddhist principle of karmic consequence, but flies in the face of taking personal responsibility for our actions. It also places an undue moral burden on the clergy who, again, are only human.

Equally troubling and equally boggling to the rational mind, the hadiths of Islam promise a higher place in heaven for Muslim martyrs who die in jihad in the name of Allah. Native American tribes as well as the ancient Greeks and Romans apparently shared a similar, perhaps less grandiose, view, considering it honorable—a good death—to die in battle, presumably while defending others. This meme still resonates in the modern military today, as well as among first responders to emergencies. Endangering or sacrificing one's life for the sake of others is held in high esteem in most ethical systems. It is valued as the ultimate in altruism and characterizes the main coterie of identified heroes in society.

On the other hand, there is the horrific vision of Armageddon. Take your pick. These dystopian end-of-the-world scenarios make certain fundamentalist subgroups strange bedfellows of competing belief systems, who otherwise agree on little else. Extremist adherents of certain religions seem to be doing all they can to bring about the end of the world as we know it, the sooner the better. They claim that such a dire future is foreordained. But we have been waiting for that second coming for a long time, like Charlie Brown and Lucy with the football, as portrayed in the Charles Schultz *Peanuts* comic strip. Maybe next time, the kickoff will transpire as prophesied.

Seeking Salvation

Salvation is a basic principle of Buddhism as well as most or all forms of theism, it seems. In a general sense, Buddha may be regarded as an agent of our salvation through his teachings, or even through a living Zen teacher. But neither Buddha nor any Zen teacher can be our savior in the sense that they are imbued with miraculous power. What we are saved from in Zen, again, is our own ignorance. A Zen teacher dedicated to the salvation of others is acting as a bodhisattva, fully engaged in mitigating the suffering of ignorance.

Buddhism recognizes Jesus Christ as a bodhisattva, an enlightening being. He is held in similar high regard as is Siddhartha Gautama before his awakening. Indeed, all true prophets of world religions would be similarly honored. An authoritative dictionary on Buddhism and Zen (Fischer-Schreiber 1991) tells us: a bodhisattva provides active help, is ready to take upon himself [herself] the suffering of all other beings, and to transfer his [her] own karmic merit to other beings (gender-appropriate inserts are mine).

The conventional phrase "enlightened being" is not as appropriate as "enlightening being." The former adjective implies a state of existence, whereas the latter gerund denotes a way of living while on the path to spiritual awakening. But if you are a bodhisattva acting for the sake and on behalf of others, it does not make you their savior. No one can save or awaken another person in Zen's teachings. Not even the historical figure Shakyamuni Buddha had this power over his followers. But he could help them help themselves in a breadth and depth that others could not.

As an aside, in Buddhist writings, uppercase initials generally signify a specific venerated Buddha such as Shakyamuni, and cosmic Bodhisattvas such as Avalokiteshvara. Lowercase usage indicates the innate potential of all human beings, including you and me, to live as bodhisattvas and to become fully awakened buddhas. But this transformation can come about only through our own efforts, under our own recognizance, so to speak. In Zen, we all have to establish our own self-awakening. Though preferably, if we are fortunate enough to find a true teacher, we can train under the sage supervision of an elder who has been there and done that, as our coach.

Bodhisattvas on the Buddhist path are supported in their efforts by all the ancestors of Zen—not through magical thinking, but through their trail-blazing efforts—as well as by the presence of living teachers who have authentic experience. We are also helped by the written record, as well as the ubiquitous presence of buddha-dharma, as evidenced in our consciousness and the surrounding environment, man-made as well as natural. All phenomena, all beings, whether sentient or insentient, manifest Buddhist truth continuously, whether they know it or not. Our challenge is to wake up to it.

Saving Yourself

As Zen Buddhists we have to save ourselves. You are your own savior. This is not an expression of hubris, but a recognition of a grave responsibility. If we pursue Zen practice in all humility, all buddhas and bodhisattvas of all times are constantly acting as our saviors. They do so by expressing the truth and directing our attention to the present moment, the only time and place in which we can be saved. To benefit from their guidance, we have to pay attention to it, which is different from believing in it. And of course, ultimately, we are all one buddha, and one bodhisattva. We are them and they are us.

Zen Buddhism: Self-Nature

It may seem contradictory that in Zen we place our trust in our own self-nature, when the very reality and trustworthiness of this self is subject to challenge. However, self is here used in the special sense of the true self or buddha-nature, rather than denoting the conventional, constructed self. This true self is the "self that is not others," the self that can do what no one else can. This concept will require further clarification, as it is a central point of departure of Zen Buddhism.

This true self is the only one that can practice "secret virtue," those selfless actions to which no one else is witness. On the other hand, the true self is set in opposition to the "secret self," the self that can sin, create bad karma, do harm to others or oneself, or commit willful errors while hiding them from others. In Zen, the only real sin is any action committed on the basis of ignorance, particularly the kind of ignorance that ignores obvious if inconvenient truths, such as the Noble Four.

Nothing is so obvious as that which is hidden, the saying goes. The secret self is a part of the constructed self, a persona based on self-striving and intoxicated by greed, hatred, and delusion, the Three Poisons of Buddhism. The obsessive-compulsive self sometimes called "monkey-mind," while natural, can become off-center, out of kilter, neurotic, even sociopathic or psychotic. These two aspects of self represent a kind of fundamental bifurcation of personality, the Dr. Jekyll and Mr. Hyde of fiction. But in Zen the emergence of our lesser angels, in response to adverse or threatening circumstance, represents a kind of categorical error. The very notion of a dual self-nature is based on a fundamental mistake.

In Zen circles we like to think that Buddha's awakening represents the pinnacle of mental health, the final expurgation of all neurosis, confusion, and mental disorders. We who follow the buddha-way aspire to the same insight, though no one would claim to have surpassed his degree of awakening to buddha-nature. However, our original nature is considered to be essentially the same as Buddha's, despite the obvious differences in time and space, cultural context, and circumstance. "Enlightened people of today are exactly as those of old" (Sotoshu 2001) as the ancient Ch'an master assures us. This original nature is not a spirit, however, but inheres in body and mind. If we recover our natural awareness through the practice of Zen and its meditation, we find the middle way in the midst of life. Surely this is the most meaningful definition of health on all levels. It embraces aging, sickness, and death as natural.

In Buddhism, our true or essential body (S. dharmakaya) is not limited to this corporeal body (S. nirmanakaya) but is interdependently connected with the whole world, and indeed the universe. The synergy of these two coming together as one is experienced as the enjoyment body (S. sambhoga-kāya). This completes the holistic tripartite body (S. trikaya) of Buddhism. It does not, however, imply or suggest a parallel construction to the holy Trinity of Father, Son, and Holy Ghost.

Further, as if this is not complicated enough, Buddhism proposes that there are likewise three aspects to the human mind (J. sanshin): magnanimous mind, nurturing mind, and joyous mind. These are offered up for cultivation in contrast to our lesser angels of selfish, destructive, and fearful minds.

If you find that you are getting lost in trying to follow the logic of all the different "selfs" being proposed here, you are not alone. It is not at all logical. Apprehension of the true self in the context of the constructed self, and the tripartite division into three bodies and minds, is not simple. It is dependent upon our ability to set aside our attachment to our imagined self as we define it to ourselves. Hopelessly circular, in other words. Like navel-gazing, but with the navel gazing back at us. But do not give up hope: if Buddha could pull this off in much more primitive times, we have no excuses. Buddha did not understand it, in any logical sense, so we should not expect to either. It is the central mystery of our existence, after all.

Trusting Zen

Zen practice inculcates a trusting nature in general, but within reason. Not exactly the Russian proverb "trust, but verify"—transmitted by the scholar Suzanne Massie to President Ronald Reagan—but close to the same caution. Later in the Metta Sutta quoted above, Buddha entreats us to cultivate this trusting nature without reservation:

So let one cultivate an infinite good will toward the whole world.

Allowing ourselves to be vulnerable in this way is founded upon a deep and abiding trust in our own self-nature. True self, variously expressed in such terms as Original Nature, Buddha Nature, Enlightened Nature, the Three Bodies or Three Minds, is distinguished from the false or constructed self. Such positive mental attitude derives from building trust in the true person, on the cushion and off. This stems from Zen's faith in the potential of human nature to transcend its egocentric limitations.

Embracing Karma

Zen's true self is not a self-existent eternal soul that survives death, transmigrating from present to future lifetimes, like the atman of Hinduism or the soul of Christianity, finally ascending to heaven. The uniquely different persona of each individual is part and parcel of the true self, founded on the simple but irrefutable observation that we are distinct personalities. I am not you and you are not me.

However, this selfsame self is connected to karma, which again is not individuated, but shared. Karmic consequence is not strictly limited to the imputed self, as constructed in our mind. We both affect, and are affected by, the actions of our family, beginning with our parentage. And by friends and neighbors, the leadership of our native country, and other denizens of the world. All influences are not equal, of course, some being proximate and predominant, others remote and less potent. This idea is examined by Peter Hershock (1999), a philosopher who draws cogent comparisons between Asian and Buddhist worldviews and contemporary Western ideas:

What is interesting about the Buddhist formulation is that while intention remains crucial in the conception of morality, it is neither reduced to choice or strictly localized. Responsibility is understood as always and intimately shared. That is, if we are born into a world in which people take up guns in anger or greed and commit conscienceless murder, it is not simply their karma, but necessarily ours. Were we free from implication in such acts, we would have been born in a world where they quite literally did not occur.

So even our intentions, which seem so personal, are not at all disconnected from our social context. Whether or not you understand or agree with Hershock's interpretation of karma, you have to agree with his assertion that no man stands alone. We seem to have lost sight of this truism in the age of the me generation, but such trends as the #MeToo movement revive the meme of strength in numbers, or togetherness. However, the action we take in Zen is not primarily on the group level but focused intensely on the personal level. Embracing karma is the first step in mitigating negative karmic effects on both levels.

By "true self" Zen isolates the individual, the "true person of no status." But this so-called individual must mature, transcending ego-individuality. The true self of Zen is simultaneously unique, and yet not separate from others.

This mindset was noted and reported by Master Dogen in an account of one of several encounters he had with senior Zen monks while traveling in China, notably monastic cooks (J. tenzo). In one instance he recounts a very old monk drying mushrooms in the blazing sun. Asked why some of the other younger monks did not take over this taxing chore, the wise one answered: they are not me.

In other words, the question makes no sense. How can others do what I do, really? Beyond that, it is my role, my personal duty, and my chosen area of practice of dharma in daily life as tenzo.

Paranoia Reigns

In my limited understanding of theism, it is apparently presumed that the individual self, being flawed at birth, cannot be trusted unless our damaged soul is healed, saved, or born again. According to this notion, we are all sinners, having been born into sin, and in need of redemption via intervention of higher powers. Unleash the demonic self and all hell breaks loose. Literally. And for the hapless soul, for eternity. If you subscribe to this belief. Those who do, believe. Those who don't are still affected.

Similarly, western rationalism, including certain memes of science, appears to regard the true self with suspicion, as hopelessly afflicted by baser impulses. The resulting characterizations range from relatively harmless imaginings of science fiction—Jekyll and Hyde, Frankenstein's monster, Doctor Strangelove, the Death Star of Star Wars—to the all-too-real-world weapons of mass destruction now so ubiquitous as to earn the acronym WMD. But these are only the tip of the paranoia iceberg.

Distrusting Self

Human beings are definitely responsible for most of the unnecessary suffering in the world. It is primarily humankind, in the literal sense of men who largely run the political world, who propagate extreme means of managing their fellows. The irrational self takes the form of nation-states, the logical extension of an imagined self to an expansive imagined group entity. As a collective self, the tribe, city-state, nation, or collaborative union of allies, stands ready, willing, and capable of unleashing hell on earth in order to defend itself and its worldview, however misguided: all at the expense of relatively innocent people designated the enemy, or "collateral damage." This is the neurotic self writ large.

While these nightmare scenarios are based on normal human survival impulses carried to survivalist extremes, they merely manifest aspects of the human psyche unhinged.

The American Psychiatric Association would appear to concur. The human self is viewed as potentially harboring nearly 500 maladjustments and counting, as defined by the Diagnostic and Statistical Manual of Mental Disorders. This unbalanced and complicated self is a potent threat to itself as well as to others, and clearly in need of intervention: long-term, even lifelong, therapy.

Whether you regard this ever-accumulating roster of illnesses needing treatment as a good thing, or as just another lamentable institutionalization of job security for the benefit of the therapists who compile the manual, you must admit that, along with other manifestations of rationalism, the sheer mass of disorders extending to all age groups portrays the untreated ego as hopelessly neurotic.

Likewise, much of the thinking in theism appears to regard the psyche as achingly vulnerable, and often enthusiastically amenable to worldly or even satanic influences. It may be true enough, but it clearly begs the question, So what? What are we to do about it?

Trusting Mistrust

One thing we are encouraged to do about our ostensible inability to rely upon ourselves is to turn to the purveyors of religious or rationalist solutions to our problems. Doing so has been a hallmark of humanity since the days of tribal cultures. Witness shamanic and other "witch doctor" traditions ubiquitous from the beginning of our collective communal history.

Currently, contemporary dispensers of traditional conventional bromides of received wisdom seem to be falling into ever greater disfavor or distrust, if we are to believe the press. People are looking elsewhere for salvation, rather than to the institutions of religion or the nostrums of science, particularly the seemingly inexhaustible medicine cabinet of big pharma.

A sense of distrust in others is often generalized, experienced as a vague intuition or hunch, a suspicion of underlying motives. As famed singer and overdose victim Elvis Presley tells us: we can't go on together, with suspicious minds. But trust is not so simple. Attributes of character and temperament that we may trust or distrust at our peril include judgment, competency, commitment, and basic honesty, as well as stated intentions. We come under this kind of scrutiny in our dealings with family, friends, colleagues, and mentors, as well as strangers, on top of questions of motive. The lure of cop shows and murder mysteries capitalizes on a public preoccupation with betrayal of trust. A person's level of commitment may be unquestionable, while their competency may be lacking. Conflicts in parenting, especially with teenagers, offer a simplified snapshot of this broader problem. Classic disagreements around chaperoning dates or adherence to a curfew—and nowadays monitoring online communications—are the stuff of family sitcoms. Teens protest that parents should unquestioningly trust them, or at least not unfairly distrust them. The confusion stems partly from a lack of clarity as to exactly which traits of the youngsters are trustworthy, and which may not be. Parents may indeed trust their kids' intentions, but not their judgment, or that of their peers.

In any case, trust in another, or even in oneself can never be absolute—that is, to do the right thing in any and all circumstances. We must reserve the right to be wrong in our relationships, as well as in regard to our own conduct. In all things, failure is the true antecedent of success. We can dependably trust ourselves to fail. There is no other way to learn.

Saving Others

If you are following Zen, the highest degree of trust must be invested in your own true self, your original self-nature, as an article of faith. This degree of trust need not extend to your Zen teacher as exemplar or mentor, however. Teachers are fallible too. But self-nature in Zen is not the convoluted ego of psychology. Nor is it the soul, salvable only through redemption via the intercession of a savior. Zen is not a form of therapy, nor is it traditional soteriology. Zen is primarily a way of taking action to correct our errors.

You may ask how Zen cannot be intrinsically soteriological (a doctrine of salvation) if it is truly a form of Buddhism? It seems that Buddhism and Zen are soteriological through-and-through since they proffer salvation via putting an end to suffering. But soteriology as conventionally understood is the province of theism, in which the soul is saved from eternal perdition. Buddhism rejects the existential reality of this soul, whether eternal or temporary. The true self of Zen is not interchangeable with the soul of theism, or the atman of Hinduism. The end of our self-inflicted suffering comes about through seeing through the true origins of that suffering, our innate ignorance, and the predomination of our own cravings, including the very craving for our own salvation.

The seeming paradox of realizing salvation without the overlay of saving our eternal soul may be resolved by considering Buddha's teaching on the true nature of a bodhisattva (Price 1990):

> Buddha said: Subhuti, all the Bodhisattva-Heroes should discipline their thoughts as follows: All living creatures . . . all these are to be caused by Me to attain Unbounded Liberation Nirvana. Yet when vast, uncountable, immeasurable numbers of beings have thus been liberated, verily no being has been liberated. Why is this, Subhuti? It is because no Bodhisattva who is a real Bodhisattva cherishes the idea of an ego-entity, a personality, a being, or a separated individuality.

Bodhisattvas realize the liberation of all beings, including themselves, by clearly seeing that all beings are from the beginning already liberated. That which binds us, preventing our liberation, is imaginary.

Deconstructing the Social

Our imputed self, characterized by our unique physical, mental, emotional, and social attributes, self-identifies as "I-me-mine." Our social self consists of extensions of this assumed self-identity, insinuating itself into the various roles we play over the span of our lifetime. It manifests in relationships to family and loved ones, friends and familiars, professional colleagues and peer groups. It is linked to birthplace, hometown, city, and nation, even sports teams and the like. Our extended families and communities are largely projections of this imagined self. At the center of this peripheral self, however, there is the authentic, originally undifferentiated self, of no particular attributes.

What are we to make of a self that has no attributes? Zen's negation of the imputed self does not mean that the self as conventionally conceived is entirely delusional. But its components: DNA, race, ethnicity, parentage, nationality, et cetera, are seen to be, if not accidents, then at best circumstantial. But if the true self has no attributes in the literal sense, then why should anyone care about such a thing? What significance could it possibly have?

Realizing the ephemeral and diaphanous nature of this constructed self, we are liberated from the very characteristics we attribute to it, whether we view them as positive or negative. Yes, I may be an aging white American male, but that does not tell the whole story. We can be neither proud, nor ashamed, of these inborn and culturally inherited traits. They can inhibit our apprehension of the true self if we let them. But they are learned, and thus can be unlearned.

Trusting in Self

In Zen we come to trust the true self, the self that is not defined by its obvious characteristics. Our reasons for trusting in this true self are far removed from the ideals of humanistic philosophy, or the self-improvement paradigms of New Ageism. Zen's trusting nature differs from the conflicted beliefs of theism which betray a deep distrust of basic human nature while putting the soul on an eternal pedestal, if reborn through redemption. Zen's concept of the imputed self may be more closely aligned with that of the models offered in modern psychology, which also studies the self. But Zen's model of the self and its natural state is unencumbered by extensive, convoluted diagnoses of ubiquitous mental and emotional disorders, let alone dependency upon medications, which can distort reality in order to ameliorate disorders, or simply to relieve pain.

In sum, Zen is highly skeptical of the conditioned, constructed, or imputed self. It is considered false to all intents and purposes. But Zen promotes a deep and abiding trust in the original or true self, to which all may awaken through direct insight. Of course, trust in oneself cannot be completely separated from a degree of trust in others. Positive relations in government, among scientific peers, clergy, and teacher-student relationships within a community of any kind are based on mutual trust. Unfortunately, in an imperfect world, social trust requires verification.

Verifying True Self

Verification of our authentic self does not derive from others, nor assumed from our Zen teacher's approval. Authentication does not magically emanate from the historical Buddha or from a cosmic buddha. Unlike the soul of theism, the self in Zen is not the gift of a deity. It does not depend upon the existence of a separate spiritual realm, or upon transcendent beings separate from physical reality. Zen insists that the physical and the spiritual cannot be separated. The way verification of this central truth of Buddhism comes about is illustrated by a poem from Master Dogen, in which he explains how zazen works to resolve this conundrum (Sotoshu 2001):

The essential function of buddhas
And the functioning essence of ancestors
Being actualized within non-thinking
Being manifested within non-interacting
Being actualized within non-thinking
The actualization is by nature intimate
Being manifested within non-interacting
The manifestation is itself verification
The actualization that is by nature intimate
Never has defilement
The manifestation that is by nature verification
Never has distinction between absolute and relative
The intimacy without defilement
Is dropping off without relying on anything
The verification beyond distinction between absolute and relative
Is making effort without aiming at it
The water is clear to the earth—a fish is swimming like a fish
The sky is vast and extends to the heavens—a bird is flying
like a bird

Brief but comprehensive, and worth quoting in full. We will not go into detailed commentary, but just highlight the points relevant to our discussion of trusting the self and not relying on others.

Verification of the truth or realizing the true self of Zen comes about through deep meditation. "Actualized within nonthinking" and "Manifested within noninteracting" may be taken loosely to indicate an entry level and deeper levels of sitting still enough, for long enough. The latter phrase is tantamount to "verification" (i.e., hitting paydirt in the midst of your practice of zazen). Definitely not through the intervention of others.

When we move beyond thinking into the neutral territory of non-thinking—not to be confused with not thinking—we arrive at the inner sanctum of noninteracting, where all entanglements, as attributes of the constructed or imputed self, are neutralized. Only then can direct realization of our true nature manifest. Meditation, zazen, is the vehicle by which we actualize this process of self-examination and transcendence. But we do not, and indeed cannot, actualize its verification. But it can become manifest to us. When and if this occurs, it naturally verifies our practice, revealing our true self.

Deconstructing Self

The constructed self, on the other hand, has to go. Or at least, get out of the way. The sum total of proximate causes and conditions, the combined temperament and character of our public persona, is just grist to the mill, in zazen. Temperament and character are regarded in psychology as inborn versus learned traits, stemming from nature and nurture, respectively. This distinction rationalizes extreme personality differences sometimes found in identical twins. Nature determines inborn temperament. Nurturing fosters learned character traits. Together they complete the unique individual. But this analysis does not yet reveal the true self of Zen.

Genetically determined traits are part and parcel of the self we construct as we individuate and mature. Genetic twins may drift apart, evolving very different personalities. Our social selves consist of compilations of labels and roles, accumulating to a self-identity that continues to evolve over time.

However, this imputed self is much like a jellyfish: clusters of components that act in concert, only seeming to comprise a single entity. Under scrutiny, they fall apart into separate constituents: the Five Aggregates (S. skandhas) and Six Sense Realms or Bases (S. ayatana). Like the analogy of a chariot, attributed to Buddha, when disassembled there is no chariot. Likewise with the deconstructed self. There is no there, there. Some assembly is required.

The seemingly independent, self-existent personality functions only when fully assembled, and even then there is something missing. What is missing is the rest of the story. For example, the trikaya.

The constructed self, or nirmanakaya, captures our living reality in the corporeal sense. It largely determines whether or not we are comfortable in our own skin. But it amounts to an incomplete construct, the definitive nature of which is called into question in Zen. In zazen, we deconstruct the construct, or more accurately, allow it to fall apart. This amounts to intentionally allowing personality disintegration to set in, which would be anathema to normal psychology. In Zen it is seen as a necessary, healthy process of tearing down in order to rebuild on a more solid foundation. It reveals the dharmakaya, or essential body. While zazen can be therapeutic, its method is not at heart a therapy. It is not a treatment administered by others "in order to reveal or heal a disorder," the dictionary definition, though it certainly reveals and heals. When the deconstruction of the nirmanakaya reveals the dharmakaya, the synergistic upshot is the samboghakaya, the enjoyment body. Enjoy!

Discovering Original Self

Buddhist spiritual insight is often called "awakening." The use of the gerund form implies a process of transformation of awareness rather than a new state that has been achieved, as suggested by the noun "enlightenment." If insight entails seeing into the ever-changing impermanence of existence— along with the insubstantiality of emptiness and the imperfection of this best of all possible worlds—then nothing actually changes, other than our awareness of our reality. Enlightenment is not a change of state, then, but a change in our awareness of the actual state of our existence: a distinction, that is, with a definite difference.

But an old Zen saying, case 17 in the Book of Serenity, a Song Dynasty koan collection, holds that there is not "a hairsbreadth's difference" before and after any such transformation. This testifies to the immense esteem in which our original "true self" is held. Yet it is the ultimate in ordinary. It is always present, just under the surface. What is transformed in awakening to it is our own worldview, not the external world itself. But thereafter, there is no separation of the internal and external.

Shakyamuni Buddha is sometimes addressed in translation with the honorific "Lord," but he is not regarded as a deity, spirit, saint, or savior. He was not, and is not, an object of worship in Zen. Nor is Buddha regarded as one who can and will intercede on our behalf in the practical view of Zen. This is why we take a do-it-yourself approach to salvation.

We each have to make the same effort Buddha made in order to awaken to our own buddha-nature. We may be "inconceivably helped by the Buddha's guidance" (*Jijuyu Zamma: Self-fulfilling Samadhi*; Tanahashi 2010) but only through direct practice and insight, realizing that "this very body [is] the body of buddha" (*Zazen Wasan: Song of Zazen*; Waddell 2017). We have the same basic equipment, the same raw materials, that he had to work with. Nothing we really need is missing.

Spiritual awakening is not dependent upon following sacred scripture, a specific practice, or a particular teacher, or even Zen, rather than another path. Zen's adamantine trust in innate buddha-nature and our ability to awaken to it considers this our birthright. But it is also seen as the result of a difficult and demanding process. This view may seem egocentric, but it is actually the opposite of ego. This buddha-potential is universally accessible to all human beings: all who are willing to put forth the effort. It clearly cannot be restricted to Buddhism, or solely to the followers of the buddha-way.

Saving Oneself and Others

Unlike the theistic view that our first priority is the need to save our own soul first, salvation in Zen has to do with saving others before oneself, which may also be considered egocentric. Who do we think we are, that we are so enlightened we can save others? Yet this terminology expresses the Bodhisattva Vow, regarded as the ultimate in selflessness. Splitting this hair further: Why would having a birthright accessible to all human beings necessarily negate its being egocentric? It could, for sake of argument, simply be equally egocentric for everyone, without regard to ethnocentric differences. Freud's notion of an ego, as an isolatable thing, shrivels under the scrutiny of Zen.

Salvation in Zen includes liberation from such dualistic dilemmas as well as from willful ignorance. Resolution of personal-social contradictions comes about through self-awakening and awakening others as inseparable bodhisattva activities. In all modesty, it is not really possible for anyone to awaken anyone else. We can only awaken ourselves, at best. But as exemplars of the method of zazen, we can help others to some degree. The least we can do is to assiduously avoid misleading others.

True self or original self-nature is not limited to the familiar and friendly, those who are like you or like me. Accumulated social traits infiltrate and infest the individual like viruses. They cling to us like barnacles on a ship. But our innate, most central self has no circumstantial, peripheral "other" in it. An ancient Ch'an poem *Hsinhsinming: Faith in Mind* (Sotoshu 2001) maintains that "in this world of suchness, there is neither self nor other-than-self." The true self retains its unitary integrity. But Zen does not assert that the self, or reality, is simply one. Rather, the transcendent nature of original self is better expressed as not-two, a venerated Zen trope.

But we do not merely scrutinize the validity of the imputed self on an intellectual plane. Meditation is said to lead inexorably to dying on the cushion. The constructed self as conceived does not survive this traumatic, transformative event. We see that all the attributes, labels, and categories we associate with our self-image are just constructions of the mind. At the farthest reaches, zazen is said to become objectless meditation (J. shikantaza). Becoming objectless, it must also become subjectless: no-self, no soul (S. anatta). The two, subject and object, are mutually defining, a complementary dyad.

Identifying with Salvation

If you self-identify as a Christian or with another branch of theism, what you directly experience in deep meditation may not conform to some of your expectations, especially those that are based on religious beliefs. Certain closely held doctrines you may hope to have confirmed, such as the validity or reality of God or the soul, or even your sense of self-identity, may be brought into question. Salvation may not appear as paradise, as promised by scripture. What it means to be saved, or born again, may not be affirmed as you preconceive it.

Your beliefs may have to be revised to accord with your direct experience. In this way your faith, in the sense of a set of beliefs, may be put to the test by your own insight. It does not follow, however, that Zen or meditation is "of the devil." Evil is also in the eye of the beholder. This mindset does not deny the presence of evil in the world. But true evil is to be found only in the actions of human beings, based upon their self-centered striving.

If rationalism is more your cup of tea, whether secular, humanistic, or a scientific blend, Zen meditation may not match your expectations from that perspective either. Your usual criteria for trustworthy truth as measurable, demonstrable, replicable, and verifiable by others will surely not be met. But you will surely experience something undeniably and authentically real, if you persist.

Trust and Transmission

Though subjective in nature, the authenticity of your insight in Zen may be verifiable by an experienced teacher. "Mind-to-mind-transmission" means that when a Zen student and teacher come to accord, both know it for sure. Many Zen stories you may have read describe this transmission event. Such exchanges comprise much of the historical record of Buddhism's lineage.

Nothing is literally transmitted from teacher to student, of course. Other than a shared, heart-to-heart communication, based on face-to-face practical experience. The student-teacher dynamic in Zen training is fraught with the same potential for misunderstanding as in any other apprenticeship. Even under the tutelage of a true teacher, one who has deep insight into Zen and is blessed with the skillful means to help others, the preponderance of responsibility for success weighs primarily on the student.

A true teacher is presumed to be already fully at home in enlightened awareness, expressed as "Mind" with a capital M. As a sincere student of Zen, you may eventually enter, or reenter, into this Mind. This is awakening to your true self-nature, which is not totally separable from that of others, including your teacher's. Both "your body and mind, as well as the body and mind of others, drop away," as Master Dogen assures us (*Fukanzazengi*, Sotoshu 2001). The true self that one awakens to is known as "buddha," the natural mind of an awakened human being. It is an article of faith in Buddhism that our fully awakened self can be trusted completely. But this does not mean that there is no room for uncertainty, confusion and error, even following such penetrating insight. It is more a matter of how one who has awakened to their buddha-nature responds to those errors. Particularly those committed by others, along with their own. If truly awakened, our response to circumstance should be completely trustworthy, informed by true compassion and tempered by wisdom. As Dogen reminds us, "When buddhas are truly buddhas, they do not necessarily notice that they are buddhas"—a dose of humility from the peak experience of an enlightened Master (*Genjokoan*, Tanahashi).

An attitude of humility regarding Zen insight is implicit in a statement attributed to Dogen that a Zen life comprises one continuous mistake. How we respond to failure is suggested in the ancient Japanese proverb "Fall down seven times, get up eight" (Reynolds 2011). We just keep on keeping on. The sixth Ancestor in China, Huineng, famously declared that he had the double vision of Zen (Price and Mou-Lam 2016):

"What I see is my own faults," replied the Patriarch. "What I do not see is the good, the evil, the merit and the demerit of others."

What did he see in others, then? How did he see their behavior, if not as their faults?

We must allow ourselves to make mistakes in many areas of life simply in order to learn. Zen is no exception and does not pretend to offer a panacea for all personal and social conflicts. But through personal introspection our perspective on the surrounding social milieu, and the futile need for our relationships with others to conform to our self-centered expectations, can come into sharper focus. Trust in mind or self-nature nurtured in meditation eventually morphs into trust, or confidence, on the social plane. We become worthy of others' trust by trusting our original mind.

DIMENSION 5.
METHODS EMPLOYED: EXPERIMENT, PRAYER, MEDITATION

To state the obvious, to be effective any method of training must be diligently employed. No method works itself, claims of the latest weight-loss regimens not-withstanding. If a given method proves to be ineffective, it must be discarded in timely fashion. But we can also quit too soon, before the effect has fully set in, as attested by the rising tide of curbside clutter on trash pickup day, featuring discarded versions of the latest and greatest in exercising devices, a steady accumulation of used treadmills and other faddish fitness equipment in the local landfills.

This principle of use it or lose it certainly applies to Zen practice. As Matsuoka Roshi once mentioned during one of his annual visits after we had both moved from Chicago—he to the West Coast and myself to the Southeast—by far the largest single group of people who take up Zen meditation in America are those who give up too soon for it to have any long-lasting effects.

Experimental methods in rational disciplines such as applied research and science are continually updated and discarded as new techniques and technology become available. Public presentation of the plastic and performing arts must also evolve in order to continue to attract audiences. Revised ap-proaches to training—method acting comes to mind—come into vogue and may hold sway for some time. But there are few fixed methods in any field that do not evolve. The field of research in design and engineering professions that focuses on improvements in methods is called methodology.

Prayer may appear to be a fixed method, but no one would claim that the content of prayer could be identical from person to person, or even from one point in time to another. Assuming that prayer works on some level for a given individual, it would have to change over time, along with their circumstances of life as they change. On the other hand, if prayer does not work for someone, then continuing to repeat the same prayer hoping for a different outcome would match one definition of insanity. In which case, the method itself would have to change, or be discarded altogether.

Refining Method

Zen meditation appears to be the same for everyone sitting in the meditation hall (J. zendo). But appearances can be deceptive. Actually, each person is doing something entirely different from every other person. The sameness is what brings out the difference, a demonstration of the principle of nonduality in Zen. While all are focusing their attention on the upright posture, abdominal breathing, and the activities of the mind—paying attention to attention itself—that is where the similarities end. Each and every one is living out his or her own living narrative with its various causes and conditions, which are starkly different from each other. No two people are breathing the same breath, seeing the same vision, hearing the same sound, or feeling the same sensations.

We do not ascribe any magical powers to Zen meditation, such as the intervention of a saint or savior called upon in prayer. While zazen is treasured as an excellent method, and assessed as marvelously effective, it does not change anything materially. All that changes is our attitude and resultant apprehension of the material world and our place in it. But that is quite enough.

Rationalism: Experiment

If you are a scientist, designer, engineer, an architect or any other kind of technician, experiment is virtually inseparable from method. Whether in the form of thought experiments, a la Dr. Einstein; a bench-test in the lab; or an initial plan, concept sketch, scale model, or maquette; the creative approach is a happy marriage of tried-and-true methods and innovative experiments.

For a scientist or engineer the process of discovery includes a mix of theory, experiment, and observation, yielding evidence. With a huge dollop of repetition. As outsiders, we imagine the birthing of a scientific theory to be a process of intense methodical thinking, in which the rigor applied to the empirical method is a determining factor in the validity of the eventual proof. In any case, we presume the method of discovery and verification in science to be a highly disciplined process, creative as well as experimental in nature, and thus intimidating to the uninitiated.

The mystery of solving a scientific dilemma is imagined by nonscientists such as myself to be a semimystical, deeply mental meditation. Plus doing the math. The science romantic's ideal is exemplified by the great physicist's archetypal "thought experiments." I read somewhere online that Einstein would dangle a pen in one hand, drifting off into a reverie, and when the pen would fall to the floor it would awaken him. Then he would pick up the pen and start over. He may have been tapping into the half-awake/half-asleep boundary states of consciousness known as "hypnogogic" and "hypnopompic" to access his higher creativity (Harman and Rheingold 1984). Entering this dreamlike, uninhibited state of mind is characteristic of Zen meditation as well. Tracking your results is less rigorous, of course, except in scientific studies of meditation itself, and certainly less likely to translate into mathematical equations.

Experimental Zen

In light of the implications of their messages, and their relative influence in society, a certain aura of intimidation surrounds both theism and rationalism at the highest levels of advanced science and religion. Intimidation is also characteristic of Zen, especially regarding the rigor and discipline of its more intensive zazen sessions. A typical Zen retreat may involve days on end of hourly bouts of seated meditation from early morning to late at night, relieved only by alternating sessions of walking meditation, bio-breaks, and intermissions for meals, which are often taken while sitting as well.

Further, the atmosphere of shared commitment to spiritual practice found in Zen monastic communities is created, in part, by vows of silence, abstention, and spiritual poverty. This monastic training is integral to Zen's formal method of researching the mind. Zen can be very intimidating, but intimidation is not necessarily a bad thing. We should be intimidated by the depth and breadth of what Zen represents. Approached as an experiment, the intimidation factor in Zen meditation is a net plus. It may encourage us to cultivate a reverential attitude toward zazen, our gateway to spiritual insight.

Zen's Happy Accident

Notably, important discoveries often unrelated to the original focus of a given experiment sometimes occur in the lab as happy accidents and serendipitous surprises. This suggests that one of the best approaches to Zen, as a rational experiment, is keeping an open mind as to where it may lead. In fact, we cannot know the outcome of our meditation practice a priori. Experimentation at its best bridges the physical and mental and embraces the emotional. This is certainly true in Zen, as well as the arts, practical applications of engineering and pure research, and applied science. The adage that the simplest, most elegant and aesthetically pleasing solution is most likely to be correct corroborates this notion, no matter the field of endeavor.

Theism: Prayer

You may feel the term "method" to be too impersonal or technical for something as intimately personal as a religious practice like prayer. Prayer may be considered a method, however, or perhaps a medium: the contact channel through which a theist communes with God. Prayer has been likened to asking God questions, meditation to listening for answers. In the history of many religions, ancient contemplative traditions honor the validity of spiritual intercourse with a higher power, sometimes known as "centering prayer." I found a pamphlet from the interfaith student counseling center of Dalhousie University while visiting our affiliate in Halifax, Nova Scotia, offering a description of this method:

- Sit quietly, comfortable and relaxed.
- Rest within your longing and desire for God.
- Move to the center of your deepest self. This movement can be facilitated by imagining yourself slowly descending in an elevator, or walking down flights of stairs, or descending a mountain, or going down into the water, as in a deep pool.
- In the stillness, become aware of God's presence; peacefully absorb God's love.

You may be familiar with this step-by-step outline, which is apparently derived from a line in the Bible, Psalms 46:10: "Be still and know that I am God." This amounts to an exercise in guided meditation, including suggestive visualizations. It is an example of meditation in its traditional definition: a subject meditating upon an object. It is also clearly based on belief in the existence of God, which is to be expected in an interfaith context. And it is clearly focused on confirming and fully realizing this belief.

From an outsider perspective, however, it would seem that prayer, centered or not, always involves direct communion with God. We might further take prayer to be communication beyond conscious thought, language, or any other intellectual filter. At minimum it suggests a two-way dialogue. Speaking in tongues may also be a manifestation of this kind of communication on a vocal but nonverbal level.

It is worth noting in passing that in the Surangama Sutra (Luk 1966) attributed to Buddha, he mentions that this kind of dialogue with the creator god Ishvara might occur in higher, or deeper, sessions of meditation. As one of the Fifty Warnings of "mara-states," or delusory experiences, his admonition is to move on, and above all do not assume that such an extraordinary event is the objective of zazen, and that you are now enlightened. In fact, quite the opposite: one more delusive relationship to set aside.

The God Experiment

It might be a worthwhile exercise to try to design a scientific experiment testing selected doctrine, which to my knowledge has not been successfully accomplished to date. Published reports of efforts to demonstrate the efficacy of prayer, for example, have not stood up to scientific scrutiny. We may propose for the sake of argument that this may be the fault of the scale and scope of the experiment. Perhaps we will have to settle for a statistical proof of such a theory, where sheer numbers become a preponderance of evidence. The emerging trend of mining mass data may provide enough sheer heft to turn mere correlation into acceptable proof of causation, regarding causality and mass prayer.

Of course, many religious folks do not view prayer solely as a means of petitioning God for help, or for tangible benefits. Contemplative prayer appears to be oriented toward entering into the presence of God as omnipresent. Prayer may simply serve as a way to manifest or express one's gratitude, faith, and reverence. Such prayer is not about outcomes, redress of grievances, or material gain. This latter motive is characteristic of "prosperity religion," including some outlier branches of Buddhism, which, perhaps, would constitute the most pedestrian form of prayer. Or worse, an example of magical thinking. For a more scholarly analysis of prayer as method we turn to Aldous Huxley (2014):

> The word "prayer" is applied to at least four distinct procedures: petition, intercession, adoration, contemplation. Petition is the asking of something for ourselves. Intercession is the asking of something for other people. Adoration is the use of intellect, feeling, will and imagination in making acts of devotion directed towards God in his personal aspect or as incarnated in human form. Contemplation is that condition of alert passivity in which the soul lays itself open to the divine Ground within and without, the immanent and transcendent Godhead.

The last classification, "alert passivity," might come closest to a description of meditation, but there is nothing passive about zazen. The suitability of the choice of terms would depend on what one means by "divine" as well as "soul" and "Ground," not to mention "Godhead." If awakening to our transcendent buddha-nature may be considered divine, the resolution of any apparent conflict as to deepest meanings of the other terms may be largely semantic. We do speak of Vairochana, the "cosmic Buddha," after all. How different is that from "God"?

Zen and Prayer

Mental guidelines for what to think about or what not to think about, whether accompanied by specific visualizations or not, may be characteristic of some forms of meditation or prayer, but are not typical of Zen meditation. Zazen does not impose any mental techniques, and in fact stresses nonthinking: neither intentionally thinking, nor actively suppressing thought. Zen does not rely on thinking.

However, the quiet suggested at the beginning, and the stillness mentioned at the end of the pamphlet's bullet points, are very much in harmony with Zen meditation. Zazen fosters settling the body and quieting the mind, entering into profound stillness on three interconnected levels: physical, mental, and emotional.

But invoking God's presence or God's love would be considered extra, somewhat superfluous, as overt doctrinal accretions to the "bare awareness" cultivated in zazen. If it appears that God enters our presence or speaks to us in zazen, no problem. But this is not the end goal of Zen's meditation. The final goal of Zen practice is beyond any kind of conceptualization, as it points to reality itself, and so is devoid of concepts of God, or prayers to a God. But this is not to argue that God does not exist.

Even prayer may eventually be abandoned by its most ardent adherents, particularly if it is tied to hoped-for but undelivered results. Prayer unconnected to preconceived outcomes would be more consonant with the altruistic aspiration in Zen, variously expressed as: may all beings be happy, from the Metta Sutta. Or, every day is a good day; every day is a happy day, per Matsuoka Roshi.

Zen Buddhism: Meditation

Matsuoka Roshi once declared that Zen meditation is the closest thing to prayer that the East has to offer the West. Unlike prayer, however, and some religious forms of meditation, zazen is not characterized as being guided by words from doctrine, or even directed talks by your teacher (J. teisho), beyond basic instructions in posture, breath, and focus of attention. We do not meditate upon any object in particular, other than the present reality. Soto Zen emphasizes upright sitting, sometimes called "quiet illumination," but prescribes no specified image or sound, no assigned teaching, no intentional thinking about any particular content at all. In this it differs from Rinzai Zen in which a koan, or illogical riddle, is often the subject of meditation.

In Soto Zen praxis theory and method are conjoined. Zen practice is only one practice, as Master Dogen reminds us in Genjokoan, recited in Zen liturgy (Sotoshu 2001):

Accordingly in the practice-enlightenment of buddha-dharma:

Meeting one thing is mastering it
Doing one practice is practicing completely

Zen's method, zazen, the most stripped-down of all meditation styles, is the operational basis of Buddhism. Reduced to its essence, zazen is simply sitting still enough, for long enough. How still is still enough, and how long is long enough, is a matter of individual discernment. If you have any doubt about it, it is not yet enough. When it is, you will know for sure.

Like Buddha, all human beings have the potential to wake up fully. We have only to penetrate through our own ignorance and confusion to recover our true self, our original nature. The way to do so is to allow all of your fantasies, interpretations, and prevarications to come to an end, leaving you with the truth, the whole truth, and nothing but the truth. Realizing that even "truth," as a thing, is just another concept until you experience Buddha's truth of self-identity with the truth. This is why it takes a considerable amount of time for most people. You may prove to be more ripe and ready.

Praying in Zen

In zazen, what has been called "choiceless awareness" comes about, in which our attention becomes independent of intentional thinking to any significant degree, let alone thinking about a prescribed subject. To rephrase a past conservative icon and POTUS: thinking is not the solution to our problem; thinking is the problem. Especially overthinking everything as we are wont to do. Soto Zen prescribes no specific content as a focus for its meditation such as the koan of Rinzai Zen, or anything else in the form of language, images, sounds, or silent prayer. In this, zazen is unlike other forms of meditation, including centered prayer, which presumes a relationship with a personal God.

We allow that a prayerful attitude, experienced as a high degree of earnestness, informs the mindset of Zen. The word "pray" sometimes appears in translations of Buddhist ritual, as in the Transfer of Merit after reciting a sutra: "We pray that this merit extend universally. . . ." It is sometimes translated as "May this merit extend universally to all. . . ." removing any confusion around the religiously laden term. As used here, prayer conveys sincerity and hope, rather than an appeal to a higher power.

This is akin to archaic English usage, "I pray thee" or the abbreviation "prithee," meaning "please," reflecting a heartfelt pleading, whether appealing to a god or the overlord of the fiefdom. In Zen, the word connotes a universal sense of yearning, rather than a specific wish that can be clearly articulated.

Meditation in Zen is not ruminating on the past, mulling over scripture, or worrying about and planning for the future, though they pop up from time to time, courtesy of the monkey mind. Zazen's prayerlike intensity does not imply that it is directed to a deity, but instead indicates a sense of urgency in pursuing the truth.

Such strenuous effort is not enlisted for material or personal benefit in this life, and certainly not in any imagined afterlife. Zen is not a prosperity religion. Zen practice aspires to realize spiritual rather than material well-being. The challenge is overcoming our ignorance, not our lack of wealth.

In order to closely examine this ignorance, Zen's method begins with the senses. The Heart of Great Wisdom Sutra says, "Given emptiness, there are no eyes, no ears, no nose, no tongue, no body, no mind." This does not deny the reality of the senses, but indicates where to focus our attention: directly on our own sensory reality. Eventually we come to understand this strange statement.

By sitting still enough for long enough, the senses themselves eventually begin to break down. We come to see for ourselves what the Heart Sutra means by all those noes, or the emptiness aspect of eye, ear, nose, tongue, body, and mind. We pray, so to speak, that this insight happens sooner rather than later, that we wake up ASAP. But the main practice of the bodhisattva path is patience, including patience with our own apparent lack of progress. Off the cushion we attend to awareness as we experience it every day, heightened by meditation. Zazen is like a magnifying glass we pull out when we want to take a closer look at our life.

Zen, Religion, and Science

Zen is regarded as a religion by some practitioners and probably by much of the uninitiated public. It is usually associated with Buddhism, one of the big four on the planet. Others consider Zen a spiritual practice, not religious in the usual sense. It fits the growing cohort of those who declare themselves to be spiritual, but not religious.

But Zen is also scientific in its open-ended, empirical spirit of inquiry, its methodical approach to meditation, and its dispassionate analysis of consciousness. Zazen can be intimidating in its physicality, much as higher mathematics can form a barrier to a novice as the essential gate to higher scientific insight. Zazen presents and confronts classic barriers of stubborn resistance and discomfort: physical, emotional, and mental. Once sitting becomes comfortable, sleep becomes a barrier to further progress.

There are no guarantees of results, not in science, nor in Zen. Leaders of some deity-based religions may promise that they can guarantee a ticket to heaven—more power to them. But everyone has to climb the Zen mountain alone. No one can climb part of it for you.

Zen is said to be unteachable, but it can be learned. Its essential method, zazen, has been refined over millennia, and fortunately can be taught. But Zen is not unlike deeper dimensions of philosophy, higher science, and theology, or the arts, which likewise cannot simply be taught, but only learned, through personal struggle. How to play a piano can be taught. How to make music cannot.

Method, Medium, and Mastery

This truism, that the deeper meanings or truths of life cannot be taught but can be learned, is acknowledged by all, certainly not invented here. Student-centered pedagogy is exemplified by the ancient Socratic method of utilizing probing questions rather than providing pat answers. But in all cases, any method works only to the degree that the student is willing to make the effort. If an athlete is unwilling to do the work, no amount of coaching will help. The 10,000 hours associated with mastering any professional discipline provides a general rule of thumb for Zen training as well. We do not want to raise the bar so high as to discourage novices, as some beneficial effects are short term. But after five years of diligent practice, we have only begun to scratch the surface of Zen, like any other demanding discipline. Dilettantes need not apply.

In the arts we define media processes as of two kinds essentially, additive or subtractive. Adding clay to an armature to build a bust of Napoleon is additive. Chipping away at stone to reveal The Thinker is subtractive. Often a combination of the two is in play in any particular project.

In zazen the medium is not material, but the fluid nature of our own mind, consciousness itself. Still, many newcomers approach Zen as additive, as if they are learning new techniques and gaining new ideas, when they are actually unlearning the misconceptions and beliefs that they already harbor, if unconsciously.

But we regard the overall process of Zen training, especially zazen, as mostly subtractive. Repetition tends to strip things down to their essence, emphasizing sameness over difference. By thoroughly examining our worldview via meditation and dispassionate observation of our daily life, we largely unlearn what we think we know, rather than learning new information. Zazen is a process of uncovering, or recovering, our original mind. This is the main reason why it takes so long to have any substantive effect. We face a dauntingly thick layer of muck and mire of learned ignorance covering the natural radiant wisdom of our original mind. It took time to accumulate and it will take time to disperse. But your time will be well invested. The return is total.

Any serious field of endeavor requires periodic review and revisions to its critical methods, incrementally improving as a work in progress, and an evolving process. It is stunning that the central method of Zen, zazen, remains fundamentally unchanged over two and a half millennia. This is a testament to its utter simplicity of design intent, the historical refinement of its subroutines, and the ongoing validation of its proven effectiveness. Zen simply finds, follows, and fosters the natural posture, the natural breath, and the natural state of mind of upright, seated meditation.

Zen's meditation approach is based on the physiology of the human body and the intricately interconnected nature of the mind. They cannot be separated, and their symbiotic nexus remains essentially unchanged after 2,500 years, even with today's vaunted improvements in diet, health, social and cultural evolution, medicine, and education. Sitting still for long periods of time may appear to fit more naturally in the context of more primitive times, given a more tribal society in a more natural habitat. But it also naturally complements modern cultural conditioning. As Matsuoka Roshi would often say: civilization conquers us. So-called civilization adds its own layers of ignorance and constraints on top of our personal conditioning and confusion. The evidence of this is only as far away as your mobile media device. Simply sitting still enough for long enough may appear too simplistic an approach in our hypercomplex context. But complexity equals necessity for simplicity.

For all that, guidelines for practicing zazen have remained virtually unchanged since their emergence in early Chinese meditation manuals. The method was handed down to the outstanding Ch'an teacher Nyojo, who passed it on to Master Dogen, who codified it in thirteenth-century Japan. But these archival documents do not include any mental techniques, as such. Zazen is more visceral than verbal, more physical than mental, more sensory than conceptual.

Of course, a Zen master may be forgiven for verbally lecturing and exhorting his followers with elegant conceptual models, visualizations, and appeals to intellectual analysis, as Buddha himself did. Or delivering the occasional inspirational talk, even during zazen. Zen is not at all anti-intellectual. It simply recognizes the limitations of the intellect when approaching the inconceivable truth.

All such exhortation, however eloquent, is recognized as mere fingers pointing at the magical moon, the reality. Our own original mind is our most reliable guide in this. Meditation is the Buddha seal, our ancestral teacher. We simply need to reestablish intimate contact with it.

Speaking of Zen masters, it is important to remember that we do not master Zen. Zen masters us.

When you practice Zen, meditation takes priority over reading scripture, deep devotion, practicing ritual, and pursuing good works. These and any other such traditionally related activities are regarded as supportive, but secondary to zazen. Meditation is ultimately more central to your practice than even your teacher. Zazen is our true teacher. However, finding and working with a living teacher is considered advisable, especially in the beginning stages of practice. It can be crucial to clarifying The Great Matter. Zen is the ultimate in do-it-yourself, but it doesn't hurt to have a qualified coach.

DIMENSION 6.
TRUTHS CLAIMED: VERIFICATION, BELIEF, IDENTIFICATION

Truth is a slippery term, I think we can all agree. One person's evidence may be ridiculed as a mere theory, or worse, disingenuous or an outright falsehood, by those holding opposing views. In spite of interfaith aspirations to rapprochement, Zen parts company with the more radical claims of some sects of theism. It bears repeating that Zen does not contradict the findings of science. According to the Dalai Lama, if such a conflict does arise, it is Buddhism, not science, that will have to be revised (Lama 2005).

Truth based on verification of evidence is of a different order than truth based on belief, it should go without saying, and without arguing the credibility of the truths claimed. Scientific truth is more generally useful to society, partly for this reason. But objective truth does not always offer much shelter from the storm. It is cold comfort for the deeper needs and fears of humanity, which is one reason people in dire straits turn to unproven beliefs, their default faith. Faith in something, anything, can be comforting, whether it is true or not.

Truth in Buddhism is of a different order. It is not based on belief, no matter how dearly held. Nor is it based on concrete evidence of an objective scientific kind, which can be verified by others. It is instead based on direct identification of the self with the truth, in the experience of each person. First-person evidence = first-person truth.

Truth Be Told

Let us clarify what we mean by truth, exactly. Master Aristotle gave a common-sense definition (1011):

> To say of what is, that it is not, or of what is not, that it is, is false.
> While to say of what is, that it is; and of what is not, that it is not, is true.

Truth is traditionally based on facts: what factually is or is not. Would it were so simple. Currently we have the fakery of "alternative facts," a flippant turn of a partisan phrase. Welcome to Wonderland. This may be a good inflection point to introduce the classic all-encompassing Indian model of logical propositions, the tetralemma, which was probably extant in Buddha's time. It goes beyond the simpler duality of Aristotelian logic to posit four perspectives on any proposition:

> (1) It is. (2) It is not. (3) It neither is nor is not. (4) It both is and is not.

There. That should settle the matter once and for all.

But what is, or is not, is based on interpretation. Whose interpretation? Our interpretation. We are witness to the consequences of mass confusion regarding competing interpretations of factual reality, in this era of "fake news." What the actual facts are is often a matter of contention. When we are presented with questionable claims, we want to see the evidence in order to judge whether it justifies our belief in the truth of the claim or confirms our suspicion of its falsity. Either is a form of verification or prevarication.

We can safely say that any conventional belief based on evidence, however skimpy, is of a different order than a belief based solely on faith. But truth based on whatever evidence is available is still a kind of belief. Using "belief" interchangeably with "faith" conflates the two, muddling clarity. The claim that truth based on evidence is of a different order refers to the degree of verification, or susceptibility to refutation, of a given claim, based on the quality of evidence. Everyday empirical claims, as well as scientific theories, are all subject to such verification or refutation. Faith-based claims are not of that order, however, as the exercise of faith rationalizes beliefs absent any evidence, and even in the face of evidence to the contrary. Facts may be stubborn things, but faith is the mule you rode in on.

Rationalism: Verification

From a rationalist perspective, evidence manifests in multifarious forms, such as indirect findings from scientific instrumentation. Most everyday evidence of the nature of reality comes from the senses or from interpretation of sense data, a theory known as empiricism. Rationalism, as a foil to theism, is subtly differentiated from empiricism. Rationalism, philosophers hold, is based on reason. Empiricism is based on evidence, primarily observed through the senses interacting with the external world. Sensory evidence, particularly of human behavior, may not always comport with reason.

Knowledge, then, is provisionally divided into two sorts: empirical versus theoretical. Theoretical knowledge attempts to explain why things are true, based on evidence. It goes beyond just the facts. Empirical knowledge is based on agreed-upon evidence, as in: we hold these truths to be self-evident. In the history of the British colonialization of North America and the founding of the Republic of the United States, an accumulation of empirical evidence over time led to the theory of a "more perfect union" social structure as a hybrid democratic republic.

A preponderance of evidence from eyewitness and expert testimony in court determines our knowledge of what happened in a particular case, reinforcing claims of guilt or innocence. Another form of widely acknowledged evidence is statistical in nature. It's not an overstatement to say that 100 percent of statewide elected offices occupied by white male incumbents constitutes de facto evidence of a good-old-boy network.

Rationalism and empiricism find common ground in the internal process called reflection, where one may come to new conclusions after pondering data garnered through the senses over a period of time. Reflection is the application of reason to evidence, giving us sufficient "reason to believe." This is a fairly accurate description of the typical mental process in meditation. But the application of reason must ultimately be set aside at the far reaches of zazen, where rational interpretation tends to inhibit or skew the direct observation of sense data. Reflection can devolve into rumination, like a cow chewing its cud over and over and over again, classic obsessive behavior.

As a scientist you place little or no trust in any hypothesis absent evidence. Peer-based independent replication is the ultimate proof, wherein lies the taste of the pudding. Absolute replication of all factors affecting outcomes is technically impossible, of course. But any theory not subject to being proved or disproved amounts to rank speculation—not very appetizing. This definition of theory means it is not simply a best guess, but a hypothesis that can be proven by sufficient evidence.

Verification in science usually requires doing the math, which disqualifies most of us. Or it may come from bench testing a theory's predictions, in which case the evidence must be accessible to the senses, directly or indirectly, or to measurement through finely tuned instruments.

But there may be insurmountable challenges to physically testing theories, as science probes ever more deeply into remote regions of the macrocosm, and minute gaps in the microcosm. Energy levels needed to recreate the conditions of the Big Bang, for example, may ultimately prove unreachable at sufficient scale. Measuring ever-more distant regions of the expanding universe reflects diminishing returns, approaching impossibility in future. We have been able to produce images of single atoms, but so far subatomic particles are detectable only by inference. Computer simulations fill the void, but have their limits as well.

Ironically but inevitably, emerging theories in such fields as particle physics and astrophysics are becoming less amenable to experiment in the real world, owing to physical limitations of extremely high-energy requirements as well as of optics and other sense-expanding technologies. Exceptions that prove the rule are the recent launches of space-based telescopes and robotic planetary probes.

Philosophers may once again speculate that the "end of knowledge" is near, or at least the end of the practically applicable side of science as we know it, on both ends of the micro and macro spectrum. But this idea has been run up the flagpole before, as has the "end of history." Both seem to be laughably premature. May it prove true. We are going to need all the tech support we can get.

Theism: Belief

A scientist or professional in any rational-based pragmatic endeavor may find their intended objectivity compromised by an unconscious belief, or bias as mentioned. Such anomalies are usually caught and corrected, we are told, via peer review or other checks and balances. A scientist may eventually be persuaded by evidence, on the testimony of peers, to abandon erroneous or dubious convictions. But people whose beliefs trump reason are unlikely to be shaken by the testimony of others, even experts who are held in high regard by society. Disrespect for scientific authority seems to be trending upward.

In lieu of demonstrable proof, even in the face of overwhelming contrary evidence buttressed by expert testimony, true believers insist that they detect irrefutable evidence of the existence of God. Again, it is difficult to impossible to persuade someone to accept something if their paycheck depends upon their not accepting it. In this case, there is more at stake than income, including professional probity, and public positions near and dear to their hearts. On the line are reputations, careers, status, and the support of fellow partisans. Pols and experts on both sides of the debate have skin in the game, of course, backed by loyal supporters and fellow travelers. But all politics is local, even when one party claims to represent God.

Inheriting Belief

We seem to adopt some beliefs as if by osmosis, all unconsciously from parents and other influences in our lives, as a natural part of our upbringing and socialization. Others are clearly force-fed through the educational system and peer pressure reflecting societal norms and mores. Today many key influencers are anonymous, holding sway over followers through social media platforms online.

Over decades, centuries, even millennia of recorded and received wisdom, shared beliefs that once may have originated from direct experience become codified and handed down through cultural evolution. Transmitted to succeeding generations as creation myth, tribal custom, or holy writ, they function much like precepts: attitudes and views held prior to experience in the present. Though disconnected from current reality, and often subliminal, they still remain powerful influences.

Received wisdom, particularly religious dogma originally based upon personal revelation, but long since rendered into impersonal doctrine, may inhibit any individual spirit of investigation into deeper insights, especially if such discoveries challenge conventional wisdom or socially acceptable norms. Ironically, blind acceptance of deeply held beliefs erects the barriers to realizing or recalling the lost, original meaning of the events they derive from.

Today, claims of revelatory epiphany, characteristic of charismatic sects, are likely to be met with skepticism, alarm and ridicule, or worse, especially if deemed contradictory to prevailing church doctrine or the political climate of the day. History has recorded many instances of persecution and martyrdom of such messenger mystics. Can anybody say: Inquisition?

With some notable examples and exceptions of the original founders of faiths, throughout religious history such claims of spiritual insight have been derogated as self-delusion, hallucination, heresy, insanity, or the work of the devil. The recently reinvestigated witch trials of Salem represent one such case in the early days of the republic. Suppression of the Ghost Dance, followed by the massacre at Wounded Knee, came later, a more nakedly realpolitik put-down of the Native American movement. But witch hunts and the Inquisition are still with us, if in different guise today: false claims and accusations of fake news and hoaxes in the political realm notwithstanding.

But getting stuck in stubborn fixed ideas is perhaps more a product of nurture than of nature. It is safe to say that we are not born with such worldviews. We have to learn them from others. If we can learn them, we should be able to unlearn them if necessary, given sufficient flexibility of mind and openness to revision. All beliefs may not be in error, but they should not go unexamined.

Belief and Birth

One persistent widely held theist belief is that our birth is attributable to the intent of God as well as that of our parents. Further, that God has a purpose in mind, a plan for our lives, his children. But Buddhism holds that we are born out of our own desire for existence, which implies that even the fetus harbors a kind of belief in the object of its inchoate desire, namely this very life. All life is driven by this fecund force, a primordial urge just to exist, including the animal and vegetable kingdoms, as well as those ambiguous boundary forms, such as viruses. In Zen, we assume responsibility not for the origin of life, but for our use of it, philosophy's greatest good.

The ancient strain of contemplative traditions in Western religions is not to be lightly dismissed. But public presentations of modern theism seem largely bereft of any emphasis on personal revelation, rendering its wisdom primarily that of the received variety: scripture-based beliefs, prescribed doctrines, and proscribed societal taboos.

From the perspective of Zen, it is curious that this should be so. If there is any area in which a spirit of inquiry should be encouraged, surely it is that of the spiritual realm. The deeper mysteries of ancient doctrines recorded in scripture are otherwise reduced to the impersonal testimony of the experience of others, however admired, revered, or even worshipped.

But on the upside, certain charismatic sects seem to value direct spiritual experience, and some evangelistic groups are reviving an interest in meditation, as well as in chanting. These protocols are traditional to Buddhism and currently common practices in Zen, which is becoming more mainstream. But they once had an honored place in mainline religious sects, long since relinquished. Perhaps we will witness their revival in our lifetime.

Buddhist chanting is not so much a devotional practice of worship as it is a recitation and remembrance of ancient teachings from Zen's countries of origin. By chanting these messages repeatedly, their meaning becomes more apparent and is assimilated by the mind far more thoroughly than by simply reading or hearing them. Chanting also has a direct impact on the body, breath, and attention. In a concrete sense, the personal physical experience of chanting comprises the true meaning of the chanting service. And on the social level, chanting helps to cohere the community.

Evidence of God

Theistic beliefs require no evidence other than doctrinal testimony, which explains their resistance to verification by third parties, and rationalizes their lack of traction in the secular rationalist community. Verification in religious matters derives instead from first-person evidence (i.e., direct experience). Descriptions of religious epiphany as recounted in the biographies of saints are of this category of evidence. There is strength in numbers in the dominant denominations, but this statistical evidence may be seen as just another case of social agreement, embracing received wisdom as the absolute truth.

The truths of theism are at odds with the truths of rationalism when they make such evidence-averse and commonsense-free claims as:

1. Darwin's *On the Origin of Species* competes with Creationism.
2. Creation was caused by fiat, God's Word (Genesis versus Big Bang).
3. Climate change, if true, is the will of God, even if caused by humans.
4. Armageddon is foreordained, rather than egregious human error.

Stubborn resistance to embracing the findings and warnings of science on the actionable items on this list just makes matters worse to those outside the faith. They paint those who insist on doctrinal interpretation with the broad brush of heedless ignorance and mindless collusion with irresponsible impulses of rampant greed. The marriage of corporate interests with the religious right makes not only for strange bedfellows, but for an ugly baby. The former stand to profit from plundering and polluting the planet in the short run, while the latter claim stewardship over the creation in the long run. But we will all share in the karmic consequences of those naively tiptoeing through the tulips and negligently whistling by the graveyard. The question Zen would ask of anyone banking on slipping out through the escape hatch and landing on their feet in paradise is What if you are wrong? Wouldn't it be better to err on the side of caution, just in case? Hedge your bet just a little bit?

Zen Buddhism: Identification

As the meditation branch of one of the four major religions of the world, Zen might reasonably be regarded as a religion, as it is by some, including some practitioners. Many Zen folk, however, would hold to the increasingly common cultural meme of self-identifying as spiritual seekers, but not really religious. Followers of Zen, if not exactly loners, do not tend to be joiners. They do not look to their spiritual practice to provide their self-identity. Any such identity comes under scrutiny in Zen. What we really are is a central question in Buddhism. "I" am not a "Buddhist." Buddha was not a Buddhist.

The foundational teachings of Buddhism's Four Noble Truths are centered around:

A definition of the problem of existence as necessarily involving change, which results in suffering.

A call to action to relinquish our own craving, which results in unnecessary suffering inflicted upon others as well as on ourselves.

A broad acceptance of the natural suffering of aging, sickness, and death as built into existence, thereby mitigating personal suffering to a reasonable degree, and leading to a cessation of damage unnecessarily inflicted upon others.

A prescription for daily practice, following the Noble Eightfold Path to realize salvation in this life, as opposed to in an imagined afterlife.

The emphasis on salvation in daily life, as opposed to after death, presents a stark difference between Zen and the reverse emphasis of some world religions. Even in Buddhism there are some who follow the teachings in this life in order to be born into better circumstances in the next go-around, probably an historical hybrid amalgam of bothHindu and Buddhist teachings.

Experiential Truth

There are many such points of departure between theism-based doctrine and the principles of Zen. The two correlate to the extent that their adherents respect personal epiphany, experiential insight that is beyond tangible evidence, but undeniably convincing. This is not in the category of miracles, but what Buddhism defines as self-identification with the higher or highest truth. Unlike objective truths of science, which may be replicated and even predicted, evidence of realization is entirely personal. Yet its authenticity is attested to by all ancestors of Zen, which testimony cannot be proven false.

Zen admittedly has a greater affinity with rationality and science than it finds with theism. But even though Zen is not a deity-based religion, it does not follow that it is necessary, or wise, for followers of Zen to debate the existence of God.

The existential question in Zen is not whether or not something actually exists, but how. Everything exists by virtue of impermanence, inexorable change. Meaning that what exists in the present did not exist in the past and will not exist in the future, at least not in the same configuration. On the other hand, everything that exists always has and always will, in a different configuration. If God exists, according to this principle, S/he also must be impermanent, insubstantial, and ever-changing, as well as imperfect like everything else in creation.

Theologians argue that God is outside of creation, not part of it. The closest corollary in Zen might be what is sometimes called the "Uncreate," mentioned in early texts from China as well as Japan. But this underlying essence of existence, or noumenon, is not separable from the surface appearance of physical existence, or phenomena. Nor is it a being, and certainly not one of divine origin. Here, words continue to fail.

Of course, it is misleading to represent all religion as centered around belief in God, gods and goddesses, spirits, and so on. It could be argued that what is really central to any and all religions are two claims; namely, that there are

    a. fundamental flaw(s) within human existence
    b. religious prescriptions providing the remedy(s)

That is, religion is largely centered around some concept of salvation, the doctrine of soteriology. This is another form of problem solving, which always begins with problem definition. The problem is that we are doomed to eternal perdition in the worst-case scenario. What to do about it? Doctrinal solutions, such as confession and repentance, are usually offered as solutions, or at least, palliatives.

Zen practice also includes repentance, as in this recitation, repeated three times for good measure:

All my past and harmful karma
Born from beginningless greed hate and delusion
Through body mouth and mind I now fully avow

But our culpability for karmic consequences is acknowledged without the overlay of a God or Savior, or an intermediary priest offering absolution. Again, the fundamental sin in Zen is ignorance, primarily ignorance of the truths of the nature of reality pointed to by Buddhist teachings. Matsuoka Roshi described the truth of Zen as round and rolling, slippery and slick. No sooner do we think we have it firmly in our grasp than it pops out, like a wet bar of soap. Whether born of rationalism, theism, or of Zen, so-called truth is elusive, perhaps especially the nondual truth of Zen.

Most of the concepts we identify with truth involve the separation of subject and object. The evidence of rationalism is objective, outside of oneself. The beliefs of theism are similarly dualistic, but inversely attempt to conform external reality to internal belief, or doctrine. In Zen, identification with the truth means going beyond dichotomies of observer and observed, beyond physical versus spiritual. We do not assert that all is one but only that the most you can say is not-two.

Identification with truth is an experience, not an idea. It means intimately witnessing the truth of the true Self, capital S, through study of the everyday self, lowercase. In doing so, we come to forget the self, identifying with the reality in which self and other are not-two. This is literally beyond belief, beyond scientific evidence, and entering directly into harmony with nonduality. Zen's credibility is based upon first-person evidence in the form of our own witness, as well as testimony from those who have gone before and claim to have been there and done that: our teachers and Zen ancestors. But the only evidence that counts is your own. The observer has always been an indispensable part of the equation in Buddhism, from Siddhartha Gautama's seminal insight under that tree to yours today.

Verification in Zen

Any substantive effect of Zen is directly experienced, rendering any description necessarily in the form of testimony. But Zen's insight is verifiable by experiment. You are free to do meditation, to study and experience Zen, and to find out for yourself. This was said to be among the last words of Buddha. In order to access the insights of Zen, it may be necessary for you to suspend disbelief for a while, to develop a more trusting nature, and to embrace—trust but verify—testimonials of other meditators such as myself, while wholeheartedly engaging its prescribed method of experimentation, zazen. If you are like me, it will become necessary to persevere in the face of little perceivable results, and with zero verification, for some time. But this too shall pass. And as in all things, your results may vary.

Buddhism and Belief

For those of us practicing Zen, belief operates on a less exalted, more pedestrian plane than it does in theism. The truth will out in your meditation, whatever beliefs you may harbor going in. Buddhist beliefs are not so much religious as they are commonsense and rational, if altruistic, based on the Bodhisattva Vow. They amount to conclusions drawn from observation and analysis. They tend to be inclusionary rather than exclusionary. The sameness between all human beings is more important, and much more determinative of our intrinsic value as human beings, than the differences.

The Zen belief that all human beings have the potential to realize their inherent buddha-nature is truly egalitarian. This being so, the potential for spiritual insight cannot be exclusive to Buddhists, by definition. People in all walks of life must share equally in this inherited birthright. Thus, in Zen, we do not necessarily self-identify as Buddhists, let alone as buddhas. On the social level, or course, if someone asks, we would have to admit the we are practicing the way of Zen, or Buddhism. But this does not imply that we have simply substituted "Buddhist" for our former self-identity as a "Christian," "Muslim," "Jew," "Atheist," "Agnostic," or "Unaffiliated."

Religious or philosophical outlook is just another in the litany of traits we may attribute to our self, as distinct from others. While gender, race, ethnicity, and the rest may be considered realities—in the sense that they are inborn causes and conditions of this unique incarnation—at the end of the day, or at the end of our lifetime, they do not finally determine our essential nature. Who and what we are is beyond labels. We take up the way of Zen as a program of action, not as a new identity. And certainly not as a program of self-improvement. This very imputed "self" is the central delusion that we all harbor, and all other delusions and misinterpretations of reality follow from this fundamental category error. It is not that there is no self, just that the constructed self is just that, a fabrication.

Our reverence for Zen's ancestors, going all the way back to Buddha and beyond, may be regarded as a kind of belief, or article of faith. There are most likely innumerable spiritually awakened beings lost to history, beginning in the dawn of prehistory. "Buddhas and ancestors of old were as we; we in the future shall be buddhas and ancestors" from Eihei Koso Hotsuganmon; Dogen's Vow (Sotoshu 2001) We are sure that the recorded lineage is not literally unbroken as claimed, and is surely fallible in its historicity, the more so the further we go back in time.

Nonetheless, we believe that our forebears were not charlatans, and that their testimony is true. While they were not perfect saints, most or all of those listed in the record were clearly sincere, genuine transmitters of enlightened truth, to the best of their ability. They had nothing to gain by deceiving others, or so we believe. There are many such beliefs in Zen, implied or explicit. First and foremost, we believe that Buddha had a genuine experience of transformative insight. We aspire to the same.

Such assertions may be characterized as basic tenets for Zen Buddhists, to whom they seem readily apparent, even self-evident, much like the truths the Founding Fathers held to be so in the United States foundational document, the Declaration of Independence: that we are all created free and equal. Of course, we can readily mount circumstantial-evidence-based arguments against that assertion.

But Zen's beliefs are not societal in nature, any more than they are religious. They do not constitute promises of future reward for good behavior in the present. They are not a form of wishful thinking. We may hope, one fine day, to finally realize our buddha-nature. But being human, we want it now.

The assurance that you, too, can be a buddha, waking up to the same insight that he and the Zen masters of history experienced, is meant to encourage, not to convince. It is not a belief, not even a claim, but an expression of faith in our lineage and their example to us. If you pursue zazen diligently, Zen promises that something notable will likely come of it. We get out of Zen what we put into it, only with a multiplier effect.

No matter how deeply felt, any given belief does not in and of itself constitute proof of its premise. Belief, or preconceived bias, has no credible place in science. Zen does not conflict with the findings of science and does not demean its empirical method. In fact, zazen emulates empiricism. Evidence in Zen may not consist of external, measurable, or easily comparable data.

However, like evidence found in the laboratory or the courtroom, the Zen experience is subject to testimony, as well as cross-examination. And we have an extensive rice paper trail. Your findings and conclusions must pass the litmus test of peer review, especially that of your teacher.

Beyond Belief

Zen asserts that its teachings, the buddha-dharma, do not really rise to the level of belief or doctrine, including the theories of reincarnation and rebirth, though some Buddhist sects emphasize these conjectures. But this statement may be misleading, or even seem disingenuous. Proponents of Zen are not interested in criticizing others, including what people choose to call themselves, or how they self-identity. The Dharma is not meant to reflect poorly on others, but to provide a mirror to the self.

It would be problematic for folks to see themselves as Buddhists, followers of Zen, or adherents of the Way, while insisting on denying certain Buddhist tenets. To pick a few: the theory of interdependent coarising; the transitory nature of all beings and conditions; and the nonduality of samsara and nirvana. These teachings are not merely semantic or conceptual frameworks, but central to what defines Buddhism as a system of thought. They may be regarded as beliefs in the pedestrian sense, as in believing that the sun will rise tomorrow. But they are not religious beliefs meant to construct a mythical narrative about the deeper meaning of existence. Dharma is operational in intent.

Perhaps the definitive difference between theistic religions and Zen is not that the former are based on doctrinal beliefs and the latter is not, but that the claims of Zen may be verified for oneself, in a way that those of theism cannot. But even this kind of claim is tricky, since theists are likely to say that their experiences indeed verify, to them, the truths of their doctrines. In much the same way that Zen practitioners might say that experience in zazen verifies their realization of the truth of emptiness, someone while praying may have a tangible sense of the presence of God. Zen's truth is not open to external verification but is grounded in internal identification. Zen masters claim that you, yourself, will know it for sure, even though the "knowing" under consideration is a kind of not-knowing. The ultimate truth is beyond knowing.

Enlightenment and Evidence

Identification of our true self with the transcendental truth of Zen, as a distinct way of fathoming reality and one's place in it, comprises "a turning about in the inmost consciousness ," as Buddha is said to have testified (Goddard 1932). That this occurs within our inmost consciousness indicates that this turning about cannot be triggered by ordinary consciousness. To enter inmost consciousness, we must take a step back from what we regard as our own consciousness, as suggested by Master Dogen in Fukanzazengi (Sotoshu 2001), while reminding us of the limitations of koan practice and study:

> You should stop pursuing words and letters And learn the backward step of turning the light on yourself When you do so your body-mind will naturally fall away And your original buddha-nature will appear

"Body-mind," representing the nonduality of body and mind, may be taken to mean that dualistic conceptual categories informing ordinary consciousness will naturally fall away, eventually. That our buddha-nature will appear "of itself" implies that it is already here, present, awaiting our awakening to it. Buddha declared this kind of truth (i.e., self-identity with truth) to be superior to unverifiable belief, as well as to findings based on evidence verifiable by third parties, scientific truth.

Identification of the true self with ultimate and unconditioned truth in the inmost consciousness must be an experience literally beyond belief, intellect, or concept, beyond evidence or measurement. Certainly beyond words and letters. The admonition "You should stop pursuing words and letters" is vintage Dogen, promoting a direct method of practice that does not rely on concepts. The prevalent form of Zen in Japan at that time was so-called "word Zen" (J. kanna) of the Linchi or Rinzai school, which emphasized meditating on assigned koans, illogical riddles meant to stymie the intellect. But the truth of Zen is inherently inconceivable, and therefore inexpressible in words, as portrayed in a sixth-century poem by Ch'an's third ancestor Sengcan, in "Faith in Mind" (Sotoshu 2001):

> No comparisons or analogies are possible
> in this causeless, relationless state
> Consider motion in stillness
> and stillness in motion;
> Both movement and stillness disappear
> When such dualities cease to exist
> oneness itself cannot exist
> To this ultimate finality
> no law or description applies

And later, at the end of the poem:

> Words! The Way is beyond language
> For in it there is no yesterday, no tomorrow, no today

Zen's revelatory insight does not qualify as an epiphany confirming a religious belief, as defined by theism, or as scientific evidence proving a hypothesis or theory, as defined by rationalism. But this does not mean that it is not real. It can be verified only in your direct experience, which requires a deep trust in, and identification with, your original or true nature: Buddhism's Zen Mind. The "ultimate finality" for Zen has nothing to do with the existence of a creator or the beginning and end of the universe and its ultimate meaning, or any other such speculative notions, however compelling. It is at once both a personal and ultimate finality, a nondual insight inclusive of the entirety of reality, transcending our dualistic conceptions of it. Thus, it is innate, something we actually already must know, if only subliminally. And it is intimate, close in time and space, like water to a fish, air to a bird.

Buddhist practice and philosophy claim to transmit a central truth, which is uniquely capable of liberating us from self-imposed bondage. Zen is not a religion of the deceased, promising paradise to believers and martyrs and perdition to the unrepentant. Zen is a spiritual practice by, for, and of the living. It promises the possibility of spiritual awakening in this lifetime, as testified to by its ancestors: the way to realizing our true identity.

A koan for you: Why did Master Sengcan, out of all the words in the vernacular vocabulary, choose the three that he did—yesterday, tomorrow, and today—to illustrate that the Way is beyond language? A follow-up koan if you get that one: Why did he list them in that order, instead of the usual yesterday, today, and tomorrow?

DIMENSION 7.
GOALS PURSUED: KNOWLEDGE, SALVATION, VOW

Knowledge may be considered a goal of all three fields. But like evidence, of starkly different flavors. Knowing and not knowing, and what we can and cannot know, clearly pertain to all. Salvation and vow, not so much. Knowledge is key in the definition of goals. Being able to know for sure, in any determinate sense, the overriding goals of advocates of theism, versus those of rationalist philosophy or science, as well as those implied in Zen, is likely to encompass the area of greatest disagreement among adherents and opponents within each field. What are you hoping to accomplish, and how far are you willing to go to do so? Most such goals as publicly reported often appear to be in direct conflict with other fields of endeavor. And just as often appear completely disingenuous in public discourse.

The push for studying the Bible in public schools is derided by secularists as a Trojan horse, intended to convert impressionable youth to Christian beliefs. Secular subjects such as evolution are criticized by religionists as conditioning children to function in a godless society. Thus, the ostensible goals of opposing sides to every issue are defined as mutually exclusive smoke screens.

Defining or redefining the goals of adversaries in the wrangle over establishing secular versus religious hegemony over the classroom may offer the most fertile ground for rapprochement: back to the drawing board, to redefine the problem before proposing solutions. For example, it is not controversial to claim that the Bible can be studied as literature, unless the faculty are died-in-the-wool proselytizers who are out to save students' souls, at the expense of a well-rounded education.

In my senior year in our small-town township high school, we studied the book of Job and Ecclesiastes, along with Greek tragedies, Ernest Hemingway, and a broadly diverse range of other literature. Admittedly this was a special honors class for what passed as the nerds of the day, not likely to be adopted as standard curriculum for most public schools. The teacher, a former WAC (Women's Army Corps) from WWII, was nationally famous and pursued by peers across the country for her curriculum. She told them to make up their own. That was the whole point.

There are many such convoluted forays in the so-called "war of ideas" waged to capture the hearts and minds of the next generation. Near-missionary zealots are often defensive about their own self-interest, and less than forthcoming as to what is at stake for them personally, all the while waxing dismissive of their opponents' viewpoint and dubious of their integrity. To see stark illustrations of this disconnect, look no further than the agencies and school boards ostensibly committed to the education of America's children, and to the protection and preservation of the world that they are to inherit, instead conscripting both parents and students into ideological campaigns.

Perhaps the only conclusion we can come to in these proxy wars is that never the twain shall meet. A first step toward détente might be to drop any pretense of commitment to a broad secular curriculum. The ongoing and unabated horror show of school shootings and antisocial social media threats of further violence illustrate the cascade of immediate consequences of the adults in the room being unable to come to accord. To reach long-term goals of harmonious communities and eventually world peace, we must first nurture personal peace.

Proponents of both science and religion claim to be working for the betterment of humankind, if on different planes: the physical versus the spiritual, respectively. The altruistic goals of rationalism and science to improve the lives of people are often assailed as antithetical to those of theism.

Programs to help people live longer or make abortions safer inevitably raise moral issues, which theists claim as their wheelhouse. Religious folk would argue that they have true compassion for others, incidentally directed more to saving their immortal souls than their mortal bodies and minds.

A more fruitful approach would be to examine the possibility of what kinds of goals both sides might share in common. You could do worse than adopting the first precept of Zen, and shared by the American Medical Association: do no harm.

We human beings naturally stress difference over sameness. Even within various specialties of such secular disciplines as health and medicine, as well as among various denominations and sects of religions, factions with conflicting agendas arise. Even within the congregation of a single church, or among members of a scientific project team, individuals often find themselves competing for recognition, as well as for diminishingly limited resources. Conflict resolution is basic problem-solving.

Zen offers meditation's middle way for the individual to settle into deep stillness on physical, emotional, and mental planes. From which standpoint, the ongoing uncivil wars may be examined more dispassionately. Out of relative serenity, the appropriate skillful action necessary to settle any skirmish may become obvious.

The goals I have chosen to contrast with Zen's vow— salvation for theism and knowledge for rationalism—may not be the most salient choices to experts in their respective specialist fields. But we can play with them, testing the theory that the differences may be more semantic than actual.

If salvation is taken as a goal of science instead of knowledge, for instance, what kind of salvation would we be talking about? Perhaps we could answer "salvation from suffering" on a relative temporal plane. If we substitute knowledge for the goal of salvation in theism, what order of knowledge would it be? Perhaps it would be expressed as certain knowledge that all may not be right with the world, but could be if we can practice a secular imitation of divine love. Eliminating world hunger for starters.

Or perhaps we can agree to agree that the fecundity and delightful design of nature our kids study in biology and botany may be accepted as part and parcel of the body-mind of God, whatever that means to the individual, rather than insisting upon a doctrinal diktat that the Bible is the literal and only dependable reference text. In this exercise, the labels may be found to be interchangeable, illuminating modifications to current patently skewed definitions associated with the terms. They are only labels. The actual goals of rationalism and theism may not be so far apart as we tend to believe.

Rationalism: Knowledge

If you are professionally engaged in a rational discipline such as education, or a specialist field of science, you may feel that your goals are not adequately expressed by the phrase "the acquisition of knowledge." A more down-to-earth goal may be expressed as "publish or perish," especially in academia. Again, the social and personal goals of right livelihood cannot be compartmentalized.

Research developed for practical applications is not usually "pure," intended for the pursuit of knowledge alone. Knowledge is often a prerequisite for more prosaic goals, such as targeting applications to profitable ends. Knowledge itself can be classified on levels ranging from the mundane to the sublime. But knowledge must be applied to have any commercial value. Knowledge is generally valued only if it is used to serve the well-being and comfort, or vanity and entertainment, of humankind. Otherwise, it has little value. "Knowledge for its own sake" may reflect a quaint throwback to times of relatively higher prosperity and relatively lower ambition. Today, we have no time to waste on it.

As an overriding goal, knowledge may be seen as an antidote to the fundamental problem of chaos. Most applications of knowledge try to exert some level of control over our world, to bring order out of chaos. This would include the ability to predict and avoid natural, as well as man-made, calamities.

Ominously, applications of technology and science seem increasingly devoted to wielding control over burgeoning populations, reflected in the nearly eighty million refugees and counting currently displaced by political conflicts. As a result, there are increasingly urgent demands for basic daily necessities, such as potable water and adequate food supplies.

Knowledge is power, as we say. Power can be applied positively, of course, to large-scale control of the environment, improving life-enhancing outcomes. But the power of knowledge based on intelligence-gathering is also central to fulfilling the demand for geopolitical and military objectives, the outcomes of which tend to be the opposite of life-enhancing. How well this will work out, as always, remains to be seen. Political failures, such as collateral damage (read civilian casualties), and missteps triggering unintended international conflicts, are increasingly blamed on faulty data (i.e., "intelligence").

Knowledge Gone Awry

Knowledge is a neutral thing. It can be used for good or ill, which is starkly in the eye of the user. One historical example of what may be considered scientific knowledge gone awry is the Manhattan Project, which developed the first nuclear weapon, the atomic bomb. This application of Einstein's pure research is one that he may have instigated by warning President Roosevelt that the Nazis were on the verge of producing such a weapon. But he was apparently deeply troubled by its development and subsequent use against the Japanese. Once that genie was let out of that bottle, it appears impossible to put it back.

We are still living in the shadow of an enormous stockpile of weapons of mass destruction, WMDs, a grim legacy of the Cold War and its strategy of mutually assured destruction, with its appropriately ironic acronym, MAD. We have just passed the seventieth anniversary of the first nuclear attack on Hiroshima, my Zen teacher's childhood stomping grounds, and Nagasaki. And we seem to have entered yet another nuclear arms race and a game of international chicken, this time with Russia. We hear again the plaintive strains of "When will they ever learn?" wafting down memory lane, Pete Seeger on the banjo (1955).

Energy Slaves

On the bright side, most of the comforts of modern life derive from rational tech innovations, mostly developed by science, mostly funded by business-oriented investors. The "internet of things" is fast becoming ubiquitous. Digital inventions, used to enhance and control daily life, may be regarded as energy slaves, as R. Buckminster Fuller defined modern appliances in general (1940). An energy slave is a unit measure of service performance. Once existing primarily in the form of actual human slaves, which, tragically are still with us in the form of international human trafficking, the relevance of the energy slave as a concept is similar to the now-outmoded measurement "horsepower."

In modern transport, the power of vehicles outstrips hundreds of horses and the digital power at our fingertips is taken for granted. A single mobile device carries a huge multiple of the total computing power that put men on the moon just fifty years ago in the Apollo 11 mission. The number of warm bodies required to provide the same level of service as do our smartphones is incalculable.

Contemporary nonhuman energy slaves take the form of computers, smart machines, mobile and wearable electronic devices, as well as robots. They are virtual slaves in that they are at our beck and call and have no choice but to serve. Ironically, people can become enslaved to their devices, in turn.

In Zen, we practice to become independent of attachments and aversions, including addictions and deleterious habits of thinking. In the modern age we must also strive to become independent of our technology. Like language, a primordial invention, we want to use tech, not be used by it.

Double-Edged Sword

Knowledge is a two-edged sword, not necessarily good or evil. It depends on how it is used. The new trend toward smart-everything is fraught with downsides such as encroaching loss of privacy and the threat of hacking and hijacking, via remote control, of our vehicles as well as interconnected home and work environments. We are witnessing our private world potentially slipping out of our personal control. It amounts to the latest twist on Hegel's dialectic, or the synthesis of form. Beginning with the existing thesis or status quo being threatened by a new technological antithesis appearing on the horizon, there follows a gradual adaptive merging of the two, the process of synthesis, into the new thesis, which in time will be disrupted by yet another antithesis. Cultural evolution is accelerated by an ever-increasing rate of change, fueled by technology and greed.

Each new advance in safety and security seems to have its own Achilles' heel. Unconstrained firearms purchased for personal and home protection are often unsecured, leaving children vulnerable. The latest home surveillance systems designed to be remotely controlled can be readily compromised by remote professional or amateur hackers. International networks are more susceptible to disruption.

Faux facades of greater security gained through greater knowledge of technology crumble into greater vulnerability, crushed under the mass of total surrender to hi-tech. Each new disruptor, each new competitive antithesis appearing on the horizon, carries the seed of its own destruction. An early low-tech example of this syndrome is the first card-accessible parking lots at one of the universities where I taught. Students quickly learned that the gate would respond to a small piece of the card, so they cut them up and sold them to other students. You cannot plan or design around human nature.

Theism: Salvation

If you are committed to a deity-based religion, you probably would agree that the most common goal of theism is some form of salvation, most crucially that of your own soul. If you are a minister, a shepherd of evangelism, or simply a caring member of the flock, your soteriological concern extends to the fate of the souls of others in the congregation as well as your own.

Most religions strive to hold individuals accountable for the consequences of their actions. But forgiveness is also highly valued, or at least paid lip service in many faiths. Such practices as papal dispensation and priestly absolution, however, disrupt and corrupt the familiar cycle of sin, confession, repentance, and redemption, codified in scripture as waystations on the road to salvation.

While this process is ostensibly internal and private, a matter between individuals and their God, or a parishioner and their priest, all too often the drama is played out in public. And occasionally becomes a melodrama performed on the daily news. It goes without saying that salvation is not possible absent redemption, which is not possible without repentance, and that confession makes no sense in the absence of sin.

All religions seem to uphold an aspiration to something ineffable, a higher and nobler truth, which as a goal is capable of raising adherents above the swamp of our baser motives and desires. In Zen, this higher reality is known as original- or buddha-nature. To realize it in this life, we train ourselves diligently in meditation.

Zen salvation consists of being saved from our own ignorance. But salvation is experienced in this life, rather than after death. And it is considered "nothing special." It is not a matter of being "born again" through accepting Buddha as our savior, but of recovering our original nature while in the midst of life. This is Zen's living salvation. Can I get an amen?

Prosperity Religion

Before leaving the subject of goals of the religious life, we will touch upon the phenomenon of prosperity religions, which enjoy considerable attention in the press and include Nichiren Buddhism. While Buddha apparently taught laypeople differently than he did the mendicant monastics in the original order, including such subjects as how to accumulate and manage wealth, he did not emphasize prosperity as the singular most important goal in lay life nor did he conflate success with devotion.

In fact, the teachings of Zen cast a jaundiced eye on the overt celebration of wretched excess that has long been a hallmark of Western and American culture. An especially onerous example is the orgy of conspicuous consumption known as the holiday season, commingled as it is with values of spiritual poverty in Christianity, which are directly contrary to overindulgence. This annual spending binge is also set against a political background of imputed values of austerity, whose proponents may talk the talk but do not usually walk the walk.

We have elected multimillionaires as president and most members of Congress are themselves comfortably wealthy, after some time in the business of horse-trading, if not when first elected to office. The value of incumbency has gone through the roof, along with the millions of dollars needed to run a competitive campaign. The cost of the best government that money can buy has skyrocketed. The Supreme Court of the United States recently allowed that corporations may be considered persons, clearing the way for them to provide unlimited contributions to political campaigns, tilting the playing field against noncorporate persons.

In a rebuke to the Founding Fathers, as well as to Engels and Marx, who all assumed revolution to be the natural response to oppression, the proletariat seem to be increasingly sheeplike, with the exception of that recent little invasion of the capital. Rather than resenting the dominance of what seems to be an oligarchy, those at the lower end of the financial spectrum tend, or pretend, to emulate the wealthy and powerful. That a limited number of individuals claim to earn millions or billions per year, while millions of others live in poverty, seems to be a given of our times.

The old adage that anyone in the USA can aspire to be president is gainsaid by the necessity of raising millions of dollars to compete, even on down-ballot campaigns. The American dream of upward mobility, the possibility of moving from the fast-disappearing middle class to the upper echelons of wealth and power, is statistically approaching zero. Choose your parents carefully.

These dismal prospects for the hoi polloi are supposedly counterbalanced by the omnipresence of the lottery, which just topped a billion dollars for the first time in its history, and its innumerable spinoffs. All of which, as investments, have a low probability of paying off, even compared to those of the sacred stock market, the Dow, which, ironically, sounds like "the Tao." While offering the chances of an ice cube in hell, the games keep the rubes coming, reinforcing the inequality gap. Everything begins to look like a casino, with the odds in favor of the house. Can't win unless you play.

Please bear with me if this is beginning to sound like a bit of a rant. It is only meant to recall the reality of our current cultural context, to establish contrast with the social teachings of Zen. My point is that while our consumer society may be a natural outgrowth of capitalism, it does not align with traditional Abrahamic doctrine as I understand it, and rampant materialism certainly does not reflect the core values of Zen. But Zen is not a crusade, and this is but a snapshot of our social situation.

Our vaunted capitalism does not necessarily stem from Democracy, or vice versa. This can be seen in the many variations of government and economics in developed and developing countries around the globe. One extreme theory has been put forth that avowed capitalists have yet another mental disorder. Others would argue that like any other system of transaction, capitalism is morally neutral. But there is an argument to be made that excess profits seem to reflect unfair income distribution derived from raiding the fair share of contributing workers, admittedly a Marxian doctrine (Weber 1947). But that does not make it untrue. The border with Mexico is a Marxian petri dish.

You may or may not agree with the growing majority of economists who argue that austerity imposed from the outside or from the top down doesn't work. In troubled economies around the globe, just as right here at home, such dictatorial control is doomed to be ineffective at best, hypocritical and exacerbating at worst. I feel safe in saying that governmental approaches, while stoking the profit-driven needs of the corporate economy, will likely fail to address the underlying personal compulsions driving mass consumption. When the going gets tough, the tough may reflexively go shopping, especially when egged on by the POTUS du jour. But that does not make it the correct, compassionate, or wise thing to do.

Austerity as practiced in Zen is self-imposed. Based on a balanced view of how much is enough, enough to sustain a moderate degree of comfort and well-being, our degree of personal consumption should reflect a pragmatic reading, and set an example of the Middle Way in action. The cutting edge of Zen can be usefully applied to such issues. Its vow of salvation through moderation is razor sharp.

Zen Buddhism: Vow

The Zen goal framed as "living by vow" may be related to the idea of salvation, but it is not directed toward saving our soul, nor the souls of others. Salvation in Zen consists in liberation from our own ignorance, which is the same underlying goal, if unstated as such, that is shared by the public and private education system in most countries of the world, including the good old USA.

The Buddhist vow to help others before oneself is open-ended and would fit the mind frame of most teachers, especially those laboring in middle and lower grades, who are known for their bodhisattva-like self-sacrifice. In the context of Zen training, the vow is actualized by exposing others to the dharma and to its method of meditation. But only if they seek it out. We do not proselytize, and we do not believe that simply by taking vows we are saved. Vows are guidelines for working out our potential liberation. Inherent in our existence as human beings, we call it our innate buddha-nature. Here, "buddha" refers to waking up completely, another unstated goal of education in general, and of all three of the fields. Waking up to the truth, that is.

You may be familiar with the Buddhist vow to save all other beings before oneself, referred to as the Bodhisattva Vow, first of the Four Great Vows. The initial stanza below is the first one I learned, the second a consensus version in use in many Soto Zen communities today (Sotoshu 2001):

> Beings are numberless; I vow to free them.
> Delusions are inexhaustible; I vow to end them.
> Dharma gates are boundless; I vow to enter them.
> The Buddha Way is unsurpassable; I vow to realize it.
>
> However innumerable all beings are, I vow to save them all.
> However inexhaustible my delusions are. I vow to extinguish them all.

However innumerable the Dharma teachings are, I vow to master them all.
However endless the Great Way is, I vow to follow it   completely.

The Four Vows encourage us to take action connected to the Four Noble
Truths. We vow to take action to resolve the dilemma of suffering existence,
for ourselves and for others. The following three cover the more personal
dimensions of Zen practice, which constitute the preparation necessary to
realize the first. Bodhisattva denotes an "enlightening being," dedicated to a
personal mission of saving others. Practical realities render the first vow literally impossible, at first blush. But living by vow requires going beyond literal
interpretations.

Zen may be altruistic, but the goals of Zen have nothing to do with changing the world in the strictly literal sense of revolutionizing the external societal
conditions in which we find ourselves. Matsuoka Roshi would remark that
the Zen person has no problem following the sidewalks, meaning that if we
are nonconformists, it manifests on a much deeper level than surface appearances. This does not mean that the Zen worldview excuse inaction in the face
of injustice, however.

While Buddhist teachings do not dictate specific ways of engaging or taking
sides in the causes of the day, many of its adherents do so, actualizing "engaged
Zen" by following their own conscience and wisdom. Instead, the tactical goals
of Zen are concerned with transforming or transcending our own existential
ignorance. If and when we do so, we will be better prepared to enter the social
and political fray without blinders, and without preconceptions. In order to
promote world peace effectively, we must first find internal peace.

Transformation necessarily begins at home, with each individual confronting their own confusion on a very up-close-and-personal level, directly
through meditation on immediate reality. We focus first on clarifying our own
heart and mind, then turning to help our fellow human beings, like the now-
iconic oxygen mask message that admonishes you to don yours first. The
process does not work the other way around. Zen is revolutionary in a ground-up,
not top-down, sense. But Zen is not a crusade. Do-gooders need not apply.

This does not mean that Zen Buddhists do not engage in good works, of
course. But it does suggest that charitable activism is not enough in and of
itself. Good works must be informed by the wisdom found in meditation,
ensuring that they are truly beneficial, or at least do no harm.

In this regard Zen can appear to be hopelessly self-centered navel-gazing.
But by stiving to change ourselves, working on our own behavior and worldview first, we become working models for change in the world, and may

even become exemplars to others. We humans cause all the trouble in the world, after all, primarily through ignorance, including, most pertinently, the widespread ignorance of the teachings of Buddhism. Zen practice trains individuals to become truly independent in terms of personal worldview, but interdependent in terms of social relationships, and to take action based on that interconnectedness. No one told us this was going to be easy.

Communal Refuge

Sympathetic altruism, as found in religious fellowship, finds resonance with Zen, where relationships among members of the community (S. sangha) are guided by a focus on direct experience of the truth of the teachings (S. dharma), primarily through meditation, but also via dialogue. In Zen centers, temples and monasteries, "good friends" in the sangha (S. kalyanamitra; J. chishiki) are defined by their singular, main, or sole interest in pursuing the dharma both for the sake of their own understanding, and that of others, which is what makes them a true friend.

Individuals in the Zen community may be interested in each other on a social level, or even in developing a deeper relationship, as is natural. But members are not generally there to meet people, but to learn and practice Zen, and so should assume that others are sincere seekers, as well. This intent informs relationships with other sangha members, namely having their best spiritual interests at heart.

Zen Buddhism shares this characteristic with world religions: an emphasis on the salvation of all. Salvation in Zen is not pictured as souls ascending to heaven after death but being saved while still alive. The last words of Buddha (Jnana 2018) are said to have included the admonition to his disciples that they should work out their own salvation, to "be a lamp unto yourself."

In Buddhism we repent our violations of precepts and take refuge in buddha and dharma, as well as in sangha. The traditional meaning of the vows is that bodhisattvas postpone their own personal salvation in deference to helping all other beings save themselves, beginning with one's own sangha.

Saved from What?

But any logical interpretation of this vow raises obvious questions such as Who needs to be saved? Save them from what? How do we save them, exactly? How many are there? How long is it going to take? Where do I begin? How do I know when I am finished? It is said that when we take the vows to heart, eternal rebirth opens before us. It is going to take a long, long, time.

Taking the vows seriously, we begin to see their inherent contradictions. Imagining that we can fulfill them in any literal sense is nonsensical at best, hubristic at worst. We have to consider a more humble take on what they may mean. If we are not even able to save ourselves, how in the world are we supposed to save others? It becomes obvious where we must begin. Salvation begins at home.

But what are we to save ourselves from, exactly? In order to save oneself from something, anything, it would seem a prerequisite to know precisely what that something is. The classic answer in Buddhism is ignorance. We save ourselves from our own ignorance. But how are we to do that?

Ignorance Abounds

In zazen we examine our own ignorance thoroughly and in great detail. But it is a tall order. This is why Zen practice takes so long to bear fruit. Our ignorance, both innate and learned, is thick and deep. Salvation does not come cheap, and it is a do-it-yourself exercise. No one can climb halfway up the Zen mountain and have someone else reach the summit for them. We each have to climb the slopes all the way to the top. There are no shortcuts. No surrogates need apply.

If we wholeheartedly enter into Zen's process of self-examination and continue in zazen to a sufficient degree, allowing our discoveries to take their full effect, we may top the summit. From personal trials and errors we may serendipitously develop the interpersonal skills, or expedient means, to help others to do likewise. But saving ourselves from our own ignorance does not necessarily enable us to help others with theirs. Insight does not magically imbue anyone with talents they do not already possess, though it may improve those you already enjoy.

Even Buddha's disciples were said to have "had it but not the use of it." Many clearly had genuine insight, but little talent or inclination to teach others. So we all simply do our best, which may not be very good. Fortunately, salvation is the responsibility of each individual. Teachers can only help.

Saving ourselves is saving all beings, as selfish and grandiose as that may sound. But believing that there are beings who need saving, and that we are uniquely capable of saving them, raises two major problems and a whole host of minor ones.

First, such a misconception misconstrues the thrust of Zen to be evangelistic and implies that others need our intervention because they are incapable of saving themselves. Second, it causes an even more grievous confusion that we can actually do for others what they can only do by and for themselves. This is the ultimate in self-aggrandizement, akin to the claim that priests can absolve the sins of others. This kind of arrogance-fed zealotry takes the focus, as well as the onus, off the individual, where it belongs. The onus is on us.

Salvation in Zen—direct verification of the true nature of your original self—lies somewhere in the middle ground between the epiphany of theistic religion and the evidence of rationalistic science. Your personal grasp of whatever kind and degree of salvation is available to you will be based upon your own evidence, garnered through your own irrefutable direct experience.

Irrefutable Experience

You may legitimately question in what sense can anything in our experience be considered irrefutable? Is it really possible that we cannot be mistaken about what we experience in zazen? It is a known issue that you can spend your whole life doing what you think is Zen meditation, while only going through the motions. You assume the posture but never get beyond the machinations of monkey-mind. Positioning Zen midway between the worldviews of rationalism and theism, the claim that direct experience in Zen is irrefutable seems indefensible. It would seem to validate blanket claims to the irrefutability of theories of rationalism and the beliefs of theism. Fair is fair.

Christian belief in the divinity of Jesus is irrefutable to a Christian. Based on the exercise of faith, it need not be either confirmed or refuted by evidence. But because in Zen we rely on experiential evidence, albeit first-person, rather than belief, we reserve the right to be wrong in the process.

But experience evolves over time. What a newcomer experiences in zazen is both the same and different from that of a veteran. The ancient Vedic mantra of "not this, not that" (S. neti neti) denotes a process of rejecting anything and everything that comes to conscious awareness in meditation, until something manifests that cannot be refuted. This "something" would be the true self of Zen.

This is the sense in which we mean that only your own, direct experience in zazen can provide irrefutable evidence of your true self, or original mind. Even the word "experience," as usually understood, cannot cut it. Ordinary experience is dualistic in nature. Nondual reality cannot, by definition, be experienced. This is the point at which we realize that words fail in the attempt to describe or in any logical way communicate, the intimate nature of realization. It simply does not compute or translate.

Zen ancestors have described the real zazen as the kind of meditation that has no particular object. The posture, breath, and attention all come together in a unified way and the mind and object finally merge in stillness, or shikantaza. Meanwhile, we may imagine that we are penetrating to the core of Zen, when actually we are still floating on the surface. But do not let this discourage you.

Master Dogen assures us in his *Jijuyu Zammai: Self-Fulfilling Samadhi* that we "will in zazen unmistakably drop off body and mind, cutting off the various defiled thoughts from the past, and realize the essential buddha-dharma" (Sotoshu 2001). We are enabled by zazen to have an unmistakable insight into what is essential, one that is not refutable by anyone else, and by the same token, not provable to anyone else. This is why Zen's insight is called intimate.

Buddhism's insight cannot claim the legitimacy of a scientific theory, let alone one that is fully proven. The underlying premise—that buddha-dharma and our original buddha-nature reflect realities—also does not constitute a belief, nor is it based upon a prelearned system of beliefs. Tenets of Zen live somewhere in the space between hypothesis or theory as testable, and belief as conviction. All three fields are based in human experience, if of different orders, and equally questionable.

Living and Dying by Vow

As a worthwhile goal for one's life, an open-ended vow to save all beings may seem counterintuitive. What kind of goal is a vow compared to, say, knowledge or control? In Zen, knowledge means self-knowledge, control means self-control. Salvation then inheres in overcoming negative syndromes and destructive behaviors of the constructed self largely through dispassionate observation, in meditation as well as in daily life. Zen's resolve, then, is simply to be unhindered by the causes and conditions of existence in our quest for liberation. Quite a resolution, New Year's or otherwise.

To be born is to be born into a situation that we definitely do not control and cannot really control in any absolute sense. As we mature into adulthood, we typically develop a sense of greater control, both over our environment and with regard to our own actions. Actions have consequences, we can all agree, regardless of our politics. But we can control our own actions and re-actions to a degree, and thus mitigate negative consequences. However, there is always the threat of unintended consequences that we cannot control, following either from acts of commission, or even acts of omission.

The ongoing dynamic of sentient existence is something about which we can do little more than act as witness. We are nearly helpless in the face of the natural progress of aging, sickness, and death, or even the daily calls of Mother Nature. To fully grasp this, next time you are meditating and nature calls, see how far you get with telling her to mind her own business and leave you alone. You are busy meditating just now. Oops! We are experiencing technical difficulties beyond our control.

Knowledge can help, in an immediate sense, to accept and lessen the impact of this fundamental lack of control. With nurture comes a kind of power over nature, if limited. But it is cold comfort in the long run. The real-world conundrum of innate mortality suggests that we abandon futile pursuit of our fancied dependency on control, and all other like conventions of knowledge, and turn our attention to arousal of the Way-seeking mind. This entails the idealistic goal of living by vow, rather than pursuing knowledge, control, or the even more elusive salvation. And least of all, enlightenment.

Mitigating Suffering

You may point to the many troubles of the world not directly caused by humans, such as natural disasters and the bloody predations of the food chain. These are not warm and fuzzy realities. But they pale in comparison with the afflictions humans visit upon others, and even upon themselves. Most of us can recall painful times when we have harmed others, intentionally or inadvertently, harming ourselves in the process. Writ large, it is clear that human population is prompting global harm in the form of pollution and climate change.

The real-world context of the Bodhisattva Vow means to "do no harm," the first ethical and moral precept of Zen. The mother of all precepts, it is the first of three "pure" precepts, and not unique to Zen. It is found, verbatim, in the Hippocratic Oath of the American Medical Association, however faithfully or erratically its members may live up to it.

It may seem oversimplified to subsume the many goals of Buddhism under three simple vows, but Zen's Pure Precepts—to do no harm, to do only good, and to do good for others—fully understood and embraced, encompass all the others. The third, not incidentally, presages the Bodhisattva Vow.

But of course, doing no harm is not a cut-and-dried proposition. It does not allow for a cookie-cutter approach. Living by vow is open-ended, not a definitive, goal-oriented set of guidelines for behavior. The true goal of living by vow may be said to be inconceivable. It is too deep and broad to define. It is more a mindset than a resolution, crusade, or campaign.

If you live your life based on this kind of vow, it may be very different from a life based on belief, or one whose deeper meaning depends upon evidence gleaned from rational reasoning. Living by vow is divorced from tangible evidence of the success of one's efforts. Living by vow is not driven by personal salvation. Nor is it a life based on applied rationalism, dedicated to the pursuit of knowledge and its application to our material safety and comfort. Living by vow is certainly not predicated upon the avoidance of suffering, as Buddhism is sometimes portrayed, or upon the mindless pursuit of happiness, which amounts to a misguided interpretation of liberation.

Universal Suffering

Zen does not countenance futile attempts to avoid suffering, other than the unnecessary kind we create by our own actions. Quite the opposite. Suffering (S. dukkha), reduced to a universal principle of change by attrition, is built into all existence, for insentient as well as sentient beings. The insentient world, up to and including collisions of galaxies, stars going nova, and all the way down to particle decay, amounts to dukkha: an ever-changing, impersonal, and universal polyrhythm of change.

From the moment of conception, we are caught up in unremitting change, extending throughout our lifetime. And even beyond death into the next life, according to the principle of rebirth. But as human beings we tend to take unwanted change very personally. And we often mount a stubborn resistance to desirable change.

Taking the Buddhist vow to lead a Zen life means meeting suffering and change head-on. This, we may say, is the ultimate in control and the only true salvation. Here is where the goal of salvation in theism finds common ground with Buddhism's embrace of karma. Surrendering one's life to God or a savior is tantamount to surrendering to buddha-dharma as a higher power, developing the "right view" of existence. But the vow is taken for the sake of others, as well for oneself. In this it is akin to the apostolic imperative, the evangelist mission of spreading the Gospel, and dedicating one's life to saving others, setting aside for now the definition of a soul. Quoting again from the sixty-century Ch'an poem *Hsinhsinming: Faith in Mind*, saving others and saving oneself are not in opposition (Sotoshu 2001):

In this world of suchness, there is neither self nor other-than-self.

If there is neither self nor other than self, then where do we find the self that is to be saved? And, again, saved from what, exactly? In Zen, we are not to be saved from our actual existential conditions, however onerous. So the question arises: Who can be saved? And by whom? When individuals embody the vow to save all others before themselves, genuinely taking this vow to heart, they become bodhisattvas, actively engaged in enlightening others, via enlightening themselves.

But again, the propagation of Zen is not to be conceived as, or confused with, yet another crusade to save the world. The advent and evolution of Buddhism may be on a different track than the arc of history, but we may harbor the hope that they are convergent paths, their arc bending toward spiritual awakening, the final and only justice. If all peoples of the world recover their original nature, societal salvation becomes possible. This possibility begins, and ends, with the vow to save all sentient beings. Including saving yourself.

DIMENSION 8.
CONCLUSIONS DRAWN: EVOLUTION, CREATION, CO-ARISING

To speak of drawing conclusions in this context—whether from the complex professions of secular rationalism, the complicated belief systems of theism, or most especially, from the teachings of Zen Buddhism—might seem inherently contradictory. How can religion, or any rational field of endeavor, including the hard and soft sciences, claim to be conclusive in any meaningful sense? We are reminded of the old joke about the field of professional economics: lay all the economists in the world head to toe, and they may circle the globe but will still not come to a conclusion. Because conclusions are the most important part of any research project, tying together the raw findings and leading to any suggested recommendations, this section will run longer than the prior dimensions.

If we compare and contrast certain conclusions from these diverse fields—especially those regarding "first causes" and "final ends"—they may seem hopelessly at odds. Conclusions drawn by theologians against those of astrophysicists, vis-à-vis the beginning and end of the universe, are seemingly irreconcilable. Unless, of course, the Word of God sounds just like the Big Bang.

For theists, God is the one and only true antecedent of the universe: the writer, producer, a rising star with top billing supported by a cast of billions. Christian and Islamist doctrines also prophesy what will come after this existence, the sequel at the end of history, after the curtain. Namely, Armageddon. This yearning for closure—how did it all begin, where is it all going to end— seems to be an obsession shared equally by the professors of theism and the priests of rationalism. It is as if existential fatigue has replaced angst, and the audience is already heading for the exits. Roll the credits.

Modern cosmology claims that there is no "before" before the Big Bang. And, one supposes, there can be no "after" after the predicted heat-death of the universe. Enter the Big Bounce theory, a modified model for the origin of the known universe, where the first bang-up cosmological event under consideration is posited as the result of the collapse of a previous universe (Guth and Tye 1980). Picture a cosmic trampoline. This bouncier view is closer to the Hindu/Buddhist vision of ever-recycling, expanding, and contracting universes, over inconceivably epochal spans of time (S. kalpa). But we human beings naturally long for closure, in both beginnings and endings.

Any and all conclusions as to first causes and final ends proposed and defended by theists, as opposed to those arrived at by rationalists, will necessarily be expressed very differently, given that they are drawn from vastly disparate premises, professional contexts, and evidence from various sources, from nonexistent, to questionable, to accepted. It is also true that experience and expression do not enjoy a one-to-one correspondence in any field. Experience is required to convince. Expression attempts to convey. In Zen, as in science, experience comes first, expression a distant second.

Further, the foundational premises of theistic religion versus those of hard science are at odds because they reflect entrenched attitudes that differentially privilege belief versus evidence. Belief and evidence are defined so differently in each field that the terms no longer share a common connotation, let alone agreed-upon meanings. In religious belief, being devoid of tangible evidence is considered a strength: "Now faith is the substance of things hoped for, the evidence of things not seen" (Hebrews 11:1). In science, concrete observation or experimental evidence is the sine qua non of any working, if tentative, "belief" in a hypothesis, theory, or law of physics. We use the term colloquially, not in the religious sense.

Most people, if asked, will tend to express their self-identity by pointing out differences in their own personality, behavior, or worldview—the catch-phrase today being "my values"—compared to those of others. This somewhat defensive predisposition to emphasize differences over shared, common traits exacerbates the natural tensions between believers and skeptics, making common ground even more difficult to find. Emphasis on difference, a cultural bias in the West, trumps recognition of essential sameness, socially and psychologically, but may simply devolve to ego-based semantics ultimately.

Upon closer examination, even the apparent differences between competing creation myths and theories of origins may also be largely semantic, and self-serving to the cause of their proponents. Evolution, for example, may be embraced as a discernible pattern in the ongoing process of creation. Creation, in turn, may be interpreted metaphorically as analogous to the Big Bang. Neither theory of "how it all began"—a question not part of Darwin's purview, by the way—satisfactorily addresses what, if anything, preceded the present universe, let alone what may succeed it. "Creation" per se is sufficiently ambiguous—connoting either a generic coming into being, or a didactic reading of Genesis, the more common association—that we may safely take some liberties with it not merely for the sake of argument, but toward a more perfect union of worldviews, so to say, via reconciliation of overwrought distinctions without differences. In the struggle for the hearts and minds of our overt opponents, if we can resist stereotyping the terms themselves, we may discover surprising commonalities between certain beliefs of theism and hypotheses of rationalism.

We might ask theologians, for example, to consider whether the prevailing physical model of the origin of the universe —running Hubble's constant backward, rewinding the rate of acceleration of galaxies expanding away from each other back to a cosmic zero-point of origin: the primordial atom, or singularity, presaging the bang, or bounce—might not offer a possible physical translation of the language in which the God of Abraham actually spoke the Word.

We might likewise solicit scientists, who otherwise have no response as to what did come before the Big Bang, that we may as well call it God, if not in the personified sense. No harm no foul since, according to science, there was no other known or knowable entity, then and there. Otherwise, aren't we just splitting cosmic hairs?

Designing Deity

Before moving on to a more focused discussion of the three selected conclusions drawn in each field, let us turn once again to the quasi-scientific, inherently rational but intuitively inspired, profession of design, where lessons learned from design-build projects shed light on the parameters of creativity.

The Genesis account of origins was at one time considered scientific, in the broad sense that it offered an explanation for the evident order in the design of organic life: Adam's naming of the animals, as the forerunner of binomial nomenclature. From a theistic perspective, if life manifests an orderly design, that design must be intentional, which necessarily presupposes a designer. This notion leans heavily on human-centric logic (e.g., the familiar "watchmaker" analogy cited by modern creationists). Of course, we may safely assume that there were no watches in the Garden of Eden.

Life, then, becomes an artifice of that designer, identified with the Abrahamic God. Darwin's theory of natural selection, however, proposed—and proved, scientifically—that adaptations in the design of species do not require an artificer. They could instead arise naturally via adaptive traits, tweaks in differential survival strategies, and resultant reproduction of progeny, all according to measurable fitness differences, passed genetically between generations.

This is not the kind of fitness we can acquire by working out. It is more like the near-perfect fit of the COVID-19 virus, and its variants, to the particular causes and conditions of our times, including an exacerbating assist from human error and venality.

An aside: watches proceeding to move clockwise, as watches are wont to do—providing a timely tautology—may presuppose a watchmaker. But the shadow of the crudest natural sundial moving in the same direction does not require a shadow maker, nor does the existence of a cloud imply a cloud maker. The mind's eye notes, of course, that there are regular, repeatable, and discernible patterns here, there, and everywhere. Why do clocks move "clockwise"? They could as easily have been built counterclockwise, which would then be clockwise. These terms will be lost to history in due digital time. God makes toilets drain clock- and counterclockwise in Southern and Northern Hemispheres. We will have to come up with another postdigital term to describe that phenomenon. But I digress.

In short, professionals in physics and biology are not interested in entertaining questions from, or mounting challenges to, the claims laid out in Genesis. However, some contemporary practitioners may feel the need to reconcile their evidence-based day jobs with their will-of-God-based religions.

The slippery slope that the Darwinian theory threatened, and still threatens for Abrahamic faiths, is that an omniscient and hopefully benevolent God is no longer necessary as the designer of Creation. Furthermore, if one of the basic premises underlying the claim of inerrancy of biblical scripture is not factual, which, if any, are? The Gospel of Thomas may be the exception that proves this rule.

From a professional design perspective, I can testify from personal experience that most, if not all, major breakthroughs in the field are the product of a group process, not individuals in ivory towers. See: God's design committee, brainstorming possibilities for future improvements to the product.

Rationalism: Evolution

Owing to the confusion still rampant in some circles regarding Darwin's elegant conclusion from his research in the biological sciences, we will wade into the weeds a bit in an attempt to clarify it. When I say "we," I mean it literally, not royally, in that I have leaned extensively via consultation with more scientifically sophisticated collaborators, but they are absolved of any sins committed by my comment. Again, these memes from science and religion are employed to set the context for those of Zen, wherein I enjoy a greater comfort level.

Those familiar with the theory of the origin of species by natural selection set out in *On the Origin of Species*, first published in 1859, recognize that it elucidates a coherent process called "Descent with Modification." Individuals within species vary from their forebears in ways that affect their capacity to survive and, more importantly, to reproduce. These are known as "fitness differences." The more successful variants are those better suited to the ever-changing conditions of life, a process known as biological adaptation. Variants in the COVID family are all-too-familiar examples of this principle.

According to natural selection, variations that are heritable will dependably be passed on to succeeding generations via genetics. Incorporating these traits, species change (i.e., evolution). Populations originally of the same single species, if separated in isolation from each other over shorter or longer times, will gradually adapt to their differing local living conditions. In time, they will differentiate sufficiently as to constitute a new species (i.e., speciation).

The theory of natural selection reveals a lovely, natural logic underlying this adaptive, ever-changing, ongoing creative evolution and speciation. Call it God's logic, if you like. Modern genetics confirms this comprehensive model of intraspecies relationships, especially as inferred from DNA. Science now enjoys a reasonable basis for what is termed taxonomic classification of organisms, called "phylogenetic systematics." The "Three Taxon" principle requires that all evolutionary relationships be stateable in the form: "A is more closely related to B than either is to C." It is comforting that scientists embrace intrinsic interrelatedness. Very Zen, though it seems to be a slippery slope into the math.

But it does not necessarily follow that any such relationship, however clear and undeniable the pattern, reflects the mental machinations of an outside intelligent designer planning, designing, and controlling the results. God may be a geometer or mathematician but did not necessarily invent them.

Darwin set out a thorough-going naturalistic explanation for the phenomena of evolution, evidence for which had already been observed, widely accepted, and appreciated as factual, but up until then unexplained. Like others before him, the great naturalist embraced as fact the principle of organic variation, based on personal observation on the voyage of the HMS *Beagle*. Like others at that time, he had the received wisdom of the *Natural Theology* of William Paley (1802), a theologian who had first introduced the watchmaker argument. For Paley, elucidation of the mind of God was the goal, a thoroughgoing theistic explanation that the young Darwin had admired. In biology, the boundaries between rationalism, naturalism, and theism had not yet ossified. The accepted paradigm of natural theology approached biology with a pious motive: evidencing the attributes of the deity from the appearances of nature.

Darwin's first eureka moment comprised analogizing changes in time with changes in geography—variation observed in species separated in space is equivalent to that seen over time—a powerful insight surpassing and supplanting theological convention. Another entailed the correlation of artificial selection—for example, manipulations by pigeon breeders to achieve different body types by selective breeding—with what he termed natural selection. In the latter, selective survival and reproduction in consequence of adaptive differences that enable it incorporates a natural process analogous to the artificial process of livestock breeders.

In his effort to discover and clarify this naturalistic basis of the creation of species, he succeeded. Evolution by natural selection was a triumph of rational observation, experiment, and analysis. It took place post-Enlightenment, a period that generally favored natural over theistic explanations. The physical sciences had long before gone over to the side of rational reasoning based on evidence, as opposed to explanation based on belief.

But if this theory of evolution was conceived by rational means, it nonetheless describes life as a continuing process, a work in progress. Except in its final sentence, and then only in later editions, Darwin's original thesis does not allude to any First Cause. That was not its point.

Returning to the "Questions asked" dimension of our comparative chart, evolution by natural selection elegantly clarifies How change comes about over successive generations, as living beings cope with and adapt to different environments, but provides no answers as to Why. It does not posit how it all began, nor how it will all end. It does not philosophize as to the meaning of it all. It is not a religious position.

Of course, most of the public opposition to teaching the extensive evidence of evolution is ultimately not based entirely on religious belief, and certainly not on science, but rather upon sociopolitical strategies, especially the part known as descent with modification (i.e., descent from an earlier species; e.g., humans from apes). Resistance to the implications of Darwin's theory of the origin of species is that humans descend from an ancestry of more primitive apes. In *The Descent of Man* (1871), he anticipated that the notion of primate origin would be distasteful to many. It was, and still is. Even the choice of the term "descent," aside from a strictly technical context, is pejorative and prejudicial.

A relatively recent manifestation of this unfortunate mischaracterization is seen in the public set-to between proponents of evolutionary biology, in Darwinian and post-Darwinian forms—spawn of the Scopes trial—and adherents of creationism, including its bastard stepchild, intelligent design.

Opponents of teaching evolution in schools dismissing it as just another theory seem to regard theories as only opinions. And after all, all opinions are equal, in lieu of any respect for evidence.

Another sore point is the suggestion that human existence itself may be attributed to chance, some sort of cosmic fluke, a chaotic accident of random, unconscious physics and chemistry begetting biology. And unconscious biology, in turn, begetting the consciousness of humanity, replacing the begats of the biblical lineage from Adam and Eve on down. These ideas challenge core beliefs that our existence reveals the intent of a benevolent God. But the theory of evolution does not challenge Genesis, any more than it challenges the Big Bang. It is a pattern clearly discernible in biological speciation, not a competing theory of First Causes.

Theism: Creation

If you self-identify as a Christian, you may concur with theism's version of the genesis of creation—that God created the world, the entire universe, by fiat—a creation myth shared by the three major Abrahamic religions, with sectarian variations, since the time of their common origin. In modern times, and in the light of modern science, some accommodations to embracing evolution as nonthreatening to theological doctrine of origins have emerged.

An insight from modern systematic biology suggests that if several species share a common feature, the first explanation we should entertain is that this is due to common ancestry, rather than convergent adaptation. Applying this principle to the evolution of the Abrahamic religions, they originally endorsed Creation by fiat, and the three branches apparently maintained this doctrine when they went their separate ways.

Most historical cultures have envisioned a creation myth, usually involving the intent and actions of a creator god, or gods. Among the world's major theistic systems, the issue of whether different faiths worship the same God, or different gods, has long been subject to debate. This raises a question. If even the legitimacy of other gods at the centers of competing belief systems can be challenged, does that not suggest that the very validity of one's own God must also be questioned?

Those who have engaged the public debate in defense of creationism have not shown any evidence that rises to the level of scientific credibility, nor developed any arguments sufficient to persuade their opponents, or to sway a skeptical audience. These are the traditional objectives of public debate, but unfortunately not what passes for debate in the political arena today, which is mostly mudslinging.

Tortuous "theories" ginned up by creationists, such as the aforementioned faux hypothesis of irreducible complexity, the idea that so many structures found in biology, such as the human eye, are of such extreme complexity that—like that wristwatch—they must have been intentionally designed and built. This position entirely dismisses the abundant evidence that complex systems arise over time from simple beginnings—to wit, the multitude of simpler organs of vision found in nature. This kind of testimonial evidence resonates only with believers preaching to the choir.

Of course, we should not cavalierly dismiss out of hand any personal testimony that is a sincere expression of closely held beliefs, such as the epiphanies of the saints, or that of eyewitnesses in a court of law. But that does not mean that we should embrace the false equivalency of privileging testimony, or doctrine, equally with scientific evidence, especially when the two are irreconcilable.

Creation is asserted by theists as an incontestable conclusion, patently self-evident. Evidence-derived theories of origins—such as the Big Bang for the present universe, and evolution by natural selection for emergent species—are likewise widely regarded as substantively verified by the science team. But unlike belief in creation, both latter theories are subject to modification and fine-tuning as new evidence is uncovered, especially when and where new biological species are discovered, or as new data is gathered from proliferating space probes. All such theories in science may be considered as provisional operating frameworks, rather than final conclusions. Creation as a theory of origins follows from myth and faith tradition, rather than from evidence. The historicity of biblical prophecy coming to pass is often cited as proof, but in turn requires a corollary belief in the authenticity of the historical record, a Catch-22 of endless regress.

Belief in a creator God dictates that existence is, by definition, the result of divine intention and therefore cannot be an accident. Clinging to this view may mask a fear that human beings do not amount to much more than some sort of cosmic fluke, a random occurrence of physical events.

From the perspective of science, the complex cascade of events leading to conscious life ranges from the Big Bang to stars going nova, releasing heavy metals and other elements into the cosmos, in turn triggering chemical events affecting coalescing solar systems, ultimately giving rise to life, which in turn, quite recently in cosmic time, gave rise to consciousness in its multiplicity of forms. This breathtaking narrative, however, appears insufficiently glorious to theists seeking deeper meaning.

Labeling existence God's creation provides that meaning. Belief in it stands as the necessary and sufficient evidence of a creator God. This conceptual loop is internally consistent, like the analogy of the watch and watchmaker. But its endorsement requires ignoring a lot of evidence to the contrary.

Creation as defined implies both an act of creation and something or someone doing the creating. These are conceptual tautologies, artifacts of our native tongue's subject-verb-object (SVO) structure, unlike God's original unitized Word. This thinking is logically circular, but finally questionable and overly simplistic. Why would God not be inclined to express her intent and to design reality precisely as science describes it? Not a once-and-forever fiat and say no more, but an ongoing dynamic dialogue?

Nonetheless no one can deny that in the colloquial sense, the universe is indeed a creation. But it is continually creating and simultaneously destroying itself in real time, moment by moment and eon by eon. Inexorable attrition, aging, decay, death, and birth are characteristic of all sentient life, including humans, illustrating the reality of the principle of impermanence emphasized by Buddhism.

We may be sure that whatever physical reality is, at any point in space and time it will be different from any other point in spacetime. You may argue that this ongoing constant change does not represent an act of creation as such, but merely reflects how the individual chairs are arranged on an all-inclusive deck. Some chairs! Some deck! The modern scientific view of the universe as finite holds that nothing can be added to it, and nothing can be taken away. It is just one big remix. But that is the heart of creativity.

Creative types and design professionals such as myself readily admit that we do not actually create anything, but only recreate, finding new combinations of preexistent components. In fine art, we basically manipulate the available media—paint pigment, for example, being a kind of highly refined mud—into compositions of colors and shapes. In communications design, we do so with preexistent words and images, such as this book. In music, we use sound. Scientists employ the language of math.

Whatever the case—whether the universe is the creation of a transcendent being or beings, or of our own mind, as some philosophies and studies of brain science suggest—it has yet to be proven, if it ever will be. Don't hold your breath: plenty of time for solving that problem in the grave.

God's Plan

It is understandable that when the complexity and the downright contrariness and capriciousness of the world exceeds our grasp, when it "surpasseth all understanding" (Philippians 4:7), the default position is to invoke the mysterious nature of the will of God. To assume that an all-powerful intelligence oversees the daily atrocities committed by human beings as reported by the news media may offer solace to some, but for the rest of us such an idea is deeply disturbing. These acts are committed by people purported to be crafted in God's image after all. Adding insult to injury, many claim to be acting in His name. It is difficult to embrace the comforting idea of a God that is loving and forgiving toward his creation in the face of such glaring evidence to the contrary.

One rationale garnered from interfaith panels with representatives of Islam and Christianity is that the world is now under the sway of Satan rather than God, and that the coming apocalypse will resolve this conflict once and for all—,which raises more questions than it answers. Why would a benevolent, all-powerful God allow such unnecessary suffering in the meantime?

As to natural catastrophes, increasingly exacerbated if not caused solely by human behavior, interpreting these events as the will of God strains credulity. Can God stop plate tectonics at a given moment and place? If he could, would he do so knowing that the accumulated stress would back up elsewhere, with potentially even greater damage to his own hapless human believers?

It is equally discomfiting that such frequent events may be totally out of God's control. This would mean that they are subject only to the inadequate interventions of humankind, the very victims and villains who commit the atrocities, come up with doctrinal rationalizations, and contribute to climatic calamity. The emotional need for believing in a God who loves and will save us all is understandable, even logical, in a psychological sense. But this must be the mother of all tough love.

However deeply held, belief does not in itself constitute evidence of the truth of said belief. Nor does faith argue effectively against evolution as a clearly discernible process whereby new species emerge and old variations vanish—including human beings—whether guided by divine will or not.

Further, belief in an anthropomorphized creator does not explain, justify, or rationalize the fear and loathing with which so many react to the suggestion of our intimate interconnectedness, through evolution and shared DNA, with so-called lower animals, especially other tailless bipeds: the great apes, chimps, gorillas, and orangutans. It has been indisputably demonstrated that we are genetically related, and, relatively recently in history, all occupying the same branch of the Tree of Life. Where, then, does this revulsion toward our bipedal cousins really come from? It is clear to anyone who can see that we are, indeed, also primates.

The most refreshingly candid and unintentionally funny translation that I have come across, of one of the ten honorifics bestowed upon Buddha during his lifetime, is "Honored among bipeds." I picture a painting of the Buddha, surrounded by apes, gorillas, chimps, and monkeys gazing up at him in rapturous veneration, like images of Jesus surrounded by lions and other wild beasts, lying down with the lambs. We are much more closely related to monkeys with tails than to other mammals, notwithstanding whatever greater intelligence we may possess. This connection is not just in our minds, but in our bodies. Look in the mirror. Does that look like a lemur? Feel that bony ring around your eyes. A giraffe, or a whale? Count your neck bones. None of this means, however, that we can hold our primate ancestors accountable for our predatory behavior.

A corollary, self-serving doctrine—God's alleged granting dominion over the earth to humans—does not excuse the godawful mistreatment humans visit upon each other and other species. Nor does it justify how we cynically abuse the term "humane" when referencing our regrettable treatment of wildlife and livestock. Fish, reptiles, birds, mammals, and hybrids make up our larger community of sentient beings. They are also God's critters, if we are. Perhaps they represent our prototypical alpha-stage versions, much like 1.0 software releases, intended to be debugged in interactive end-user interface, via descent with modification, resulting in the acme of life that is the human being, in all its glory. Seriously, a sense of humility is in order.

Taking It to the Schools

Another issue in scientific circles is reconciling one's religious beliefs with ethical obligations to maintain one's professional objectivity, especially in public and private education. The most fraught cases arise at the elementary, middle, and high school levels, where the hearts and minds of the next generations are at stake. At the higher level of university and college studies, the concern shifts to ideological indoctrination. Employment, tenure, and reputation are some of the impelling incentives.

At least one motivation of those attempting to discredit the theory of evolution by promoting the creationism mantra is to gain and maintain control of public school curricula, a long-term objective of the religious right. Clearly religious and political rather than pedagogical, this agenda is driven by ideological creed as well as greed. Today's schoolkids are tomorrow's voters after all.

A laughable compromise offered by a former "compassionate conservative" POTUS: Why not teach both sides of the debate? was widely derided as yet another Trojan horse intended to sneak Bible study into public schools, in the guise of an ostensibly "fair and balanced" approach. This kind of disingenuous deception is characterized in Zen as the behavior of a "wily fox." Coincidence?

The so-called "wedge strategy," courtesy of the Discovery Institute, intends to leverage influence over education as well as promote the rubric of "intelligent design" itself and attempts to bring that old-time creation wolf in sheep's clothing into the secular curriculum. Grandstanding politics smoke-screen a conservative Christian crusade to reshape the youth of America in His image, as alluded to on the almighty dollar bill, "In God We Trust," circa 1955, Eisenhower administration. The schoolboard campaign to politicize the vax-and-mask program for preventing spread of the COVID pandemic as a conspiracy is the most recent variant of this particular viral epidemic. Other by-now-familiar examples include stuffing the courts with conservative Christian candidates.

Armageddon-inspired campaigns to save America take precedence over relatively trivial, temporal concerns, such as the ongoing worldwide pandemic, not to mention climate change lurking just over the horizon. Both of which are actually embraced, in some quarters, as confirmation of the biblical apocalyptic narrative and vision for the future of not only America, but the world. Bring it on.

This manipulation of the commonweal to conform to ideological aspirations of religious factions is clearly in 180-degree opposition to the intent of the Founding Fathers, and the doctrine of the separation of church and state. It also flies in the face of the harmonious community ideal of Zen.

Zen Buddhism: Coarising

The Twelvefold Chain of Interdependent Coarising (figure 4), one of the fundamental teachings of Mahayana Buddhism, will require some unpacking. The construction "interdependent coarising," sometimes rendered "co-origination," indicates its interactive, nonlinear nature. Whereas "chain of causality," a traditional interpretation, implies an overly simple, linear cause and effect. We offer this alternative for your consideration, in contrast to our selected conclusions for rationalism and theism: evolution and creation, respectively. Owing to the scope and intricate detail of reasoning in Buddha's teaching, we will have to wade into the weed patch again. The chain is traditionally connected to karmic consequence over several lifetimes. It links the personal sphere of sentient being to the universal cycles of existence. Welcome to the Twilight Zone.

This ancient model of the biology of sentience from early India is not unrelated to the dynamic laid out in the theory of evolution. They both penetrate into the fog of prehistory and the dawn of humankind. Thus have I heard: there are multitoothed and baleen whales because there were at one time proto-whales with regular jaws, because there were hippo-like critters that learned to live in the water, and so on. In the first edition of *Origin*, but corrected in later revisions, Darwin considers the bears swimming about in Yellowstone lakes with mouths wide open to catch fish. He guesses that "the habit, long continued" might produce whales. Just so.

Further how questions that may be similarly addressed: How the Elephant got its Trunk; How the Rhinoceros got its Skin; How the Camel got its Hump. Perhaps God invented evolution as the preferred method of realizing his vision, and—heaven forfend!—improving upon it over time?

The Four Noble Truths present a model of how things are, take it or leave it. And some suggestions as to what we can do about it, the Noble Eightfold Path. This formulation, the Twelvefold Chain, deals more with how things came to be the way they are. And more pertinently, how sentience continues to come into being, every moment of every day. As such, it is a highly articulated description of the ongoing processes of birth and growth, as well as life and death. Much like evolution.

But the links in the chain do not set out a belief about universal genesis, other than proposing that existence arises from a kind of primordial ignorance, the first link in the chain. Buddhism is not concerned with establishing yet another competitive creation myth. And Zen regards any first cause as essentially unknowable. What caused the Big Bang? Who or what preceded God?

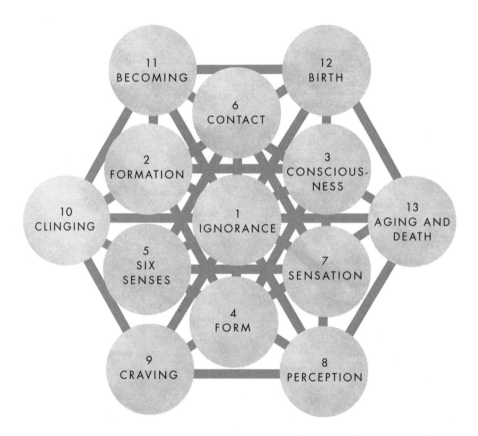

FIGURE 4. Twelvefold Chain

LIFE CYCLE	LINKS IN CHAIN
A. Prior life	1. Ignorance
	2. Impulse
B. Present life	3. Consciousness
	• Name and form

LIFE CYCLE	LINKS IN CHAIN
	4. Six senses
	5. Contact
	6. Sensation
	7. Perception
C. Fruits in present life	8. Craving
	9. Clinging
	10. Becoming
D. Future life	11. Birth
	12. Aging (sickness) and Death

In this teaching, attributed to Buddha, the twelve links are usually listed in sequential order as above, taking place over a period of three lifetimes at a minimum, to complete the entire cycle of rebirth. I was told by Shohaku Okumura Roshi that Perception, number eight in the list, was subsumed under Sensation in the initial version, rendering the chain in twelve links. But since Perception is called out separately as one of the Five Aggregates—namely Form, Sensation, Perception, Impulse, and Consciousness, another classic teaching of the Buddhist system—it seems reasonable to include it. And, since a raw Sensation would not likely result directly in Craving without first passing through the filter of Perception, where it registers as pleasant or unpleasant, I decided to position it between these two links. With Perception logically following Sensation, this revised model of the chain consists of thirteen links all told. Think of it as an upgrade. A baker's dozen.

Arising within primordial Ignorance, as a leftover from a prior existence, a subliminal Impulse toward awareness leads to the emergence of Consciousness. This enables the discernment of Form (S. rupa) as the Six Senses (S. sadayatana) come into play, and later Name (S. nama), as we acquire our native tongue after birth. Picture this first series as the embryo growing into the fetus.

Contact between self and other begins in the form of inchoate sensation emerging in the womb, refining into Perception, again fully developing following birth. This leads to acquiring the bitter fruits of Craving, including both attachment and aversion, which leads to Clinging to the pleasant and avoidance of the unpleasant. Clinging, in turn, drives Becoming, as the impetus to the next birth, which, like this present lifetime, ends in Aging and Death, with Sickness thrown in for good measure along the way.

Following inevitable aging, sickness, and death in future life, the cycle loops back to its origin in Ignorance—the primordial swamp of not-knowing—from which all existence arises. The Buddhist principles of rebirth and karmic consequence operating over successive lifetimes are implicit in this model but may not seem obvious or germane to you at first blush. In fact, the very idea may seem inordinately pessimistic.

But Buddhism is neither pessimistic nor overly optimistic. It is unabashedly realistic. This model, like the Four Noble Truths, simply frames the facts of our existence and the provenance of our personal causes and conditions, whether we accept it or not. It is what it is.

While the specific sequencing of the links may appeal to our love of algebraic logic, they are not meant to comprise merely a circular template of linear cause and effect, nor simply an expanded, more complex version of dualistic causality. Each cause is an effect, and each effect is, in turn, a cause.

The chain is, instead, a model of the intricate interconnectedness of all determinate causes and conditions of sentient existence, and their mutually interactive influence on each other. In modern parlance, they are all linked to each other, like so many related subjects in a robust search on the internet. Click on any one link, and it brings up all the others. The semantic model illustrates this interrelatedness three-dimensionally and is intended as a mnemonic to help you remember its form.

Conclusive Ambiguity

Zen Buddhism's conclusion of interdependent coarising embraces ambiguity to a degree that renders the theory itself inconclusive in its basic formulation. It concludes, and is comfortable with concluding, that reality itself is inherently inconclusive. That is, existence is a work in progress.

Buddhism posits that when we speculate about when and where it all began, we confront an endless regression into the foggy mists of the eternal past. Likewise, when we attempt to predict where and when it will all end, we ignore the magnitude of information missing from our calculations. And ignoring is the root of all forms of ignorance, whether willful or innocent.

Science can focus sharply on proximate causes, and in some cases confidently predict outcomes, both positive and calamitous. Religion can offer hope in the presence of great indecision and fear. Zen calls upon us to embrace the ambiguity, and to keep our doubt at a keen edge. Why should we fear the future when it is only a continuum of the past? Why fear death when we do not fear birth?

As a theoretical construct, the chain is similar to the model of evolution, in that it points not to incipient beginnings or ultimate finalities, but to a natural progression of adaptive stages of maturation, through which all sentient beings progress from birth to death and beyond, via genetic inheritance.

To put a finer point on it, the appearance of any logical pattern or sequence becomes evident only after the fact. Generally, adaptations in nature as well as human endeavors are temporary solutions to immediate problems, stumbled upon by random tinkering until something clicks: basic trial and error. In biology, the tinkering arena is the gene pool. In design, one example is seen in the slow evolution of window shapes in the annual redesign of the Volkswagen Beetle, my first automobile purchase. Then there was the "Never!" ad showing a Beetle with a two-toned paint job. But I digress again.

The twelve links, it is said, require at least three lifetimes to traverse the complete cycle. This entails the Buddhist tenet of rebirth, which differs from Hinduism's doctrine of reincarnation as popularly defined. We will not parse these concepts too deeply here. Suffice it to say that rebirth holds that the being reborn is not the same as the one that dies but is connected through a karmic bond something like DNA, but not material. Reincarnation, in contrast and in brief, posits a transmigrating self-existent entity, atman. This self-existent self survives death and takes on another life, donning and discarding new bodies much as we change our clothing, in an ongoing tandem series of life-times. The atman is not to be confused with the soul of Christianity, which did not emerge as a cultural meme until a half millennium or so later.

For human beings, biological and phenomenological life transitions, represented as links in the chain, mark the emergence and evolution of our personal conscious awareness, potentially culminating in our own spiritual awakening. This propitious prospect, personified in Buddha's experience, comprises the highest potential for evolution of the human mind, in effect breaking the chain, running the sequence backward through the links to the original primordial ignorance, so to speak.

Creation and Zen

In all fairness it should be noted that along with the Twelvefold Chain, the concepts of creation and evolution should not be oversimplified as linear, one-directional cause-and-effect concepts. Both of these ideas posit multiplex, multidimensional matrices, made up of many moving parts.

But in Zen, creationism, as such, is scarcely ever discussed, let alone debated, denied, or asserted as a concept or a belief. Tribal India surely had its share of creation myths. But Buddhism does not hold that some cosmic Buddha or some god created the Universe, who thereafter created Buddha. The figures Ishvara and Brahma may be analogous to a creator god in early Hinduism. But according to Buddha, finding yourself in deep dialogue with such an entity in meditation is, while not a full-blown hallucination, then at best an incomplete stage along the path of full-blown realization. It must be said that Zen followers do not self-identify as buddhas, let alone as God. We did not create this mess.

Any such proposition regarding first causes would find its place among those unfathomable conjectures that Buddha himself is said to have refused to answer or to debate, such as how it all began and how it will all end. He considered such speculation to be specious, and irrelevant in the face of the immediate and urgent causes and conditions of suffering—specifically aging, sickness and death—impinging upon our brief human lives. We have no time to waste on idle speculation.

Zen and Evolution

Belief in creationism or opposition to the idea, then, is not really relevant to Buddhism, and so is not a subject of Zen dialogue. Evolution by natural selection, as a reasonable explanation of the origin of species, is also not up for debate in Zen, if for opposite reasons. Evolution is not to be dismissed as rank speculation. Natural selection through adaptation seems irrefutable, given the overwhelming preponderance of evidence. As a natural process, evolution is a present, provable, and predictable pattern, clearly observable in life. But it does not compete with the gospel of creation as a first cause, and thus, constitutes no threat to the doctrines of theism.

Further, evolution is not capable of explaining such nonbiological phenomena as nuclear fission, or the Big Bang, other than in an idiomatic sense, as in the "evolution of science." Nor is it concerned with or relevant to such matters. But a major challenge to Darwin's explanation of evolution was that the physics of the day allotted far too short a time span for life to originate and evolve. Only after the discovery of nuclear fission as the source of solar energy was Darwinism accorded a practically endless time frame to work its magic. So far, no single theory of rationalism or science explains everything.

Unlike the default position of theism, which is simply: "the will of God."

Though somewhat irrelevant to the pragmatic purposes of Zen, evolution may suggest a useful model for the progress of human intelligence over time, and even across species, if you will. We may take Buddha's insight as the high point of evolution of human intelligence, reaching a formidable peak at that time in history. Much like the process of speciation, his experience arose out of the interface of conflicts with his lived realty and is regarded as the cumulative result of many lives, as in evolution.

It follows that if you or I were to awaken today, it would count as a new, updated peak experience of mind. As Matsuoka Roshi once said: your enlightenment will be even greater than Buddha's! When asked what I think he could possibly have meant by this startling statement, I say that perhaps the intervening 2,500 years count.

Could the arc of enlightenment be cumulative, over generations? Remember that Buddha is revered—not worshiped—because he made his discovery without benefit of an enlightened mentor. He didn't have a Bodhidharma, a Master Dogen, or a Matsuoka Roshi to talk to.

Zen's awakening may be considered the highest peak experience of consciousness in natural or manmade evolution, confined to human awareness. But this does not rise, or sink, to the level of belief. We will willingly stand, or sit, corrected in the face of credible evidence contradicting Buddhism's teachings. In this open-ended mindfulness Zen remains agnostic but is quite scientific in its empirical mindset and method. In science, a parallel process of evolution of the species may be discerned in such events as annual physics conferences expanding on quantum theory. They get bigger and better every year.

Balancing Theory with Method

The teachings of Buddhism and Zen may be relegated to hypothesis or theory rather than belief, though with more due respect than found in the cavalier way that some creationists dismiss evolution as "just a theory." Like the patterns of natural selection discovered by Charles Darwin, Zen's teachings are based on first-person observation, evidenced as testimony in the written record.

They were discovered and codified by Zen's ancestors, beginning with Buddha and twenty-eight patriarchs over a millennium in India, twenty-plus generations through seven centuries or so in China, another seven centuries in Japan for thirty-plus generations, and three or four American generations in the West so far, beginning roughly around World War II. And that is just

Soto Zen's lineage alone. Unknown numbers of other masters comprise the Korean, Vietnamese, and other transmissions throughout East Asia, including the robust Tibetan legacy.

But theory without method is as incomplete and impotent as method without theory. These teachings, by adapting to the times, have spread to innumerable followers worldwide today. But the essential method for assimilating them has remained the same, from Buddha's experience on down to yours or mine: simply sitting still enough for long enough in upright seated meditation.

Evolving Zen

Zen finds no contradictions with the findings of science, such as evolution. Zen practice, like some hypotheses in science, focuses our attention on process, the natural dynamic of daily life. It also concentrates on the process of the mind itself, particularly in meditation. The science of Zen is to experiment with our own mind in meditation, observing its machinations dispassionately, much as folks in lab coats observe whatever phenomena are under the microscope at the moment.

The traditional name for the overall process in Zen is called awakening, which has sudden, as well as gradual, characteristics. If and when it happens, it must be sudden, as just the moment before we were still confused. It must also be gradual, as it took all of universal time and space evolving to get to this present moment. Two things can be true at the same time. In Zen, innumerable myriads of things are all true at once.

But Zen's goal is not achieving a state of enlightenment, whether sudden or gradual, as is popularly believed. Setting a specific preconceived goal, such as "enlightenment," inhibits the open-ended approach necessary to thoroughly examine ongoing reality with an open, unbiased mind: true for Zen, for science, and for religion.

Actively engaging in simply observing the mind as it evolves through a natural process of awakening is already enlightened behavior. We are enlightened to the fact that something is missing in our own lives, our understanding, our worldview. Turning our attention to the source of the problem—the way we react, or overreact, to our own senses and mind— affords us the best chance of finding out what is truly missing.

Consciousness itself is the subject of Zen study. Consciousness is the medium and the message (McLuhan 1994). Zen meditation is consciousness studying consciousness through consciousness. Verbal thinking gives way to nonthinking. Doing surrenders to nondoing. Duality opens to nondual reality, beyond language, beyond concept.

Embracing Complementarity

From the dispassionate perspective of Zen, both creationism and evolution may be seen to be complementary concepts, if not of equal import or scope. The former may be understood as simply coming into being, the latter as not strictly limited to biology. As theories of how things come to be the way they are, both may be seen as compatible with the Twelvefold Chain of Causation, with the caveat that it is focused on the life cycles of sentient beings.

This generic usage of creation as causation does not imply a creator, however. The creation, this universe, manifests from the overwhelming thrust of the desire to exist, the life force itself, inclusive of all sentient beings. Desire, in Buddhist mode, precedes birth, and even survives death, but not as an entity, as a force.

Evolution may be analogized as the engine, or at least the transmission, of the vehicle of nature, trucking along via natural selection, or if you insist, an engine of God's will. This organic mechanism drives the interface of living beings with each other, as well as with the nonliving world. It shapes the creative destruction of what was, replacing it with what is. Until the next cycle, wherein what is again becomes what was.

In a broader sense, what was is what still is. That is, the world is finite. We cannot add to it, or take away from it, in any ultimate sense. It, our world and the universe at large, is the original transformer, forever regenerating itself, recombining parts like recombinant DNA. It is the ultimate recycling machine.

This is the "what" of our reality, the primal question of Zen. Evolution describes the "how" of rational science and sentient existence, its method of natural selection, through genetic change and diversification of living species. Creation is theism's attempt to explain the "why" of it all. The will of God defines the intent of existence, particularly that of humanity. We are only human, after all.

Intentional Creation

Summarizing our proposed alternative, nondual theory of how things got to be the way they are, and are likely continue to do so, in brief: some source of primordial, inchoate intent—God, Nature, the Universe; take your pick— continually regenerates reality in ongoing creation mode. Interacting fundamental forces, mutually modifying causes and conditions, engage in a multiplex interface with disparate, impermanent, and imperfect insentient and sentient beings. Human witness to this all-encompassing process is necessarily limited to and filtered by the six senses, including discriminating mind, which imposes conceptual, often erroneous, interpretations upon incoming sensory data.

Strict proponents of rationalism may protest this use of "intent" as sloppy or specious, even grievous misdirection. But some investigators claim to detect intent in sentient beings lower on the food chain, a hypothesis that appears to be accumulating solid evidence. But most would probably not allow an assumption of intent in the case of viruses or bacteria, let alone the insentient world. Nonetheless, this is a human-based—ergo human-biased—interpretation of the limits of intent.

Adherents of theism attribute the existence and intent of the universe to the will of God. But the universe may reasonably be regarded as an expression of the cumulative intent of all creation. If we claim an intention underlying the universe, how can we deny that the universe, itself, has intent? A primitive impulse simply to be, to exist. A massive work-in-progress.

According to my scant understanding of Buddhism's cosmology, the existence of the universe does not require, or even suggest, the presence of an outside independent creator, directing events based on willful intention, or controlling change through magical intervention. Whatever the origin and intent of existence itself, the fundamental operational dynamic of human life, indeed of all sentient life, is parsed in some detail by the Twelvefold Chain. It is as feasible a framework as any.

A Buddhist teaching, "The Theory of the Momentary Appearance and Disappearance of the Universe," also called "The Theory of Instantaneousness" as discussed in Master Dogen's *Hotsu Bodaishin; Establishment of the Bodhi Mind* (Nishijima and Cross 1994) holds that the entire universe, the whole shebang, appears and disappears every moment. But this moment is extremely brief, a micromoment, the smallest unit of time (S. ksana). If so, and an intelligent designer is in charge, they may have obsessive-compulsive disorder, starting and stopping and starting again at so short an interval, such a high frequency, that we cannot perceive it. Like the monitor on your computer or the early cinescopes at 16 cycles per second, we see seamless continuity, a delusion.

Theoretical Zen

Some clarification may be in order as to the sense in which the term "theory" should be read, especially regarding Zen. Colloquially, it means something like a best guess: I have a theory about who stole my wallet. In the context of a theory of gravity or the theory of evolution, it takes on a more substantial meaning as a reasonable and well-confirmed explanation. While any and all empirical or scientific claims are ultimately open to revision, pending future discovery of contradictory evidence, no one in the scientific community would take seriously the idea that the theory of gravity in relativity, or of speciation in evolution, will be significantly revised in our lifetime. They may be amended over time with the advent of new data but are not likely to be totally refuted in favor of an altogether different explanation.

It is precisely this confusion about the meaning of theory as a best guess, versus a well-confirmed explanation, that proponents of creationism try to exploit, by asserting that evolution is only a theory, merely Darwin's best guess. Given all this, it may be problematic or confusing to mention hypothetical or theoretical constructs from Zen in the same breath with theories of science. We must clarify the specific meaning we ascribe to theory, as it is used in Zen.

Any theory or tenet of Buddhism or Zen is not one that can be proven, in the sense that a scientific theory may be. Nor is it simply a best guess. Instead, the tenets of Zen rest in a middle ground, validated by first-person direct experience. Examples are Buddha's extensive teachings on lay householder relationships, which would represent the sociology or behavioral science of the time. Others would be the rules and regulations governing monastic mendicant behavior.

Zen teachings are not religious beliefs, nor intended to be used as items of debate in the public arena, but practical propositions to be tested, both on the cushion and in daily life. It is probably best to regard teachings of Zen, and perhaps those of all major religions and philosophies, as hypotheses based on the testimony of our forebears, to be verified through first-person experimentation. Once we have tested and proven them out for ourselves, we might venture to share them with others.

All this talk about the connection of Zen to rationalism and science may creating a false impression. Zen may be more scientific than religious, but there is no conceivable experiment or observation that would negate Zen. We constitute perhaps the oldest tribe of practical experimenters. But the historicity of its provenance, the veracity of our claims, are not subject to scientific verification. It simply doesn't matter if Shakyamuni's awakening took place under a Bodhi tree or not. Or if it was or was not Venus, or a star, and if so which star, that triggered his awakening that fateful evening. Other religions could found several denominations based on these questions. It doesn't even matter whether or not the historical Buddha existed, though we discern an historical religious movement beginning at about that time, spreading and evolving from the west unto the east. In fact, there is no concrete east or west, north or south. The only thing that matters in Zen is your experience.

Zen Nonsense

Zen's methodology differs from the empirical methods of science, defined as systematic collection and analysis of data, primarily through the senses. Or, these days, increasingly through instruments. The instrument employed in Zen is the body in zazen. Zen meditation focuses immediately upon the sensory process itself, calling into question the very data received by the mind through the sense organs. The Six Senses of Buddhism are deemed to be unbalanced, biased in favor of survival.

The senses are closely and critically examined in zazen, as referenced in the Heart of Great Wisdom Sutra: "Given Emptiness, there is no eyes, no ears, no nose, no tongue, no body, no mind; no seeing, hearing, tasting, touching, thinking." Then for good measure: "No realm of sight . . . and all the rest . . . no realm of mind consciousness" (Sotoshu 2001). Note that the koan of Emptiness is a game changer for the senses. Apparently there is a thoroughgoing denial of the senses, at least as we conceive them—not that they are absolutely nonexistent, but they are also not exactly existent and not in the form that we perceive them to be.

Buddha is said to have remarked that the sixth sense, discriminating mind, imposes a false stillness on reality, a kind of built-in damper on perceptual chaos. On the plus side, this sixth sense enables urgent, instantaneous life-or-death judgment calls. If all is in crazy motion, we may be distracted and lose track, perhaps even endanger our life. Incoming information is supposedly parsed in a timely, unbiased, clear, and complete way. But this false stillness challenges the assumption that the interpretation of sense data by the discriminating powers of the mind is accurate, let alone 100 percent of the time. Optical illusions are instructive in this regard. The double-take reverses our first take, which turns out to be a perceptual mistake.

Evidence of the other senses, as we think we know them, is similarly skewed, assumed to be incomplete and therefore inadequate to the challenge of developing insight. Tactile feelings, sounds, tastes, and smells are likewise obviously relative and elusive, short lived and ever changing.

The process of maturation of raw awareness begins early in life. In Zen, we turn our attention away from the outer to the inner world, so to speak, while recognizing that they are not truly separate. The interface between the two is, in fact, the senses, and the first focus of zazen, which is transsensory.

The "oceanic awareness" Sigmund Freud (1989) described as characteristic of the consciousness of the infant in the crib, a state of near-total helplessness, begins to give way to what is called individuation, analyzed extensively by Carl Jung (2014). The child learns to differentiate itself from its environment, to discriminate "mom" from the background noise.

Brain science reminds us that the field of sensory stimulation in which our consciousness operates is extremely dynamic. There is nothing that is not moving, if at different frequencies. We perceive reality as constant and continuous, in spite of rampant fluctuations. We register relative movement, as it manifests against relative stillness. In zazen, sensory dualities merge into a more comprehensive nonduality, in which they are seen to be complementary, not independently existing elements in opposition to each other.

Reasoning Perception

Conventional reasoning informs our experience of perceptions and conceptions alike. It must likewise be challenged, owing partially to the built-in bias toward survival of the self-constructed self. Reasoning alone may not fully take into account this skewed orientation. Bias is blind to bias. The mind's penchant for conventional reasoning reflects upon and informs our experience of sensory awareness, revising, reinforcing, and reifying our grip on reality. This is illustrated quite literally by the role binocular vision plays for arboreal apes, swinging from limb to limb. It serves as well for terrestrial apes, judging distance to their prey. Not to mention hairless apes, driving on the expressway.

But this default mode of knee-jerk interpretation must be set aside in meditation to foster a gradual deconditioning process. The built-in bias of monkey-mind toward reification of the self-constructed self is basically a defense mechanism. It defends against loss of identity, and ultimately loss of life.

In place of unquestioning acceptance of sensory data as is, or relying solely on reason, Zen adopts a method of observation that places both under the microscope. We simply sit still enough, for long enough periods of time, that the natural process of sensory adaptation becomes all-encompassing and profoundly deep, eventually transcending the senses altogether, ergo, "no Six Senses" in zazen.

You may remember from your high school biology class, when you first used the microscope, what astronomers also know about peripheral vision: for best resolution, you were taught not to look directly at the object at the other end of tube. Rather, you turn your head slightly and pick up the image off-center. It is seen in much sharper focus.

So too in Zen. We don't look at the koan of the present moment head-on, but rather a bit askew, as if from an obtuse angle. We simply sit still enough, for long enough, so that we can see it clearly, out of the corner of the eye, so to speak.

Thinking itself is considered the sixth of the senses in Buddhism, the brain on autopilot, an automatic functioning of the autonomic discriminating mind, the operative interface of the brain with the external sense organs. Relying upon our faculty of reasoning and reflection must be left behind, subsumed under adaptation or absorption, in order to enter into the inmost sanctum of awareness, which, like our own wormhole, bridges our inner and outer worlds, the personal and the communal.

Compassionate Community

Harmony is the key ingredient in community, according to Zen. If we can find harmonious accommodation between the now-divided camps of people of faith in science and those of religion, it will go a long way toward a broader rapprochement of the rationalist and theist worldviews. Who knows—even our so-called political leaders may have to get on board, if not out in front of this parade.

The community of Buddhist practitioners began in India some 2,500 years ago as a group of monks, who after some years, and during Buddha's lifetime, welcomed women into the club. As the group grew, and their understanding of the role and responsibility of human beings in relation to the animal kingdom deepened, the meaning of community expanded to embrace all living beings, including animals, eventually even the vegetable kingdom. The tenet emerged that all life is intimately and intricately interconnected with human life. Thus the first of the Ten Grave Precepts of bodhisattvas urges us to affirm life—do not kill.

Thich Nhat Hahn, the famous Vietnamese Zen master who died recently, coined the term "interbeing" (1987) to capture this aspiration in contemporary generic terms. This all-inclusive embrace came to characterize Buddhism's worldview, its altruistic wish that all beings be happy. But of course, that all beings should be happy with existence as it is, rather than as we might wish it could be. Whether this happiness is the result of a beneficent God, or not, is very much beside the point.

From the perspective of Zen, the concrete miracle of reality requires no conceptual overlay of a creator. But to argue the nonexistence of said creator would be to fall into the mistake of dualistic thinking, a distinction without a difference. The view known as atheism represents the complementary pole to theism, its darker doppelganger, so to say. Arguing against the existence of God is 100 percent dependent upon a concept of God, just as not thinking is a form of thinking. Atheism is sometimes said to be the strongest form of theism.

But Zen steps aside from and stands outside this dualistic debate, to point to the middle way. This is analogous to thinking versus not-thinking begetting nonthinking, Dogen's coinage for the original mind. Whether God exists, or does not exist, does not alter the concrete reality, the basics of our human existence, set forth as the Four Noble Truths in Buddhist teachings.

Further, the operative meaning of existence and our place in it does not depend upon the resolution of this belief-based dilemma. Any more than the existence or nonexistence of God, or heaven and hell, determines and dictates morality. This may have been one of the early rationales for the doctrinal threat of even greater suffering in store, after shuffling off this mortal coil and leaving this "veil of tears." This world (S. samsara) provides entirely sufficient suffering, thank you very much. We don't need no stinking threat of hell to make us do the right thing. In Zen, morality does not derive from the threat of punishment in hell, nor the promise of reward in heaven, but is practiced for its own sake, as well as for the sake of others. The first Pure Precept—do no harm and following the golden rule—pretty much cover the bases.

NAVIGATING THE MIDDLE WAY

Much of the confusion, chaos, and civic unrest arising today in the face of the pandemic, accompanied by a precipitous spike in millions of unemployed, aggravated by police violence and overseen by inept and self-dealing political leadership, represents the worst-case scenario in living memory for most of the citizenry. The lack of cogent, credible leadership appears to reflect conflicting worldviews based on religious belief (e.g., the apocalypse to come) or scientific memes conflicting with politico-economic concerns (e.g., the confusion as to how, when, and where, and to what degree, to continue antipandemic measures or relax them). Prevailing class distinctions and inequality, exaggerated in direct proportion to the crisis at hand, do not help. Compassion is not communism, nor is it capitalism. Add the traditional Four Horsemen of pestilence, war, famine, and plague, all fully operative somewhere around the globe, and it is difficult to deny that Armageddon may indeed be upon us. Not to mention the looming tsunami of climate change, playing havoc with what used to be the normal, relatively predictable seasonality.

Some take the view "Not to worry, all will be well." Or that "Oh well, the apocalypse is foreordained, no matter what we do." Which would be irrelevant, if such mindsets were not used to excuse the action or inaction of leaders occupying crucial positions of power, from which they tend to block any timely reaction to crises that may affect their constituents' bottom lines or ideology. The view that whatever happens reflects the will of God watching over us from above becomes a self-fulfilling tautology when it persuades us to ignore the warnings of science, postpone any inconvenient action on the personal or political front, and to trust only those who play to our particular brand of faith.

Others hope salvation will magically appear in the form of silver bullets from science. The authors of science fiction play on this theme, from both sides of the Pond. British science fiction tends to take a negative view of science as a net barrier to solutions, whereas American sci-fi is traditionally positive— that effective technological solutions will emerge from the lab in time to save the day. But then the United Kingdom has had a little more tenure in the school of hard knocks and time to develop a justified skepticism, as they have witnessed the empire on which the sun once never set shrink back to its original boundaries as a small island nation.

Such views are often biased in favor of selfishly rational, but socially destructive, cultural-political-economic objectives. These include, at absurd extremes, supposed miracle cures, such as injecting bleach or taking horse medicine to kill a virus, while dismissing scientifically developed vaccines as products and agents of sci-fi-worthy conspiracies.

The most insidious and self-defeating of these arise from flagrant conflations of two social forces, those of church and state combined. That makes for an ugly baby, birthed as it is in a toxic mix of undemocratic zealotry on the part of the voting flock, and unrelenting hypocrisy on the part of their governmental enablers.

Meditating versus Medicating

It is by no means a panacea, but Zen's humble prescription for sitting in zazen, still enough and for long enough, holds out hope for coping with the whole catastrophe. There is only one letter's difference between meditation and medication. But the "smallest distinction sets heaven and earth infinitely apart," as the ancient Ch'an poem *Hsinhsinming: Faith in Mind* reminds us (Sotoshu 2001). Medication is clearly the dominant default cultural go-to for curing what ails you, or covering up the symptoms. Of course, you would not ask someone with a broken arm to grin and bear it. Nor should you ask persons with broken brain chemistries to just deal with it. Antidepressants properly applied may render the sixth sense a useful tool, rather than a screaming monkey.

Advocates of Zen and other traditions have long claimed that benefits to health and well-being flow from meditation. Positive effects have been documented in contemporary experiments by medical researchers. The connection is obvious to one of the many ongoing debates raging in America today, specifically that over the state of healthcare, which has been laid bare by the pandemic. With a vital connection to the overall economy, the healthcare system occupies a central place in the tug-of-war between the powers that be. Healthcare delivery personally affects everyone in modern society. Because of this, impersonal political policy determined at a distance can have a direct effect on up-close and personal health, and resultant quality of life.

This is one example of the Buddhist principle of the interconnectivity of all beings, as applied to the social dimension. But interconnectivity has a downside as well as an upside. It can be a source of interpersonal delight, but also a source of emotional unease, as well as a force-multiplier of epidemics and pandemics. Ease of air travel enabled the original transmission of viral vectors in the early spread of HIV, attributed largely to one particularly itinerant and sexually active flight attendant. Resistance to immigration becomes a form of quarantine, not just an expression of cultural unease. Too much interconnectivity can foster the NIMBY response. Another such concern attaches to social media, where digital connectivity is apparently, and ironically, exacerbating a pervasive sense of personal alienation.

Another source of unease today is that personal problems with well-being are increasingly addressed by self-medicating; read: doping. And not only in professional sports—just watch television news programs, where the audience is apparently predominantly geriatric. The endless list of drugs for every imaginable ailment or discomfort is straining the ability to come up with new names for them. Yet the legal ability to advertise prescription drugs dates back only to the Reagan administration.

The new normal for many, perhaps including yourself, is trending toward daily dependency on drugs. Illegal drugs, as well as over-the-counter prescriptions blessed by doctors and psychiatrists, are employed to treat everything from boredom to hyperactivity, attention deficit to insomnia, and digestive regularity to sexual impotency, to name just a few of our modern maladies. On the parenting front, the debate is shifting from what Johnny should be doing, to how much Johnny should be dosing.

Freedom from Dependency

You may enjoy a healthy degree of freedom from this chemical dependency, for whatever reasons, such as genetic benefits of nature, or a nurturing lifestyle that renders you relatively immune. Others may not be so lucky.

But regardless of your personal situation, you must be aware that socially sanctioned drug dependency has reached epidemic proportions, fueled by marketing campaigns of Big Pharma. This questionable trend is further impelled by an ever-expanding list of adult, adolescent, and childhood mental and personality disorders, as identified by the American Psychiatric Association, now approaching 500-plus identified syndromes. If you are in the business of curing maladies, of course, the more the merrier, positively impacting the bottom line.

Wherever you fall on the spectrum spanning progressive and conservative ideology, the direction of public health appears to be increasingly driven by profit motive rather than by the seminal precept of the American Medical Association: first, do no harm. But in the context of healthcare as defined by insurance companies and other vested interests, certain health benefits commonly attributed to Zen, such as improved vitality and happiness, mental peace and emotional serenity, can sound hopelessly innocent, painfully naïve.

But it this very quality of innocence that has gone missing in a culture marked by cynicism. Zen suggests that we return to a more trusting outlook, one based on assuming personal responsibility for our own health and well-being, and moderating our appetites. Only then can we begin addressing the social dimensions of healthcare and holding corporate entities and their leadership responsible for their transgressions. In other words, if we are not doing all we can to stay healthy on a personal level, we undermine our credibility on the social level. Smoking tobacco is the fading poster boy for this truism. In taking responsibility for your own holistic health, zazen is the most you can do.

Your first reaction to this idea may be one of skepticism or even derision. Personal responsibility is given a lot of lip service by politicians and other defenders of the status quo, belied by their own taxpayer-funded gold-standard healthcare insurance and other perks. But we must note in passing that no mention of moderation is ever made in their public utterances. In today's consumerist cult of growth, that would be antibusiness, and therefore un-American.

But Zen does not promise a panacea, nor does it set meditation directly in opposition to medication as a substitute for medical science, or for traditional therapies, whether physical, mental, or emotional. Zen does not recommend a Buddhist form of Christian Science. However, if you practice with diligence and sincerity, and come to understand how zazen works, it should enable you to better decide these matters for yourself. If you balance meditation with necessary medication, you may have a much better shot at actualizing the quintessential American values of life, liberty, and the pursuit of happiness, if not in the materialistic sense. Again, Zen is not a prosperity religion.

Navigating the middle way between the complex currents of stresses impinging upon us from all sides requires that we begin to see through the contradictions inherent in our dualistic approach to life, and its ever-increasing polarities. Moving from a belief-based worldview that God will take care of us, or a smug overconfidence in science to come to our rescue at the eleventh hour, to an embrace of the relative ambiguity of reality, will not be easy. But the razorblade of Zen is sharp enough to cut through this particular Gordian knot.

In theism our personal relationship to our creator is of central concern. In science the observer is seen to directly affect or bias that which is being observed. In Zen, the personal sphere of nondualistic worldview has always included the observer, thee and me, into the equation. From this perspective, including the observer in that which is observed, the three fields have much in common. The vaunted objectivity of science can itself be interpreted as a kind of imaginary belief. In the soft sciences, it is a given that there is no such thing as true objectivity. The subjective framework of the researcher has to be taken into account in translating findings into conclusions and recommendations. Belief in a loving God may similarly be severely tested by real-world events. Each of our realities constantly flows, momentarily arising, abiding, changing, and decaying, however disparate the lenses through which we choose to view it.

Instead of applying a preconceived viewpoint, Zen simply directs our attention to the present reality, however messy, but in a holistic, all-inclusive way, setting aside for the moment the social sphere of partisan politics, good and evil, right and wrong. We question as well as such neat personal distinctions as objectivity versus subjectivity, the absolute and the relative, mind and object, and so on. All of which turn out to be extraneous, if highly refined, filters imposed upon direct experience.

Both sides of any perceived duality may be equally true, but neither tells the complete story. Just as there is no cold without heat, no dark without light, there is no conservatism without liberalism, no generosity without venality, no justice without injustice, no compassion without wisdom. One person's privilege is another's constraint. You cannot give someone something without taking something away, and vice versa. These dualistic takes on reality remain mired in relativity. Even the relative taken together with the absolute is still incomplete in Zen's holistic worldview.

Debating Reality

Many of the positions taken in public debates as reported in the media illustrate extreme differences in certain worldviews in general, herein oversimplified as rationalism aka science, versus theism aka religion. These public positions as reported do, however, capture a relatively accurate snapshot of the contentiousness of our current social scene. Snapshots in time, regarded as our immediate past, can set the stage for introducing a new departure—a compassionate culture—our future based on Zen. Not likely to happen. But it could happen, at least for you, if only on an intensely personal level, which in turn would inevitably affect and alter your engagement with society. Through the ripple effect, the personal dimension subsumes not only the social but also the natural, perhaps even the universal, dimensions of existence: a single drop of clear water, dropped into the center of the pond of nascent Zen life, creating concentric waves to the horizons.

Four Spheres of Zen

In terms of spheres of influence, we may assign Buddha to the personal, Dharma to the universal, and Sangha to the social spheres. All partake of the natural, as does our tripartite approach to meditation through posture, breath, and attention. We rediscover the natural upright sitting posture of our forebears, following the wisdom of the body. We follow the breath, returning to its natural rhythm. We pay attention to everything until we recover our original, natural mind. And of course, the three overlap in an interactive, holistic whole while retaining their individual integrity (figure 5).

Whatever professional or spiritual way we take up in life, we practice it in the middle of the entirety of existence. Sitting in meditation, we find momentary sanctuary in the personal sphere, our own bubble, if you will. But it shares a boundary with the social sphere, which overlaps the natural, and ultimately extends to the universal. Our actions can have some effect from the inner sphere to the outer, and major impacts can intrude from the outermost spheres of the universe, from nature and society, directly into our personal lives. Can anyone say Cretaceous-Paleogene? Mass extinction can happen again, but it is increasingly likely that we may make the planet uninhabitable all by ourselves, thank you very much. A dualistic view of heaven and earth is part of the problem.

To contrast prevalent dualistic views with Zen's middle way, we have only to consider conflicts between radically conservative theism aka fundamentalism, and radically materialistic rationalism aka reductionism. In the latter we find the objectionable premise that life, including humanity, is merely a fluke of chance, via a kind of reductio ad absurdum. In the former lurks intelligent design, creationism dressed up as a theory ostensibly worthy of challenging that of evolution. Of course, the twain shall never meet. Again, evolution has nothing to do with first causes, and intelligent design can present no credible evidence of its proof.

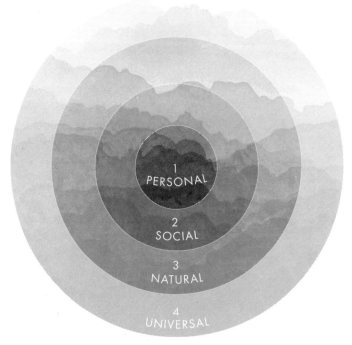

FIGURE 5. Four Spheres of Zen

Another of the extreme resorts of rationalism—the tendency to attribute all behavior, however altruistic in appearance, to an underlying survival value—seems far too simple. Applying such linear logic in an attempt to relegate all spiritual inquiry to rank superstition, or New Age mysticism; or attributing conscious intelligence to mere biological function, reducing biology to chemistry, chemistry to physics, and physical existence itself to essentially a random accident, may be seen as attempts to take the mystery out of life, to reinforce the self-centered view that we know everything that can be known, or is worth knowing. How many times has the end of knowledge been claimed? Matsuoka Roshi once remarked that there are some people who can talk themselves out of existence.

The scientific worldview called "reductionism" is defined according to the Oxford University Press as

> the practice of analyzing and describing a complex phenomenon in terms of phenomena that are held to represent a simpler or more fundamental level, especially when this is said to provide a sufficient explanation.

The irreducible complexity of theism, and the simplistic reductionism of rationalism turn out to be obverse extremes, opposite sides of the same coin. We live in "two different worlds" as in the old standard song. The sufficiency of any such simplistic explanation is challenged by the fact that the evidentiary picture is ever-changing. Although the same patterns of change seem to reappear over and over again—much like the merry-go-round of habitual, obsessive-compulsive thinking—like snowflakes they are never exactly the same in any two instances.

Of course, in the context of political resistance to stubborn and inconvenient facts found by scientific analysis, and funded by vested interests, it is hard to blame the rationalist for coming down on the side of science as the only reliable source of data. Perhaps the most pernicious example of politically coopting the rational is to be found in the public debate around climate change, denying humankind's culpability in the face of irrefutable evidence. The success of such campaigns depends upon the average Joe's reluctance and lack of time to dig into the actual data. It is frightening.

Human nature is stubborn, resisting change in the face of relentlessly changing circumstances, particularly when bottom-line calculations are thrown into the mix. It becomes difficult to accede to or even recognize evidence that is contrary to our preconceived reality, especially when our own paycheck or our "values" depend upon our not allowing it. When blunt facts threaten our position in the social hierarchy, from the president on down, or our pride in being an independent American in the international hierarchy, intransigence in the face of contravening evidence becomes the default.

The eight dimensions of the three fields represent stark distinctions with real differences. Questions addressed by theism, rationalism, or Zen; problems defined on social or personal levels; attitudes nurtured within the field, internalized or externalized; entities, concrete or tangible, in which adherents' trust is invested; methods employed individually or in groups; goals pursued in this life or the next; and conclusions drawn based on objective evidence, subjective belief, or first-person experience, represent only the tip of this tripartite iceberg. We may be forgiven for feeling that no reconciliation of the three worldviews is possible. But let us not give up hope. Keep sharpening that razorblade.

RECONCILING SCIENCE
WITH ZEN

In the following, please permit me to recap and summarize some of the main themes of the text above. The core concepts may be redundant, but bear repetition. Different takes on similar issues may help clarify the radical departure from the norm that is Zen.

Most informed observers would probably agree that Zen can be classified as finding its position closer to the extreme of rationalism on the spectrum, with theism at the opposite end. Even in its initial period of burgeoning in India and its spread through China into Korea and Japan, this would probably hold true, though religion and science were not conceived of as distinctly separate. For that matter there was no hard-and-fast official wall between church and state. Today, we may comfortably embrace the findings of science and Zen as similar in their method and to some degree, their worldview. Notwithstanding that they may have irreconcilable differences as we have seen, particularly as to what is considered sufficient evidence or proof of a claim. Their imputed opposed goals of avoiding, versus embracing, natural suffering can also benefit from reconciliation.

Science's standard model of the fundamentals of physics evolves over time with the advent of new data, achieving higher and higher approximations of the way the universe actually works. But whether it can ultimately explain the Theory of Everything is arguable. And whether its outputs can be effectively deployed in time to save us from the overwhelming confluence of manmade and natural disasters looming is, as always, TBD: yet to be determined.

We might even propose that the arcs of science and Zen are somewhat convergent, trending toward an overarching, comprehensive understanding of both duality and nonduality. Duality, as the norm and meme underlying public discourse, needs no further explanation to our purpose. Nonduality, a fundamental principle of Buddhism, can be applied to all dimensions of existence, including the physical. It is exemplified in science by relativity's measured conflation of matter and energy, $E = mc2$. The nether world of quantum physics apparently reveals a new frontier of ambiguity and uncertainty.

Zen teachings do not propound theories about objective reality absent an observer, as the modus operandi of science typically attempts. Buddha's observations of the world and his place in it were the whole point and import of his insight, as it will be of yours. In all disciplines of unbiased research, Zen included, it is a truism that there is no objectivity, or actual separation of subjective and objective.

In Zen, we are all assigned the role of central observer of our own reality, perhaps the ultimate mode of rational problem-solving. As in the design profession, the immediate task is really problem definition, rather than prematurely leaping to a solution. The theory is that if we truly and thoroughly define the problem at hand, the solution will be implicit in that definition. We each reinvent Zen.

We are also, each and every one of us individually, the final judge of whatever progress we may make in employing Zen's central method, zazen. Matsuoka Roshi would often say that zazen should be the "comfortable way." Of course, it takes a considerable amount of time just to become physically comfortable with the sitting posture. Becoming mentally and emotionally comfortable with expending the time and effort necessary to explore Zen's deeper effects takes even longer. It also requires the development of great patience, particularly with our perceived lack of progress, experienced and expressed as "plateauing." Along the way we may expect to run into a great deal of resistance on both personal and social levels. Your friends and family may not understand or appreciate your dedication to this inexplicable practice. But then who really understands the obsession with science? Or religion?

In explaining the task of critical self-examination in meditation—much like the lonely scientist late at night in the laboratory, or the saint in the wilderness—we often find we are at a loss for words. We lack the eloquence to adequately articulate what we are actually doing in zazen, let alone why. The "how" of it is pretty straightforward: we simply show others the method of zazen. It is up to them to work the method.

Such deeply disturbing ambivalence might threaten to sound the death knell for any experiment in science or form a test of faith in religion. But Zen's truth is directly accessible to anyone willing to invest the time and effort required to get past expectations of measurable results, to go beyond thought and language, and to relinquish their own opinions of what they think reality is or should be. Einstein's expression that scientific insight is "helped by a feeling for the order lying behind the appearance" recalls a saying from Taoism: something to the effect that as long as we are caught by desire, we see only the manifestations (of reality). But freed from desire, we confront the Mystery, capital M. So the answer we find in Zen, as well as Taoism, is a deeper question.

In Taoism as well as Zen, "manifestations" constitute the superficial, relatively fixed appearances or forms of our perceived reality. But this built-in facade masks their essence, the underlying mystery, the dynamic nature of emptiness. Form as emptiness makes visible and visceral the essence of matter as energy. They cannot be equated, as they cannot be separated to begin with. Form is innately emptiness, emptiness innately form. The two terms are mutually defining, like hot and cold, light and dark. What we realize in Zen is precisely the personal ambiguity of duality and nonduality.

In Zen, we rely on simple, direct observation, giving up our usual reliance on trying to think our way through everything. Objectless meditation, or "just precisely sitting," is Zen's way of getting beyond the limitations of our discriminating mind and tapping into our intuitive wisdom. Appearance or form is what we think we know. Emptiness is the truth beyond what we think we know and can know, ultimately unknowable in conventional terms: in other words, the higher order underlying apparent chaos.

Knowing the Unknowable

What we can know through direct sensory experience is not usually so beyond the pale that it precludes philosophical or scientific examination. But such analysis is always looking back in time, reflecting upon previous experience, if only of the past immediate moment. This suggests that preconceptions stemming from past experience can affect not only our interpretation of present experience but may even color or distort our immediate perceptions not only of sensory data but received social wisdom.

An example can be found in the way we interpret the behaviors and motives of those with whom we have had prior dealings, pleasant or unpleasant.

If you have not seen someone for more than a minute, do not assume that they are still the same, the saying goes.

But expectations and stereotyping tend to trump this open-ended and open-minded attitude. As Baba Ram Dass advised in an extended talk to one of my classes at the University of Illinois in Chicago in the 1960s, if you insist that the cop be the cop, the cop has no option other than to be the cop. If, however, we can see beyond the badge and into the humanity behind it, we can drop perceiving the cop as a cop, at least for the moment. Only then does the officer have the leeway to stop playing the cop. Same for the perp, of course. Similarly, theories strongly felt to be true or false may influence the way a scientist interprets data from an experiment. Observed phenomena can be interpreted in incompatible ways that are relatively consistent with the raw evidence. To choose between equally valid explanations, other considerations come into play: the simplicity or beauty of the solution; agreement with related theories; and again, desired outcomes the scientist may favor, consciously or subliminally.

Rules of thumb can also influence the judgment call, such as that the simplest and most elegant solution is most likely the correct one. Or the way a similar situation was resolved in the past. Owing to the impossibility of replicating all of the contingent causes and conditions, the absolute replication of the results of any experiment is not physically possible. But as long as they fall within the range of predictability, they may prove useful. Close enough for jazz, as we say.

Being in the Moment

Using journalism's formula for covering the bases the reader needs to know on any newsworthy event—who, what, where, when, and why, and sometimes how—helps differentiate Zen's focus from that of rationalism or theism. While answers to the other questions may fill in important background context, the foreground of present reality comes into sharp focus as a "what."

In the context of the present moment and our individual place in it—in which the natural sphere has forcefully taken precedence over the personal in the form of a viral threat impinging upon everyone's daily routine—Zen poses the greatest conundrum of all: What is this? What is the meaning of this in its broadest and deepest sense?

Asking the "what" question is not intellectually pondering the meaning of life, the "why" of philosophy. Not why it is happening from a theistic framework of sin and redemption. Much less does Zen venture into the province of theology and wonder who is behind the present reality as first cause. It does not speculate as to beginnings and endings found in creation myths, nor as to astrophysics or biology. It does not consider precisely how the world works, which is the wheelhouse of applied and pure science. Zen simply asks, "What, finally, is this very existence?" It takes in its presently abnormal, irrational, and rational dimensions—which is that an alien virus is conquering Earth with an unwitting and unwilling assist from its host, humanity.

Clinging to our carefully constructed self and to our learned mode of learning falls away in zazen. Gone are its division into dualities: mind as interior subject; body and environment as exterior objects. In contradistinction to intriguing intellectual insights, that which arises from direct contemplation of consciousness is experienced on a gut level, much like the visceral thought experiments of Dr. Einstein. Waking up is not "all up in our heads." Objectless meditation is also necessarily subjectless.

Becoming Objectless

Of course, our findings in Zen are of a different order from those of Einstein and other scientists. They are not amenable to measurement, mathematics, or demonstrable proof. But this does not mean that they are not real. Or that they are trivial or insignificant. In the case of your own personal insight, only you will know for sure. Counterintuitively and counterculturally, in Zen meditation we abandon the very idea of having any specific idea, or goal, in mind.

Dealing with duality in its many forms: subject vs. object; mind vs. body; self vs. other; easy vs. difficult—et cetera ad infinitum—is intrinsic to any learning process. But dealing with duality is also intrinsic to the inverse unlearning process of Zen. Language, the main medium by which we learn, is in itself dualistic. This is illustrated by the well-known oxymoron: this sentence is not true. If this assertion is indeed true, then what it asserts cannot be. If what it asserts is untrue, then the sentence is true, contradicting what it asserts.

The tetralemma (see: Wikipedia), four premises of logical propositions that stem from early Indian thought, deals with this seeming contradiction. It states that with reference to any logical proposition X, there are four possibilities: affirmation, negation, both, and neither. Something either is OR is not; OR both is and is not; OR neither is nor is not. That covers the logical waterfront. However, much of what we experience in Zen and may want to share with others is not at all logical. Stepping outside its four-cornered box we discover the fifth possibility: none of the above.

"Why" and "how" questions elicit a narrow answer of who, in the case of theism, and causality, in the case of rationalism, respectively. This does not mean that these worldviews lack the potential to transcend their own limitations. Any useful branch of mathematics, it is said, must ultimately transcend its axioms to remain usefully relevant or vital.

The "what" question of Zen suggests answers of a different order than the "why" and "how" questions. It requires stepping back from our usual safe place and seeing the bigger picture, from 30,000 feet as we jet-setters say today. "Why" and "how" may seem to be bigger questions than "what," with its apparently narrow focus on present reality, but this ignores the tenet of Zen's Three Times—past, future, and present—being embraced within the eternal moment.

Questions and Answers

Naturally we hope and expect to find final answers to the important questions that we ask. Any real answer we find in Zen, however, appears as yet an even deeper question. The primordial mystery of existence itself may be accessible to experience, but cannot be fully grasped by our thinking mind.

One reason is that thinking takes time. Discrimination is always looking in the rearview mirror at what has just occurred. It can never catch up to the present moment in spacetime, which, after all, is where and when we confront the mystery, the fundamental question of existence. As Master Dogen puts it, again in the Genjokoan: "Here is the place; here the Way unfolds" (Sotoshu 2001):

> When you find your place where you are, practice occurs, actualizing the fundamental point.
> When you find your way at this moment, practice occurs, actualizing the fundamental point.

This illustrates the open-ended question in Zen: homing in on this place at this moment. It bears repeating that in Zen as well as in science, the questions we ask are at least as important, sometimes more so, than any pat answers we may find. Great scientists ask the great questions. A mediocre scientist, if there is such a person, may pursue questions for which the answer is findable, but relatively unimportant, even if commercially viable. It goes without saying that asking the wrong question is not likely to lead to the right answer. But it might.

Answers represent those things that we can know or think that we already know. But what we don't know— indeed, what cannot be known in any ordinary sense—is our focus in Zen. Zen is an endless and endlessly fascinating Q&A without relying on the A.

Those of us who represent, propagate, and promote Zen practice and its teachings find no essential conflict between the findings of science and those of Zen. If in future a conflict does arise, it is Buddhism that will have to adapt, according to His Holiness the Dalai Lama (Goleman 2008):

> I have often said that if science proves facts that conflict with Buddhist understanding, Buddhism must change accordingly. We should always adopt a view that accords with the facts. If upon investigation we find that there is reason and proof for a point, then we should accept it. However, a clear distinction should be made between what is not found by science and what is found to be nonexistent by science. What science finds to be nonexistent we should all accept as nonexistent, but what science merely does not find is a completely different matter. An example is consciousness itself. Although sentient beings, including humans, have experienced consciousness for centuries, we still do not know what consciousness actually is: its complete nature and how it functions.

Zen practice challenges us to go beyond conventional thinking, beyond belief, beyond received wisdom, beyond even common sense, beyond what we may regard as objective evidence. We are not simply substituting one system of thought for another (i.e., that of Zen Buddhism in place of beliefs of theism or tenets of rationalism). Zen's method transcends thought itself but does not throw the world of ideas entirely under the proverbial bus; again from the *Hsinhsinming* (Sotoshu 2001):

> To move in the One Way do not reject even the world of senses and ideas.
> Indeed to accept them fully is identical with true enlightenment.

This wonderful admonition carries the essential message of Zen to the householder, as well as to the monastic, I think. Today more than ever we need creative application of the senses and ideas to our personal practice, as well as to the public propagation of Zen. In the American cultural context, this will mean setting aside and getting beyond some of the received wisdom, such as restricting belief systems of theism and inhibiting biases of rationalist skepticism. We will need some wiggle room.

GETTING BEYOND BELIEF

Zen Buddhism does not require that we subscribe to a system of beliefs, as do most theistic religions. Nor that we frame our reality in a rational system of concepts, as does most rationalist thought, in science as well as philosophy. All such systems are based upon a set of beliefs about human nature, and its place in the grand scheme of things, whether within a rationalist or theistic frame. Zen appeals to our most primal desire to wake up fully to the nature of reality—rational, belief-based, or not.

Our desires are usually attached to outcomes we want to pursue, and averse to those we would like to avoid, to belabor the obvious. These innate, often subliminal and instinctual, desires directly affect our apprehension of sensual data. Unconscious interpretation can mask the underlying essence of direct experience. For example, falling in love requires a certain degree of suspension of disbelief. Disregarding the less attractive dimensions of the object of our affection—such as the biological processes taking place in the GI tract and the inevitable aging, sickness, and death—is essential to our vicarious enjoyment of the romantic storyline. This illustrates an interference principle of learned beliefs conflicting with immediate desires that are often driven by nature. An obvious example is the function of hormones impelling us toward procreation of the species, which we interpret as falling in love. How could we otherwise participate in the fantasy of our newly beloved's absolute perfection?

Perception is subliminally impacted by such impulses and further distorted by conscious desires. Zen's motivating desire to comprehend true reality—a goal largely shared but pursued differently by all three fields of rationalism, theism, and Zen—is compromised by more prosaic desires.

We all want to feel "normal," unless our usual normal is a kind of torture. We seek assurance that our experience conforms with the experience of others, taking comfort in the agreed-upon givens of our shared reality. We want to be sane, in other words. But Zen distrusts this definition of sanity.

We also wish to avoid pain, the alleviation of which is the direct or indirect goal of many scientific endeavors, a primary objective of rationalism in general, medical science in particular. We also wish to pursue pleasure. And perhaps above all, we strive to maintain the status quo, depending on how and whether it operates to our advantage. The status quo, such as it is, may redound to our benefit in the form of privilege, for example, or conversely to our disadvantage in the form of injustice. It depends.

In a well-known Zen trope, the ocean provides an analogy to this self-centered perception. To a fish, the deep is very different from what it appears to a human being. To a bird it is something else again. Yet it is the same ocean. Then again, the ocean is never the same from one moment to the next. Nonetheless, it means something different to each class of sentient beings. It can be their home, a source of life, or it can become a life-threatening tsunami. In any case, like the ocean, we develop and adopt a series of cherished beliefs regarding the meaning of our existence and our place in it.

Understanding Meaning

Someone once said that practicing Zen is pursuing the understanding of meaning. This construction may appear contradictory, circular or redundant, upon first consideration. But there are many dimensions of life that we understand—such as how to conceive a child—the full meaning of which we cannot know. Anyone's birth—our own, or that of our children—remains a total and deeply profound mystery.

Similarly, the most meaningful experiences in life—such as the death of a loved one, even if their time has come—no one, not even Buddha, can claim to fully understand. Understanding and meaning are not of the same order. Nonetheless, for our Zen practice to comprise a practical pursuit of the understanding of meaning, it must begin with the present moment in which that meaning is coming to fruition.

The central meaning of life, the crux of philosophy, is also a central question in Zen. But Zen's approach to understanding meaning begins at home, in meditation, focusing on direct apprehension of our life in all its wild complexity. Only when we have settled into our own personal comfort zone—physically, emotionally, and mentally, especially regarding our own aging, sickness, and death—can we be in a position to sally forth into the world armed with wisdom and compassion. But this suggests that our presumed understanding of the meaning of our own existence may have to have changed. We no longer have a dog in this hunt. But our dog definitely has, or is, buddha-nature.

Plumbing the Mystery

Zen promises that overcoming our own limited perspective makes it possible to apprehend the true nature of reality, whether expressed as the Great Mystery, "the order lying behind," to borrow Einstein's coinage, the presence of God, or as emptiness itself. Simply stated, what we already know—the familiar—is the form. What we seek to find—the unfamiliar—is the emptiness. What we seek to know, in other words, is already inherent in what we know.

A corrective to our usual concept and mode of perception as necessarily involving a subject observing an object is offered up in Dongshan's *Hokyo Zamma: Precious Mirror Samadhi* (Sotoshu 2001):

Like facing a precious mirror, form and reflection behold each other.
You are not it, but in truth it is you.

A well-made mirror reflects everything equally, without distortion. The form, the subject—the observer as well as the observed—merge in mutual nonduality, recalling Meister Eckhart's saying (see Wikiquote):

The eye through which I see God is the same eye through
which God sees me;
my eye and God's eye are one eye, one seeing, one knowing, one love.

Without resorting to referencing God, Zen directs our attention to the nonduality of self and other—rather than to a concept, a definition, or a description of what the "other" may be—implicitly questioning what this so-called "self" may be. Zen's answer to the conundrum of existence is to be found not in the Bible or any other scripture, including Buddhist teachings, but right here and now in the ever-arising present moment.

Aspiring to Buddha-Nature

We all want to believe that deep down, at base, the self, our human nature, is naturally compassionate. That fundamentally we are all humane, even altruistic, capable of great self-sacrifice. If this hopeful image were truly so, simply peeling away our layers of ignorance, delusions, and misconceptions would allow anyone to reconnect with the root goodness that is already there: the remainder of our essential nature, stripped bare of self-centered and cultural accretions. But this may be overly optimistic, a form of wishful thinking. Lurking at the root of human nature is the survival instinct, as for all beings, coiled and ever ready to spring, baring claws and fangs, as we have all borne witness.

Of course, we can point to the many well-documented altruistic acts of humanity, as well as those of so-called lower animals. Even female bats—reputedly the species of origin of the current plague, replacing the loathed rats of the bubonic—have been found to share food with others not of their own bloodline. It seems that observance of the positive "affirm life" of the first precept's prohibitive admonition "do not kill" is not limited to humanity. All life affirms life, while privileging species.

But none of this means that human nature is innately selfless. Altruistic or even heroic deeds may represent the transcendence of human nature, rather than its definitive core character. Compassion may not be an intrinsic component of what it means to be human.

In Buddhism, our original awakened nature must be realized, before we can have true compassion. We can practice compassion, of course, just as we practice playing the piano long before our performance becomes truly musical. In Zen, we trust that all human beings have the potential to realize their innate compassion and wisdom, but do not believe that it is a given to be taken for granted. This is one reason why Zen is so difficult. It does not deny the active presence and effectiveness of motives and impulses beyond our control.

Indeed, Zen suggests that our greater and lesser angels are largely dependent upon the circumstance of the moment. We are saints or devils, bodhisattvas or demons, depending largely on what is happening in the immediate now, or what has just happened in the immediate past. Or if we are inclined to carry a grudge, or are plagued by PTSD, the distant past holds sway. Revenge is a dish best served cold. We often act before thinking things through, and even after having given things a great deal of thought, to no avail. Actions based on impulse or reasoning may not have the intended effect.

This is why we aspire to buddha-nature, not human nature, in Zen. In a very real sense, our all-too-human nature must be transcended, the conventional self must be relinquished, in order to accede to the buddha brand of wisdom.

Perfecting Compassion

Siddhartha Gautama was definitely human. In fact, his awakening depended on this fact, according to Zen. Birth as a human is the ticket to awakening. In realizing Buddhahood, he did not merely realize his essential humanity, he surpassed it. He was not the only truly human being in his milieu, obviously, but he was the only one who was fully awake. His spiritual awakening included the recognition that everyone else was sleepwalking "Like a dream, like a fantasy" (Senzaki 2005). This realization informed his compassionate impetus to teach others.

In order to be compassionate to others, you must already be filled with compassion. It cannot come from outside nor can it come from a mental disposition, or solely from conscious effort. If compassion is a reality, it already exists. It cannot depend upon you, your actions, or even your intent.

Actualizing true compassion coarises with life-changing insight, revealing the compassion inherent in our very existence. We come to see that we exist by virtue of the compassion of the universe, in its support of all life. Intrinsic to this insight is that we and all other beings are inseparable from each other as well as from the larger universe which is, after all, our true home.

Anyone realizing the universality of compassion as a built-in characteristic of existence already has immeasurable compassion: indeed, all of the compassion that there is to be had. This renders compassion ready at hand and easily available to share with others. It is not a rare commodity, being universal, as it is, in its distribution. Genuine compassion thus embodies an apparent paradox: we have to be in possession of it in order to be enabled to share it. but this is true of even the most mundane commodity. We cannot share the wealth unless we have wealth to share. Compassion is true wealth.

We can try to behave more compassionately to others, of course. But if we are not intimately aware of innate compassion, our efforts may do more harm than good. Compassion must be balanced with wisdom, the ability to intuit the effective thing to do in each situation, which calls upon a kind of situational awareness, as opposed to an exercise in situational ethics. Compassion sometimes looks like cruelty, tough love. It is seen in a mother's strictness with her child, or a Zen master striking a student with a staff or a stick, the "blow of compassion" (J. kyosaku).

Zen practice offers many ways, or skillful means, of intentionally developing compassion. Traditionally, this is done through observance of the Six Perfections (S. paramitas), translated as Generosity, Precepts, Energy, Patience, Meditation, and Wisdom (figure 6). Each of the six are similar to compassion, having an apparent external form as well as a less obvious internal essence. True compassion is not so much a matter of acting compassionately—generously, ethically, patiently, energetically, and wisely on behalf of others—but recognizing that as human beings we are already the ultimate beneficiaries of a compassion that is universal and absolute. All other sentient beings also owe their life to this immanent compassion, but they may not have the capacity to realize it. Human beings alone are considered capable of this kind of insight.

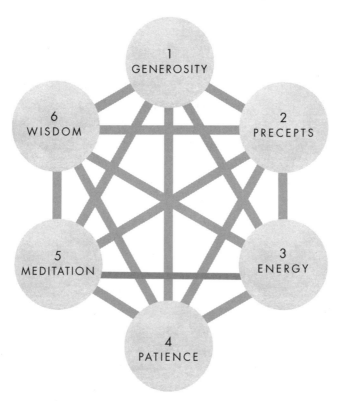

FIGURE 6. Six Perfections

Birthing Buddha

To be born as a human being is considered exceedingly rare in Buddhism, the population bomb notwithstanding. Other sentient beings far exceed the population of human beings, of course. Insects alone are estimated at some seventeen times our mass, viruses three times as massive in total. But the ecological impact of the human race is feared to be causing extinction of species at alarming rates. In

Buddhism, the place of human beings in the food chain is more in the center than at the top. Zen shares the view that our central position is one of responsibility, of stewardship. Human beings are considered uniquely capable of spiritual awakening, whether in this lifetime or over the span of several. It may be that the nearly eight billion people on Earth represent the cumulative rebirth of all human beings to date. But that is a bit too speculative. You do the math. Human birth is held in high esteem because it is considered the absolutely necessary pivot point (J. yoki), the nexus or essential confluence of causes and conditions necessary to realize spiritual insight. Human beings have sufficient self-awareness and intelligence to wake up to the facts of existence as articulated in the Four Noble Truths, and the capacity to realize their own buddha-nature. This is why even Buddha's awakening was ultimately dependent upon his humanity. We also maintain that the event transcended normalcy. In a very real sense humans benefit from being the prime recipients of compassion, manifested in our existence as the only sentient beings who have the unique ability to wake up fully. This is expressed succinctly in Hakuin's *Zazen Wasan; Song of Zazen* (Waddell 2017):

> Like water and ice, without water no ice, outside us no buddhas.

Repaying Our Debt

This pivot-point benefit is our birthright as human beings but also represents a grave responsibility, as well as a call to action not to squander the opportunity. Having buddha-nature does not make us lords of the universe, nor does it justify raping and pillaging the planet and its lesser beings. Broadly paraphrasing the canon, our proper place is at the middle level of Buddhism's Six Realms, the perceptual planes of existence occupied by all sentient beings. Heaven and hell at the top and bottom are self-created, as are the middle ones of the angry gods, humans, animals and insects, and hungry ghosts in this model. Zen teachings do not attribute the creation of the universe, or life, to ourselves as authors, but we do assume responsibility for our own behavior and its consequences. This is the essence of the karmic view of causality.

A Zen trope from the historical collection of anecdotal exchanges, otherwise known as koans, points to the obvious: in order to have such a thing [enlightenment], you must be such a person. And its corollary: [But] If you are such a person, what interest would you have in gaining such a thing?

The punchline of this saying indicates that what we may be seeking outside ourselves cannot be found there. If you were already such an enlightened person, what interest or motive could you possibly have in pursuing enlightenment? In order to find it, we have to stop seeking it. The paradox is in our mind, not in Zen. As my grandmother would sagely advise when we were looking for something we had misplaced: "One thing is for sure: it will be in the last place you look for it."

Buddha did not merely develop compassion, the capacity to suffer along with others, the literal meaning of the term. In other words, to "feel your pain," to quote a recent POTUS. Siddhartha was apparently aghast at the suffering he witnessed every day of his life, and so became estranged from existence itself. The world was too much with him (shout-out to Wordsworth). This was his fundamental koan, or impelling dilemma.

He is said to have sat down in desperation that night 2,500 years ago, resolved to die if need be, in order to resolve this debilitating dilemma. Fortunately for us, he did not die but woke up to the meaning of suffering, and so was able to fully embrace it. He also possessed the skillful means to transmit this insight to others, though he expressed ambivalence that there was actually anything to teach. His final deathbed message to the members of his community was essentially: do thou likewise.

This is our personal challenge, and sharing this practice and method with others is our social mission in Zen. But there is no guarantee that others will be open to the dialogue, or ready to do the work to overcome their own ignorance. Zen is not a crusade, not even a campaign. The possibility of world peace may depend, in all humility, on all humanity embracing the compassion and maturing the wisdom of Zen. People are buddha—potentially awakened—but do not know it. This is the uncertainty principle in full flower.

Sweating the Big Stuff

In Zen, we find confirmation of this very uncertainty. Different schools or sects promulgate divergent interpretations of the teachings attributed to Buddha. In such debates, Buddhism seems to be all about philosophy. But in Zen we do not debate Zen. It is a take-it-or-leave-it proposition.

Buddhist philosophy takes on a soteriological slant in its Bodhisattva Vow to save all beings, and thus may be classified as religious, at least in intent. But we do not proselytize. And we can legitimately claim that certain nonreligious philosophies have grown out of Buddhism, like humanism. After all, Buddhism's raison d'être is not saving souls from eternal damnation but saving living human beings from their own ignorance, thereby saving the world from unnecessary suffering driven by ignorance.

In Zen practice, particularly while on the cushion, we set aside our proclivity to get bogged down in details and instead sit with an open question, an all-inclusive assessment of the present moment. But zazen is not obsessive navel-gazing, as some may suppose. From open-ended unembellished observation we may hope to overcome our biases and register afresh the unfiltered, unanticipated incoming data. We follow the conventional wisdom: don't sweat the small stuff. And its corollary: it's all small stuff. We allow that the true solution to the problem of existence cannot be foreknown.

Allowing the Inevitable

This attitude of allowing—enshrined as the heart of wisdom by those Zen masters of music, the Beatles, in one of their mega-hit songs, "Let It Be" (1970)—is intrinsic to the acceptance of our own personal suffering. But complacency in the face of the suffering of others is not Buddhist. The ancient definition of "suffer" as meaning "to allow" is encapsulated in a saying attributed to Jesus (Matthew 19:14):

Jesus said, Suffer the little children come to me, and do not hinder them, for the kingdom of heaven belongs to such as these.

One would assume that the kingdom of heaven belongs to the innocent, those who are at least as innocent as a newborn child. Newborns are not considered completely innocent of desire in Buddhism. They are guilty of the primordial desire to exist, or they would not be born. But recovering our original nature or buddha-mind is tantamount to recovering the innocence of childhood, only with the full maturity of adulthood.

This is our mission, the main reason why we promulgate the teachings of Zen and propagate the practice of zazen. These may be considered truly altruistic activities if uncorrupted by self-centered striving. Like the old proverb, variously attributed, I am told, to Lao Tsu, Confucius, and Maimonides, among others, again demonstrating that historicity is inversely proportional to antiquity: "Give a man a fish, and he will eat for a day; teach a man how to fish and you feed him for a lifetime." If we transmit the method of Zen, we have done our best.

All we can teach others is zazen, but it is the true basis of Zen insight. As Matsuoka Roshi said, "Sharing the Dharma is the most we can do for ourselves, or for others" (Matsuoka 2006):

When he awakened, the Buddha saw into the true nature of all things, and his heart was full of compassion for all living beings. The purity of his mind and heart and the compassion he felt made his whole being incapable of hurting himself or others. In Zen, we strive to be the same. . . . As our minds are calmed with the vision of the true nature of existence, or of life and death, and our hearts become filled with the compassion of the Buddha, we too, will become incapable of anything but the purest acts towards ourselves and others. In Zen, there is no authority outside of ourselves to judge us, but as we become enlightened and live our lives as Buddha each day, we naturally act in harmony with the compassion in our hearts and with the knowledge of the Buddha-Nature that is in our minds. The Buddha-Nature that is within each of us is the authority that guides. It finds expression in our lives as our minds become empty of the self from meditation, and as the mind is no longer a hindrance to our true nature asserting itself.

Sensei commented on the way compassion operates in Zen: "Compassion is not driven by fear of a judging God; but is taken up on our own recognizance." The method of exercising our own recognizance in Zen is zazen. Each time we sit in meditation we take up this commitment again. The benefits that come to us through Zen are real. Those who receive these benefits naturally yearn to share them with others, a result of what is known as opening the heart of compassion, considered tantamount to gaining true insight. Our attention turns from obsessing over ourselves to recognizing the plight of others. In broadening our embrace of suffering, our own is diminished proportionately. This is what Sensei means by the "purest acts" toward others. They are non-dualistic in nature, untainted by considerations of risks and rewards, or of self and other as winners and losers.

This transformation in worldview—opening the heart—is considered much more difficult of attainment than enlightenment or insight itself. The two go hand in hand and reinforce each other. The suffering of others comes to be felt as clearly as we feel our own. But even more poignantly, in that there is little that we can do about it on an existential level. "I feel your pain" is a genuinely authentic expression in Zen and Buddhism. Buddha, the fully awakened one, and Avalokiteshvara, the Bodhisattva of Compassion, are the avatars of seeing, feeling, and hearing the suffering of the world.

CUTTING THROUGH THE CLUTTER

Matsuoka Roshi once said that in zazen we should just keep cutting through everything that comes to mind, like the edge of a razorblade. It may seem far too simple to suggest that just sitting still enough for long enough can bring about any meaningful change in your life, especially in cutting through the vagaries and uncertainty of the current crisis. But the pandemic, and peoples' reaction to it, simply reinforce these basic teachings of Buddhism and Zen, such as that life is fragile and temporary. The natural sphere—in the form of a virus—has intruded upon the social and personal spheres of our existence. The most natural thing to do about it is to turn to meditation.

In zazen we return to the natural sitting posture. This is the upright alert posture that human beings have been employing since prehistoric and tribal times, sitting around the campfire or waiting silently for prey on the hunt. We follow the breath until it returns to its natural rhythm, filling us with oxygen, our main source of vital energy. In turn, the stilling of posture and breath naturally still the mind until we recover our natural state of awareness, long forgotten but hauntingly familiar, as the childlike consciousness we were born into. When zazen is allowed to take its natural course, our posture, breath, and attention all come together in a unified way. This is what my teacher would frequently refer to as "the real zazen."

If you are of a theistic bent, you may consider this method of Zen to be a kind of prayer, but one that is holistic, whole body-and-mind engagement, a heartfelt effort to "hear the true gospel," the true dharma. If you tend to lean to the rationalist worldview, you may regard it as a kind of all-inclusive bench test, an experiment in directly studying the machinations of the mind, uninhibited by preconception.

When we brandish the razorblade of Zen in the traditional form of zazen, familiar dimensions fall away, including those of space and time. Measured time is seen for what it is: a mere concept, an invention, however useful. Space is seen to be infinite and yet intimate. Personal, social, natural, and universal spheres all interpenetrate, mutually influencing and interacting with each other. The Zen model of reality is all-inclusive and not at all separate from all manner of beings within it, including human beings and yes, even viruses. The true nature of spacetime as well as that of Zen is indivisible and inconceivable. Entering into the real zazen means entering into real time: emergent and continuously unfolding in the present eternal moment, like a smoke ring. It means immersing ourselves into real space: the landscape of our real life, inner and outer.

Imagining Future Imperfect

The future emerging out of our past may be regarded as a form of potential energy, charged with the kinetic force of consequences from actions we take in the present. But we enjoy no guarantee of achieving perfection. In fact, Buddhism candidly assesses existence itself as imperfect from our human perspective, as it is also impermanent and insubstantial. But this should be a source of relief for us, rather than a source of anxiety, as suggested in the ancient Ch'an poem *Hsinhsinming* (Sotoshu 2001):

> To live in this realization is to be without anxiety about non-perfection.

Zen does not offer us rose-colored glasses or hold out any spiritual candy for trick-or-treat. But it enables us to entertain the possibility of moving toward a personal resolution of any conflicts, real or imaginary, between spirituality and science, or between theism and rationality. Your Zen practice may help to bring about a more rational approach to your personal take on theism or religion. And it may engender a more spiritual appreciation of rationalism or science. We enter the mean between the extremes sitting in Zen meditation. Your revolution in worldview may then extend naturally, from your personal realm to the social realm and beyond. Your "eye of practice," mentioned briefly by Master Dogen in *Genjokoan* (Sotoshu 2001), opens wider and wider

It may be that we privileged citizens of the world are reaching a point of spiritual maturity after a couple of centuries of international individuation and striving. Perhaps we are coming out of a phase of humanity's extended adolescence, marked by excesses of craven consumption and self-absorption.

Like Buddha, who had become so refined by self-gratification that he was basically jaded, perhaps you have begun to see through the unsatisfactory nature of a life pursuing material comfort. This is the hallmark of true renunciation. According to Zen, self-renunciation is the necessary first step, followed by self-awakening, then self-clarification. You have to do all three stages yourself, perhaps with an assist from a teacher and a Zen community. But we do not have to pivot all the way from extremes of self-gratification to that of self-mortification. Buddha assured us that there is no need to go there. The middle way is the most extreme standpoint, and simultaneously the most balanced.

Religion of the Future

The current predominance of established sectarianism and organized religion in the United States, said to be unusually high compared to other countries, may be optimistically but perhaps naively interpreted as a symptom of a natural process of national maturation. That we turn to traditional sources of religious succor or rational relief in tough times is to be expected. But that we find ourselves no longer satisfied with the prescriptive messages of those institutions is also understandable. Turning to other sources offering a more direct approach, as a consequence, is highly predictable and much to be encouraged.

This trend is reflected in the growing self-identification of many as "spiritual but not religious." You may place yourself in this camp. But the self-identified religious right disagree with this worldview. They are not likely to yield their position, nor their grip on domains of public discourse, without a fight, even if they, too, are feeling nagging doubts. Consider the struggle for hegemony over curriculum and funding in public and private schools. This crusade to shape the minds and hearts of the next generation could go either way, or one of several. Reason may prevail, but religion might also triumph, but only as long as they are at odds.

One reaction to self-doubt is to see strength in numbers. We may end up with the blind majority leading the blind minority, or vice versa. And most likely end in inflicting unnecessary suffering on others in our zealotry. Unnecessary suffering is the only kind that can come to an end, according to Buddhism. Wisdom is to distinguish the unnecessary from the necessary.

Whichever way these conflicts in the public arena are resolved, the eternal truths of existential suffering in Buddhism—the inevitability of aging, sickness and death—will not be contravened. They are woven into the very fabric of existence. This is the future focus of humanistic religion.

Surviving in an Unnatural World

Much of the social suffering we witness in our neighborhoods and around the globe may be attributed to overreacting negatively to inconvenient realities. We like to think that we can avoid, minimize, or at least postpone effects of natural and man-made disasters visited upon us and our loved ones. This in turn predictably causes more unnecessary suffering, both to ourselves and to others, our unloved ones.

Helped along by the unintended consequences of unnatural selection (i.e., the untoward and unheeding interventions of humankind), we inflict unintentional but willful damage, driven by our best intentions paving more and more roads to hell. Like so many well-intentioned bulls in so many china shops, the side effects of our environmental, hormonal, and medical ministrations end up producing evermore resistant strains of bacteria, and evermore virulent viruses. So many ways to make Mother Nature angry.

The uptick in destructive weather patterns that deniers desire to wish away is a prescient and pressing example. The United States is now witnessing ten times the frequency of tornadoes as the rest of the world, as just one example. It is as if a vengeful God is using his giant power erasers— hurricanes and tornadoes—to selectively erase large swaths of this country, wiping them off the face of the Earth like a mistake in drawing up the plans. Maybe the Old Testament, and certain contemporary televangelists, are to be believed. Maybe it is the Designer going back to the drawing board. Apparently, it is only going to get far worse before it gets better.

But the picture is not all gloom and doom. For example, we may anticipate a continuing increase in overall life expectancy fed by victories of medical science over some, if not all, of the physical diseases afflicting humankind. Some scraps of medical mercy may even be extended to our long-suffering nonhuman wards.

Also in the offing may be a greater ability to predict and prevent natural disasters, along with enhanced warning systems and shortened response times. Increased mitigation of aftermath damage through wiser anticipatory design may result. Destructive effects on local infrastructure, populace, and decline of civilization may be reduced. But if the climate itself is at a tipping point, there is little that a comparatively puny human race can do about it. We are like mites on the fleas on the planetary dog.

Future generations will be the primary beneficiaries or victims of any such scenarios, sunny or gloomy, which, in the widening scope and increasing frequency of symptomatic signals, beggar the imagination. Our visionaries have always vacillated between competing utopian and dystopian prognostications of how it will all end: with heaven on Earth, hell in eternity, or simple oblivion. But as long as we survive as a species, the basic issues of our existence as imperfect beings in an imperfect world will still obtain. This is why the findings of Buddhism are always relevant and timely, its conclusions and recommendations increasingly urgent. Zen is always contemporary.

If cooler heads prevail, we may yet be witness to the advent of the long-wished-for fabled Utopia. Peace on Earth is surely possible even without a Second Coming. But only if we human beings are willing to be realistic about it and take up the hard work of personal transformation.

There is no time to waste. But actually, it takes no time at all to wake up to reality. Whatever the initial investment in time required on your part, it is bound to be worth it and to offer a great return. After all, as Sensei would often say, "What else can you do that will give you your whole life back?"

BIBLIOGRAPHY

American Psychiatric Association. 2013. *Diagnostic and Statistical Manual of Mental Disorders (DSM-5®)*. American Psychiatric Pub.

Aristotle. *Metaphysics* 1011 b25.

Beatles. 1970. "Let It Be." Track 6 on *Let It Be*. Apple, EMI and Twickenham Film Studios.

Bielefeldt, C. 1990. *Dogen's Manuals of Zen Meditation*. Berkeley: University of California Press.

Boyd, N. M., and J. Bogen. 2021. "Theory and Observation in Science." In *Stanford Encyclopedia of Philosophy* . Edited by Edward N. Zalta. Stanford University. Article published January 6, 2009; last modified June 14, 2021. https://plato.stanford.edu/archives/win2021/entries/science-theory-observation.

Collected Wheel Publications. 2014. *Collected Wheel Publications Volume XXVII: Numbers 412–430*. Sri Lanka: Buddhist Publication Society.

Carson, R. 2002. *Silent Spring*. 40th anniv. ed. Boston: Houghton Mifflin Harcourt.

Chang, G. C. C. 1971. *The Buddhist Teaching of Totality: The Philosophy of Hwa Yen Buddhism*. New York: Routledge. https://doi.org/10.4324/9780203706732.

Cleary, T. F. 2005. *The Book of Serenity: One Hundred Zen Dialogues*. Boston: Shambhala.

Coleridge, S. 1798. "The Rime of the Ancient Mariner." In *Lyrical Ballads, with a Few Other Poems*. J. & A. Arch.

Darwin, C. 1859. *On the Origin of Species by Means of Natural Selection, or, The Preservation of Favoured Races in the Struggle for Life*. J. Murray.

———. 1871. *The Descent of Man and Selection in Relation to Sex*. John Murray.

"Definition of Reductionism." 2021. Oxford: Oxford University Press. Lexico.com. Accessed Januar 16, 2022. https://www.lexico.com/en/definition/reductionism.

Dixon, D. 1981. *After Man: A Zoology of the Future*. St Martin's Press.

Dōgen, E. 1995. *Moon in a Dewdrop: Writings of Zen Master Dogen*. Edited by Kazuaki Tanahashi. North Point.

———. 2010. "On the Endeavor of the Way." In *Treasury of The True Dharma Eye: Zen Master Dogen's Shobo Genzo*, translated and edited by Kazuaki Tanahashi. San Francisco: San Francisco Zen Center.

Dylan, B. 1964.*The Times They Are a-Changin'*. Columbia Records.

———. 1975. "Shelter from the Storm." Track 9 on *Blood on the Tracks*. Columbia Records.

Einstein, A. 1918. "Principles of Research." Address by Albert Einstein to the Physical Society, Berlin, for Max Planck's sixtieth birthday. https://www.site.uottawa.ca/~yymao/misc/Einstein_PlanckBirthday.html.

Elliston, M. 2021. *The Original Frontier: A Serious Seeker's Guide to Zen*. Atglen, PA: Red Feather.

English, J., and G. F. Feng, ed. 1989. *Tao Te Ching*. Vintage.

Fischer-Schreiber, I., F. Ehrhard, and M. Diener. 1991. *The Shambhala Dictionary of Buddhism and Zen*. Translated by M. Kohn.Boston:

Boston: Shambhala.

Freud, S. 1989. *The Ego and the Id*. New York: W. W. Norton.

Fuller, R. B. 1940. "World Energy: A Map by R. Buckminster Fuller, executed by Philip Ragan." *Fortune* 21, no. 2 (February): 7.

Fuller, R. B., and K. Kuromiya. 1981. *Critical Path*. New York: Macmillan.

Goddard, D. 1932. *A Buddhist Bible: The Lankavatara Sutra: Chapter IX*. Vermont: self-published. https://www.sacred-texts.com/bud/bb/bb16.htm.

Goleman, D. 2008. *Destructive Emotions: A Scientific Dialogue with the Dalai Lama*. New York: Bantam.

Guth A., and S. Tye. 1980. "Phase Transitions and Magnetic Monopole Production in the Very Early Universe." *Physical Review Letters* 44:631–35.

Hahn, T. N. 1998. *Interbeing: Fourteen Guidelines for Engaged Buddhis*m. Berkeley, CA: Parallax.

Harman, W. W., and H. Rheingold. 1984. *Higher Creativity*. J. P. Tarcher.

Hegel, G. W. F., H. C. Brockmeyer, and W. T. Harris. 1869. "Hegel's Phenomenology of Spirit." *The Journal of Speculative Philosophy* 2 no. 4): 229–41.ew

Hershock, P. D. 1999. *Reinventing the Wheel: A Buddhist Response to the Information Age*. Albany: State University of New York Press.

———. 2004. *Chan Buddhism*. Honolulu: University of Hawaii Press.

Holt, J. 201. "Why Does the Universe Exist?" Filmed March 2014. TED video, 17:08. https://www.ted.com/talks/jim_holt_why_does_the_universe_exist?.

The Holy Bible, King James Version. 2022. Cambridge ed.: 1769. King James Bible Online. www.kingjamesbibleonline.org.

Huxley, A. 2014. *The Perennial Philosophy*. Chapter 16 Prayer. McClelland & Stewart.

Jnana, Y. P. 201. "Dwelling as a Lamp unto Oneself–Attadipa sutta." The Way of Bodhi. May 22, 2018. https://www.wayofbodhi.org/attadipa-sutta-dwelling-as-a-lamp-unto-oneself/.

Jung, C. 2014. "A Study in the Process of Individuation." In *Collected Works of C.G. Jung, Volume 9 (Part 1)*, edited by R. Hull. Princeton, NJ: Princeton University Press. https://doi.org/10.1515/9781400850969.290.

Kapleau, R. P. 2013. *The Three Pillars of Zen*. New York: Anchor.

Kuhn, T. S. 1970. *The Structure of Scientific Revolutions*. 2nd ed. Chicago: University of Chicago Press.

Lama, D. 2005. *The Universe in a Single Atom: The Convergence of Science and Spirituality*. Harmony.

Luk, C., trans. 1966. *The Surangama Sutra*. Rider and Company.

Matsuoka, Z. S. 2006. *The Kyosaku: Soto Zen Teachings Archive Volume I*. Atlanta: Atlanta Soto Zen Center.

———. 2011. *Moku-Rai: Soto Zen Teachings Archive Volume II*. Atlanta: Atlanta Soto Zen Center.

McLuhan, M. 1994. *Understanding Media: The Extensions of Man*. Cambridge, MA: MIT Press.

Nhat Hahn, T. 1987. *Interbeing: Fourteen Guidelines for Engaged Buddhism*. Berkeley, CA: Parallax.

Nishijima, G. and C. Cross. 1994. *Master Dogen's Shobogenzo Book 1*. Windbell.

———. 1996. *Master Dogen's Shobogenzo Book 2*. Windbell.

———. 1997. *Master Dogen's Shobogenzo Book 3*. Windbell.

———. 1999. *Master Dogen's Shobogenzo Book 4*. Windbell.

Paley, W. 1802. *Natural Theology: or, Evidences of the Existence and Attributes of the Deity*. . J. Faulder.

Pine, R. 2001. *The Diamond Sutra: The Perfection of Wisdom*. New York: Counterpoint Press.

Pirsig, R. M. 1999. *Zen and the Art of Motorcycle Maintenance: An Inquiry into Values*. New York: Random House.

Price, A. F., and Wong, M. L. 1990. *Diamond Sutra and the Sutra of Hui-Neng*. Shambhala.

———, trans. 2016. "The Platform Sutra of the 6th Patriarch, HuiNeng." Buddhism.org. July 24, 2016. http://www.buddhism.org/the-platform-sutra-of-the-6th-patriarch-hui-neng/.

Reynolds, G. 2011. "Fall Down Seven Times, Get Up Eight: The Power of Japanese Resilience." Presentation Zen. March 2011. https://www.presentationzen.com/presentationzen/2011/03/fall-down-seven-times-get-up-eight-the-power-of-japanese-resilience.html.

Sahn, S. 1999. *Only Don't Know: Selected Teaching Letters of Zen Master Seung Sahn*. Boston: Shambhala.

Schoetz, A. 2017. "Tetralemma: A 3,000-Year-Old Method for 21st Century Decisions." LinkedIn. September 18, 2017. https://www.linkedin.com/pulse /tetralemma-3000-year-old-method-21st-century-andreas-schoetz.

Seeger, P. 1955. "Where Have All the Flowers Gone?" *Sing Out!* magazine.

Senzaki, N. 2005. *Like a Dream, Like a Fantasy: The Zen Teachings and Translations of Nyogen Senzaki*. New York: Simon and Schuster.

Silent Thunder Order. *Zen Practice at Home*. Atlanta: Atlanta Soto Zen Center.

"sin, n." 2021. *OED Online*. Oxford: Oxford University Press. December 2021. https://www. oed.com/view/Entry/180030?rskey=uYc3X7 &result=1

Soto Zen Buddhism International Center, ed. 2002. *SOTO ZEN: An Introduction to Zazen*. Sotoshu Shumucho.

Sotoshu Shumucho. 2001. *Soto School Scriptures for Daily Services and Practice*. Tokyo, Japan: Soto Zen Text Project.

Stevenson, R. L. 2006. *Strange Case of Dr. Jekyll and Mr. Hyde and Other Tales*. Oxford: Oxford University Press.

Suzuki, D. T. 2009. *The Lankavatara Sutra A Mahayana Text*. Motilal Banarsidass.

Tanahashi, K, and P. Levitt, eds. 2013. *The Essential Dogen: Writings of the Great Zen Master*. Boston: Shambhala.

Uchiyama, K. 2004. *Opening the Hand of Thought: Foundations of Zen Buddhist Practice*. New York: Simon and Schuster.

Van Biema, D. 2007. "Mother Teresa's Crisis of Faith." *Time Magazine* 170 (10): 35–43.

Waddell, N., trans. 2017. *Complete Poison Blossoms from a Thicket of Thorn: The Zen Records of Hakuin Ekaku*. http://www.thezensite.com/ZwhenenTeachings/Translations/Song_of_Zazen.htm.

Warner, J., and S. Okumura, eds. 2001. *Nothing Is Hidden: Essays on Zen Master Dōgen's Instructions for the Cook*. Weatherhill.

Weber, M. 1947. *The Theory of Social and Economic Organization*. New York: New York Free Press.

Wikipedia, s.v. Big Bounce. 2021. Accessed September 7, 2021. https://en.wikipedia. org/wiki/Big_Bounce.

Wikipedia, s.v. "Language." 2022. Accessed January 6, 2022. https://en.wikipedia. org/wiki/Language.

Wikiquote, s.v. "Meister Eckhart," 2022. Accessed January 16, 2022. https:// en.wikiquote.org/wiki/Meister_Eckhart.